GRATIAN

THE TREATISE ON LAWS
WITH THE ORDINARY GLOSS

STUDIES IN MEDIEVAL AND EARLY MODERN CANON LAW

Kenneth Pennington, General Editor

Editorial Advisory Board

STUDIES IN MEDIEVAL AND EARLY
MODERN CANON LAW

VOLUME 2

Gratian
The Treatise on Laws
(Decretum DD. 1–20)

translated by Augustine Thompson, O.P.

with the Ordinary Gloss

translated by James Gordley

and an introduction by Katherine Christensen

The Catholic University of America Press
Washington, D.C.

NIHIL OBSTAT
R. P. Alanus Duston, O.P., J.C.D.
Censor ad Hoc

IMPRIMI POTEST
R. P. Johannes Flannery, O.P., M.D.
Prior Provincialis Provinciae Ss. Nominis Jesu
die 4 Novembris 1992

IMPRIMATUR
Reverend Msgr. William J. Kane
Vicar General for the Archdiocese of Washington
July 22, 1993

The nihil obstat and imprimatur are official declarations that a book or pamphlet is free of doctrinal or moral error. No implication is contained therein that those who have granted the nihil obstat and the imprimatur agree with the content, opinions, or statements expressed.

This volume was typeset by the translators using WordPerfect 5.1 Word Processing Software on the Linotronic System of Loyola Graphics, San Francisco, California.

The plate included in this volume, from Munich, Bayerische Staatsbibliothek, Ms. Clm. 23552, fo. 1, at D. 1 c. 1, with miniatures attributed to Nicolò di Giacomo da Bologna (XIV cent.), is reproduced with permission of the Staatsbibliothek.

The paper used in this publication meets the minimum requirements of the American National Standards for Information Science—Permanence of Paper for Printed Library Materials, ANSI Z39.48–1984.

Library of Congress Cataloging-in-Publication Data
Gratian, 12th cent.
    [Decretum. D. 1–20. English]
    The Treatise on laws (Decretum DD. 1–20) / Gratian, translated by Augustine Thompson, O.P. : with the Ordinary gloss, translated by James Gordley ; and an introduction by Katherine Christensen.
    p. cm.—(Studies in medieval and early modern canon law : v. 2)
    Includes bibliographical references.
    1. Canon law—Sources. I. Thompson, Augustine. II. Gordley, James. III. Christensen, Katherine. IV. Title. V. Title: Ordinary Gloss to Decretum DD. 1–20. VI. Series.
LAW <CANON Gratian 1993>
262.9'22–dc20   93–19237
ISBN 0–8132–0785–1 cl
ISBN 0–8132–0786–x pa

CONTENTS

As outlined in the Summa Magistri Rolandi (for a more complete summary of each distinction, see Introduction, pp. xxi-xxvi):

TRANSLATORS' PREFACE

Gratian's *Treatise on Laws* incorporates passages from authors of different periods with widely different Latin styles. While we have attempted to produce a smooth, readily intelligible English version that avoids Latinisms, we have also tried to stay close to the forms and structure of the original language. One reason is fidelity to the nature of legal material. Although many passages were from sermons, letters, and theological treatises, Gratian treats them as legal sources. Thus the words used and the formal structure of the language often have legal significance. Moreover, the Ordinary Gloss often clarifies obscurities and ambiguities in the *Treatise*, and so we have preserved these in our text. Also, as explained in the Glossary, we have sought consistency in translating certain technical vocabulary by always using certain English words.

Our translation was made from the Roman edition of Gratian and the Ordinary Gloss (1582). We chose that edition not only because it became the authoritative version for later canon law, but also because there was no obvious alternative. There is neither a satisfactory critical edition of the medieval Gratian nor a single base manuscript. There is an edition of Gratian by Emil Friedberg (2d ed., 1879), but we thought it would be unwise to use it. Friedberg created a hybrid text that is neither the Roman edition nor any medieval manuscript used by the medieval glossators. Consequently, this text cannot be used with the printed version of the Ordinary Gloss. We have, however, included in our backnotes the significant discrepancies between the Roman edition and that of Friedberg, explanatory commentary, and references to scholarly literature. The backnotes are found at the end of the *Treatise* and shown by raised numbers in the text of Gratian and by raised numbers in parentheses in the Gloss. The Greek canons reproduced in the notes follow the identical text of both editions with all its idiosyncrasies.

Medieval manuscripts of Gratian usually included an introduction, which outlined and summarized the text of the *Decretum*. In the same spirit we have included in our table of contents the summaries of the first twenty distinctions as they appear in the *Summa Magistri Rolandi*, one of the earliest outlines of Gratian's compilation. A more comprehensive outline can be found at the end of the Introduction.

We have also included in our notes many of the comments made by the Roman Correctors in their edition. Our notes also reproduce the lists of parallel passages in the major pre-Gratian compilations: Anselm of Lucca, Burchard of Worms, the *Polycarpus*, and Ivo's *Decretum*, *Tripartita* (both recensions), and the *Panormia*, as these appear in the Roman and Friedberg editions. These have been checked and corrected, where possible, using the available editions listed in the bibliography. We also include references to modern editions and usable English translations, when these exist, for the patristic sources. We believe them of interest, even though Gratian generally took his material from earlier compilations, rather than directly from the fathers.

The translation of the Gloss presented different problems. Its Latin is more consistent, pithy, and lawyerly than that of the *Decretum* itself. Our translation attempts to preserve this flavor. For reasons that are explained in the appendix, "The Jurists in the Gloss," we have left the abbreviations of the jurists' names found in the Gloss in their original abbreviated form.

We have converted the medieval citation system of the Gloss into modern notation. Medieval citation of the Roman law was by the incipits of the title, law, and, where applicable, paragraph. For example, Book 1 Title 2 Law 2 Paragraph 13 of the Digest of Justinian (abbreviated "ff.") would be cited as "ff. de orig[ine iuris]. l[ex]. necessarium § post originem." We cite it as Dig. 1.2.2.13. When the medieval version of the Roman law, the so-called "Vulgate," differs from the modern critical editions of Theodor Mommsen and Paul Krueger, we cite the Vulgate afterwards in brackets. We do the same for the Code and the Institutes. In citing the Novels, we give the modern numbering first, then in brackets the medieval Latin version known as the *Authenticum*, which was divided into "Collationes." Medieval versions of the Code included passages of the *Authenticum* interspersed with Code provisions. These are cited, for example, as Auth. *Navigia* post Cod. 6.2.18 (for the passage beginning with the word *Navigia* that appears after Book 6 Title 2 Law 18 of the Code). Along with citations to texts after a law there are also passages "ante" (before) and "inter" (within).

Similarly, we have converted medieval canon law citations into modern form as illustrated below. Comments by Gratian are cited, for example, *dicta Gratiani post* D. 4 c. 3, for a comment appearing after capitulum 3 of Distinction 4, or *ante* D. 4 c. 3 for a comment appearing before. Since the Roman Correctors numbered the sections in the capitula of the *Decretum* differently than Friedberg, and since we preserved their numbering in our translation of Gratian's text, we have included their numbers in brackets after the Friedberg numbers in the citations whenever the citation is to a portion of the *Decretum* that we have translated.

The modern forms of citation are as follows:

Roman Law

Institutes: Instit. 1. 1. 1.
Code: Cod. 1. 1. 1.
Digest: Dig. 1. 1. 1. 1.
Novels: Nov. 1. 1 [Coll. I. 1].

Canon Law

Decretum
Distinctiones: D. 1 c. 1.
Causae: C. 1 q. 1 c. 1.
Tractatus de Poenitentia: *De poen.* D. 1 c. 1.
Tractatus de Consecratione: *De cons.* D. 1 c. 1.

Liber Extra: X 1. 1. 1.

INTRODUCTION

The text presented in English in this volume is the introductory section of a textbook on Church law from the Middle Ages. In the hundreds of years since it first came into circulation in the middle of the twelfth century, this textbook, formally entitled the *Harmony of Discordant Canons*, has helped to shape the thinking of lawyers and legal scholars, clergy including popes from Alexander III to John Paul II, and, however indirectly, lay people of all standings. For the canonist, it was long the starting point of study, a fundamental text to be mastered and made an integral part of one's mental furniture. Its contents had to be reckoned with by merchant and theologian, politician and pastor. The modern scholar cannot genuinely understand the high medieval Church without coming to terms with its nature and its influence.

As a central text of western Christian ecclesiastical law and lawmaking, the *Decretum*, as it was (and is) commonly called, was drawn upon by Aquinas, Dante, and Chaucer, publicly denounced and burnt by Luther (although appreciated and used by Melanchthon and Calvin), sniped at by John Donne even as its traces lingered in the legal traditions of his Anglican Church.[1] In print by 1472, lovingly and rigorously reedited in the sixteenth century amid the tensions of the Reformation, the *Decretum* continued to guide the work of canonists from Rome to Maryland, Mexico City, Manila, and Macao for another three centuries, and retained a quiet influence within the evangelical tradition of church law as well. It was a major source for the codification of Roman Catholic canon law promulgated in 1917 by Pope Benedict XV and, through it, the 1983 revision of Pope John Paul II.[2]

Usually referred to during the Middle Ages simply as the *Decreta*, more frequently as the *Decretum*,[3] this text was not commissioned by any pope or bishop. Rather, it was originally the work of an individual scholar of genius and modified by later scholars who followed his lead, all seeking to make sense of the law of the Church and to teach it more effectively to others. The text of the *Decretum* presents an understanding of its subject

---

[1] Aquinas used Gratian frequently; Dante placed Gratian with Aquinas in the fourth heaven, the sphere of the sun (*Paradiso* X, 103–6). Chaucer assumed much of the *Decretum*'s teaching, especially on marriage; cf. H. A. Kelly, *Love and Marriage in the Age of Chaucer* (New York: Cornell Univ. Press, 1975), ch. 3. Luther is usually remembered as having burned the *Extravagantes*; papal legislation was his particular *bête noire* among canonical materials. But the *Decretum* went into the flames as well; cf. Luther's letter to Georg Spalatin describing the famous 1520 book burning, in his *Letters* 1, Works 48, tr. G. G. Krodel (Philadelphia: Fortress, 1963), pp. 187–88. On the reform tradition's relationship in general to Gratian, see below, f.n. 30.

[2] The *Decretum* has no legal status in the Roman Catholic Church today; it ceased to be authoritative with the promulgation of the 1917 Code, which has in turn been superseded by the 1983 Code. Gratian's text remains of great historical interest and often sheds light on the thinking behind modern canons (cf. P. Gasparri and J. Serédi, *Codicis Iuris Canonici Fontes*, 9 vols. (Rome: Typis Polyglottis Vaticanis, 1923–39), for the place of the *Decretum* among the sources of the 1917 Code; unfortunately no parallel work is available as yet for the 1983 Code). But it could not now be cited as "the law" in an ecclesiastical court.

[3] S. Kuttner, "The Father of the Science of Canon Law," *The Jurist* 1 (1941), 15.

from the first half of the twelfth century, drawing on the accumulated traditions of the Church from apostolic times. The commentary, the "Ordinary Gloss" (*Glossa Ordinaria*), which accompanies the main text, was written about three-quarters of a century later, and reflects both the growing legal sophistication and the ecclesiastical concerns of the intervening years. The excerpt translated here, Distinctions 1 through 20, constitutes a treatise on the nature of law and lays the foundation for the subsequent discussion of particular topics.

The medieval law student, lay jurist, or cleric would have approached the *Decretum*, if not with a conscious knowledge of its history, at least with a sense of its structure and its underlying preconceptions. Modern students must try to reconstruct that sense for themselves, as well as seek to understand the people and circumstances contributing to the shaping of the *Decretum* and its Gloss, and the significance of the text in the life of the medieval and early modern Church.

Gratian and His World

From its earliest days, the *Decretum* has been linked to the name of one Master Gratian, but of this individual, the father of the science of canon law, little can be said with certainty. Canonists' folklore, some of it recorded only centuries after Gratian's time, describes him as a (Camaldolese?) monk of the monastery of Saints Felix and Nabor in Bologna and a teacher in that city, medieval western Europe's greatest center for the study of law. Traditions of varying (and sometimes dubious) reliability called him a papal legate, a legal consultant, even a brother of the Parisian theologian Peter Lombard (he was not). Modern scholarship can confirm very little of this; contemporary records are almost entirely silent. (A scrap of evidence suggesting that Gratian ended his career as bishop of Chiusi remains a tantalizing riddle.)[4] Even the assertion of Gratian's monastic status raises questions. By the first half of the twelfth century, teaching law would have been considered rather generally to be a peculiar and unsuitable occupation for a monk, yet to some scholars, the strong emphasis on and detail concerning monastic affairs in the *Decretum* powerfully suggest a reflection of its author's concerns. Moreover, the tradition is very old, appearing before 1170.[5]

In the end, what may be said with reasonable security about the author of the *Decretum*? Gratian was a scholar and probably a teacher at Bologna, possibly a monk, and honored in his own time as *magister*. His work on the *Decretum* was most likely done in the second quarter of the twelfth century; the most recent materials incorporated into the text are canons of the second Lateran council of 1139, and they are only imperfectly integrated, as if a last-minute addition. The traditional date for the appearance of the earliest form of the *Decretum*, c. 1140, remains as good as any. As for Gratian himself, by the 1160s other canonists refer to him as already deceased.[6] Bologna is a city full of tombs of eminent jurists, but there is none for him, only the occasional commemorative tablet, including one erected through the filial piety of canon law historians in the mid-twentieth

---

[4] S. Kuttner, "Research on Gratian," *Proceedings of the Seventh International Congress of Medieval Canon Law, Cambridge*, ed. P. Linehan, Monumenta Iuris Canonici, Series C: Subsidia 7 (Vatican City: Biblioteca Apostolica Vaticana, 1988), pp. 8–9; J. Noonan, Jr., "Gratian Slept Here," *Traditio* 35 (1979), 145–79, explores the history of trying to determine what is actually knowable about Gratian.

[5] Cf. *Summa Parisiensis*, ed. T. P. McLaughlin (Toronto: PIMS, 1952), p. xvii.

[6] P. Landau, "Gratian (von Bologna)," *Theologische Realenzyklopaedie* 14:1/2, p. 124.

century.[7] Gratian's real monument is, and has always been, his "harmony of discordant canons," the *Decretum*.

Monastic or not, as a twelfth-century European churchman, Gratian lived in a world of energy and ferment, both practical and theoretical. The bright confluence of religious, political, social, economic, intellectual, and cultural developments that the American medievalist Charles Homer Haskins christened the "renaissance of the twelfth century" included several currents crucial to the nature and reception of Gratian's work. In religious matters, there was a strong emphasis on renewal and reform. The pastoral realm saw the reassertion of spiritual priorities that followed the gradual settlement of the eleventh-century conflict over lay investiture (which had itself seen renewed attention to the sources and organization of Church law); there was fresh energy and intensity in new monastic communities like the Cistercians. These reformers shared a concern and desire to return to and be guided by the good *mores* of the past. All this was taking place at a time when political developments in many parts of Europe were calling for clearer, more nuanced thinking about the relationship between spiritual and secular authority, about where, practically and precisely, one had to draw the line between what belonged to Caesar and what to God.

Of great importance among these developments was a renewed stress on law as an attribute and instrument of kingship, especially in the light of the revival of the study of Roman law. Around the year 1100, a man named Irnerius began lecturing in Bologna on the volumes of Roman legal sources, which had been compiled in the sixth century A.D. by order of the emperor Justinian and became known as the *Corpus Iuris Civilis*. Although the arrangement of these sources was disorderly and the sources themselves sometimes contradictory, study of the *Corpus Iuris Civilis* restored to western Europe the full heritage of Roman law and introduced medieval Europeans to a legal system more profound and lucid than any they had previously known. A great law school grew up in Bologna, attracting students from throughout Europe.[8] This development, in turn, was only one element in an intellectual milieu that encompassed the use of dialectical method and the rise of the universities, of which Bologna was among the earliest.[9]

It is important to recognize the significance and place of law, particularly ecclesiastical law, in the world of medieval European society. Law was more than a set of limits, prescriptions and penalties. It defined communities, and individuals' membership and specific places within them. In fact, one's relationship to law could be a positive element of one's status; the nobleman was subject to more legal obligations than was the villein, the male than the female, the cleric than the lay person. Ecclesiastical law had an especially charged character, at once numinous and, to anyone accustomed to modern conceptions about the role of the Church (indeed religion in general) in society, remarkably hard-edged. While "integrating human jurisprudence into the divine order of salvation,"[10]

---

[7] The text of which is printed in *Studia Gratiana* 1 (1953), xv–xvi.

[8] M. Bellomo, *L'Europa del diritto comune*, 5th ed. (Rome: Il Cigno Galileo Galilei, 1991), pp. 125–38, English translation: *The Common Law (Ius Commune) of Europe*, tr. L. Cochrane, Studies in Medieval and Early Modern Canon Law (Washington, D.C.: Catholic Univ. of America Press, [forthcoming]); K. Nörr, "Institutional Foundations of the New Jurisprudence," in *Renaissance and Renewal in the Twelfth Century*, ed. R. L. Benson and G. Constable (Cambridge, Mass.: Harvard Univ. Press, 1982), pp. 324–38; C. Donahue, "Law, Civil–*Corpus Iuris*, Revival and Spread," *Dictionary of the Middle Ages* 7 (1986), which includes an excellent bibliography.

[9] See S. Kuttner, "The Revival of Jurisprudence," in *Renaissance and Renewal in the Twelfth Century*, pp. 299–323.

[10] S. Kuttner, *Harmony from Dissonance*, Wimmer Lecture 10 (Latrobe, Penn.: Archabbey Press, 1960), p.

using the tools of the law to foster the salvation of souls, canon law also served to define and regulate the Church as a distinct and fully constituted (though humanly weak and flawed) society. The Church was not separate from secular social structures but also very clearly not just a part of, much less subordinate to them. The Church maintained a complete legal structure of its own, asserting full disciplinary powers over the clergy and extensive ones over the laity as well. Some of the most basic concerns of everyday life, almost everything having to do with marriage and wills, for example, fell, by common consensus, within the jurisdiction of the Church.

The Decretum: *Sources, Structure, and Method*

It was the accumulated law of the Church which Gratian set out to collect, organize, and rationalize, in a form which would facilitate its study and reference to it, in accordance with the most advanced scholarly techniques of his day. The past provided the materials of Gratian's *Decretum*; the present provided his intellectual tools and motivations and a society for which the work filled a need.

The body of material Gratian inherited ran from the Decalogue to the enactments of contemporary councils and included Scripture, the writings of the fathers, papal letters and decretals both genuine and spurious, and rulings of a millennium's worth of councils and synods large and small, all over the Christian world. Nonetheless, the modern reader must not imagine Gratian as a twelfth-century version of a jurist with a decent research library at his disposal, with (more or less) complete texts in scholarly editions of patristic writings, papal letters, sets of conciliar canons, etc., as well as a mass of learned commentary on the interpretation of Scripture and on earlier periods of Church history, to help him see his materials in context. Scholars can only speculate on the precise contents of Gratian's bookshelves, but every student of medieval thought must take into account that an author's knowledge of any given text might well come, not from having the whole work in front of him, but from a *florilegium*, an anthology. (One exception is Scripture, which at any point the author might be citing from memory and with less-than-perfect accuracy.)

Canon law material particularly presents difficulties of this nature, for much of it circulated in the form of collections. Some of these derived from earlier collections (more than one, in some instances), some combined genuine texts with new concoctions given venerable attributions. All of them were made in specific circumstances to meet specific needs, by people who felt perfectly free to edit as they did so, and more often than not, probably could not have checked their sources if they had wanted to.

Canonical collection building and adaptation in the earlier Middle Ages seems to have flourished in situations both of growth and consolidation and of uncertainty and conflict. The most hopeful days of Charlemagne's efforts to shape a Christian empire had seen intense interest in canonical sources and the formation of the collection called the *Dacheriana*, which blended texts sent from Rome (the *Collectio Dionysio-Hadriana*) with Frankish canonists' resources, while tense, bitter episcopal quarrels under later Carolingians in the mid-ninth century provoked a flurry of treatises and collections, including the legendary *Pseudo-Isidorian Decretals*. Legislation emanating from Rome mingled with local statutes and customs in messy eclecticism and evident inconsistency, with the occasional

45; reprinted in *The History of Ideas and Doctrines in the Middle Ages* (London: Variorum, 1980), p. 13.

scholar or tidy-minded bishop trying to make a coherent synthesis.[11] The Investiture Controversy set adherents of both sides to poring over the inherited tradition in search of justification of their own positions, ammunition against those of their opponents, and, at last, common ground upon which an honorable peace might be made. Initial attempts by the victorious papalists to prune the tradition back to old, Roman-derived material were soon wisely abandoned in recognition that the passage of time had seen changes in the Church's structures and needs which newer, local enactments effectively addressed. Diversity remained, but so did a dissatisfaction at its disorder.[12]

Precisely what of all this inherited material Gratian himself was actually using has been the subject of considerable, if not entirely conclusive, study. In general, the scholarly consensus seems to be that Gratian worked from a fairly small body of sources, relatively recent collections that one would reasonably expect to be available to a canonist working in north-central Italy in the 1120s to the 1140s: Anselm of Lucca, the *Panormia* of Ivo of Chartres, the *Tripartita*, the *Polycarpus*, the *Collection in Three Books*, Alger of Liège's *Liber de Misericordia et Iustitia*, plus some form of Isidore of Seville's *Etymologies*. (The dating of some of these collections reinforces the conviction that Gratian was working in the second quarter of the twelfth century.) Whether he used Pseudo-Isidore directly or through an intermediary remains an open question.[13] One can easily imagine how very recent material might have found its way into his hands; medieval bishops commonly brought home copies of canons they had agreed to at councils and synods, sometimes under specific orders from the presiding metropolitan or pope to have them copied and distributed (cf. D. 12 c. 17 in the text).

Gratian's materials were thus in no sense exceptional. The genius of the *Decretum* lay in how he selected, organized, and analyzed them. Certain tendencies of selection have been noted by specialists: Gratian used a good deal of Pseudo-Isidorian material, especially for procedural matters, and his authentic papal letters are mostly early (Leo I, Gelasius I, Gregory the Great, Nicholas I), with comparatively little from the Gregorian Reform tradition. (He does, however, cite almost all of the patristic authorities and texts that the Gregorian reformers used.)[14] He parts company from earlier collections in his extensive use of western patristic texts, particularly from Augustine of Hippo; such material makes up about a third of the *Decretum*.[15] Among the councils, canons from Iberian, Italian, and Frankish regional gatherings appear alongside those of the great ecumenical councils of the imperial Church.

The *Decretum* exists today in much the same form it had by the late twelfth century. Its 3800 individual texts, or *capitula* (sing. *capitulum*) are arranged in a rather complicated structure. (In this, too, Gratian goes his own way; a straightforward division by subject matter was more usual among earlier collections, when there was any evident organizing

---

[11] R. E. Reynolds, "Law, Canon, to Gratian," *Dictionary of the Middle Ages* 7 (1986) is the best account in English of the pre-Gratian collections; see also G. Fransen, *Les Collections canoniques*, Typologie des sources du moyen âge occidental 10 (Turnhout: Brepols, 1973/1985).

[12] On the Investiture Controversy, see B. Tierney, *The Crisis of Church and State, 1050–1300* (Englewood Cliffs, N.J.: Prentice-Hall, 1964), pp. 33–95, 116–26 provides a convenient summary and the key texts; now see also U.-R. Blumenthal, *The Investiture Controversy* (Philadelphia: Univ. of Penn. Press, 1988).

[13] P. Landau, "Gratian," pp. 124–30, concisely summarizes current thinking on much of this.

[14] Cf. Tierney, *Crisis of Church and State*, pp. 57–84.

[15] C. Munier, *Les Sources patristiques du droit de l'Église*, Univ. of Strasbourg dissertation, 1954 (Mulhouse, Switz.: Salvator, 1957).

principle at all.) The first section (of which the text translated here is the opening part) consists of 101 distinctions, sets of capitula grouped around a particular point. The first twenty deal with the nature of law and authority; the rest take up other general points about Church discipline and orders. The second section is made up of thirty-six fictional cases or *causae* (sing. *causa*), designed to pose an interlocking set of questions about a given legal situation. Some are elaborate to the point of striking the modern reader as far-fetched, a sort of ultimate story problem, but every twist and turn proves significant as each question is dealt with in a series of capitula. In Causa 33, the third question is abruptly handled in a different manner, in a series of seven distinctions known collectively as *De Poenitentia* (on penance). The third section of the *Decretum*, which follows Causa 36, is known simply as *De Consecratione* (on consecration) and consists of five distinctions dealing with sacraments and worship. It should also be noted that scattered among the capitula are about two hundred texts drawn from Roman law sources, and almost one hundred and fifty texts labeled "palea"; the term itself is mysterious (literally, it means "chaff," and even medieval canonists seem to have been perplexed about it), yet the texts themselves are of the same sorts found in the capitula.

Over decades of careful study of the *Decretum*, however, scholars have become convinced that the text as we have it is not the text as Gratian himself put it together. There is no "original," no autograph copy, no *Ur-text*, but a combination of internal evidence and comparison of a number of early manuscripts suggests several points at which Gratian's plan was altered. It seems likely that the division of part I into distinctions was not Gratian's doing; he referred to that section, in another part of the text, as "tracta-tes."[16] The division of part II into causae is original, as are the explanatory rubrics, the headings which proceed each capitulum. (The latter are clearly part of the line of argument.) But *De Poenitentia* and *De Consecratione* (i.e. part III), the Roman law texts that are taken from earlier canonical sources, and the paleae are all apparently later additions, although they were added very early in the *Decretum*'s history.[17] In the case of the Roman law texts, the implication is that Gratian intended to present a canon law completely independent of secular sources, however important or venerable; in the paleae one can see a collection of texts Gratian might have used, but chose not to, only to have his successors decide they were worth citing after all. Scholars have suggested that these additions were intended either to introduce modifications or to fill in gaps, as the book was used in actual teaching.[18] To summarize, the *Decretum* as it left Gratian's hands consisted of the texts found in the distinctions (divided somehow differently) and the causae, without the Roman law texts or the paleae these now contain. The rest is the work of others.

Grounded as Gratian was within a tradition, it is in the realm of method, and specifically method on a remarkably large scale, that his accomplishment shines. The *Decretum* is a collection of sources, and as such, one among many, but it was also intended as a textbook and a teaching program, designed to set forth (and make comprehen-

---

[16] The arrangement into distinctions may be the work of Paucapalea, one of Gratian's students; cf. Landau, "Gratian," p. 126.

[17] *De Poenitentia* is distinctively theological according to Karol Wojtyła (John Paul II), "Le Traité 'De Poenitentia' de Gratien dans l'abrégé de Gdansk Mar. F. 275," *Studia Gratiana* 7 (1959), 355–90 at 389; Landau, "Gratian," p. 125, observes that *De Consecratione* lacks Gratian's usual "textbook-like commentary."

[18] Cf. K. Pennington, "Gratian," *Dictionary of the Middle Ages* 5 (1986), p. 657.

sible) an internally consistent system of law. This required not only organization, but analysis, and analysis that could come to terms with the serious problem of disagreement among the sources. The centrality of this problem in Gratian's thinking is manifest in the title he gave his work: *Concordia Discordantium Canonum*, the harmony of discordant canons. That title gives the key to Gratian's approach.

In the modern western world, intellectual elites thrive on controversy, and challenge to authority of any kind is more likely to be praised than criticized. Medieval scholars loved an argument, too, but their fundamental attitude toward authority, whether of individuals, institutions, or traditions, was one of respect. Confident of their own skills and powers, they were also conscious of belonging to a community that reached across time as well as territory; they knew the value of their heritage and were appreciative of the holiness and learning of their spiritual and intellectual ancestors. So for them, disagreement among their authorities was a matter of genuine concern. Not all of these authorities were considered to be of equal weight, of course, and in his treatise on law Gratian discussed how canonists could determine an order of precedence among them (cf. D. 9 c. 6). But such guidelines alone were not always enough to deal with discrepancy or a flat contradiction.

This concern was not confined to the field of canon law. A major task the professors of Roman law at Bologna set for themselves was to reconcile every text of the *Corpus Iuris Civilis* with every other. They were only partially successful. Yet their task was easier than that of Gratian and his successors in canon law. Whatever their contradictions, the Roman law texts were the product of one legal culture and were edited and arranged, however imperfectly, in a single collection. Gratian's texts came from far more diverse sources: the Bible, centuries of Church councils, the letters, sermons, and treatises of the fathers, papal decretals, even penitential manuals.[19] Moreover, for their society, the stakes were higher—spiritual and eternal.

By the time Gratian was writing the *Decretum*, the problem of discordant texts had already produced a measure of havoc in theology, exemplified by the firestorm that resulted when Peter Abelard had lined up contradictory authorities on various theological questions in *Sic et Non*, and with cheerful insouciance (his enemies would have said culpable recklessness) invited his readers to employ the newly popular logical tools of dialectic to reason through the tangle to their own conclusions. Abelard had not been entirely reckless; his prologue to *Sic et Non* is full of sensible comments about textual corruption, difficulties attached to unusual forms of language, the possibilities of error, a change of mind, even tentativeness of opinion in an author, and the ultimate authority of Scripture.[20] Gratian would (and possibly did) agree with every word. Yet the open-ended format was considered dangerous, and Gratian did not use it.

What he did do was present his sources, one by one, and when discrepancy or contradiction appeared, he inserted his own commentary, in sections referred to as *dicta* (literally "sayings," in this translation printed in italics), in which he suggested how the authorities might be reconciled, or how one was to be held preferable to others: how, ultimately,

---

[19] One must remember, however, that some texts would have come to Gratian only embedded in other collections, not in their original contexts.

[20] Peter Abelard, *Sic et Non*, ed. B. Bayer and R. McKeon (Chicago: Univ. of Chicago Press, 1976); for a translation of the pertinent passages, see B. Tierney, *The Sources of Medieval History*, 5th ed. (New York: McGraw-Hill, 1992), pp. 178–81.

the discord could be resolved. The addition of these dicta was a true novelty and set Gratian's collection apart from most other canonical collections before and after. The final stage of the dialectical process was left not to the students' wits but to the *magister*'s experience and wisdom. Some of the principles were obvious enough. General councils outranked their regional counterparts; popes outranked bishops, even great and saintly ones like Augustine, and so on. An opinion on some specific and limited matter, from however eminent a source, might not deserve the status of a general rule, needing to be applied in all or in greatly different circumstances. Above all, pride of place went to the Scriptures, the inspired word of God, the touchstone of everything else. (In fact, Gratian cited Scripture primarily in the dicta, in making judgments about other sources.)[21] But beyond obvious rules were points of judgment, as in the dicta following D. 12 c. 11, where Gratian suggested that outdated customs were better abrogated. In the text he was introducing, c. 12, Augustine advised that when a custom was not sanctioned by Scripture or the authority of the universal Church it could be changed, not only if it were onerous, but also when habits varied as to time and place. Gratian's view has even broader implications as an approach to the question of change in human communities.

Gratian was not the first to seek to reconcile discrepancies and conflicts among canonical sources. Ivo of Chartres, in the wise and learned prologue to his canonical collections (written about 1095), had sought to lay out principles of jurisprudence which would address the problem.[22] Bernold of Constance had been moving in a similar direction in *De Excommunicatis Vitandis*, and Alger of Liège had demonstrated the possibilities of harmonization on a small scale in *De Misericordia et Iustitia*. Gratian's *Decretum* represented the next step forward, a comprehensive effort to standardize the canon law beyond what had previously been attempted.[23]

The importance of the achievement was soon recognized. The papal chancery assumed knowledge of the *Decretum* among its correspondents within a few years of the work's appearance. Summaries and abbreviations of the text began to appear almost as quickly. Without any formal "reception," or any official adoption by the Holy See, Gratian's *Decretum* became the standard textbook in the field and the first part of what canonists came to know, along with the collections of subsequent papal decretal legislation in the *Liber Extra*, the *Liber Sextus*, the *Extravagantes*, and the *Clementinae*, as the *Corpus Iuris Canonici*.[24] Manuscripts of the *Decretum* may be traced to copyists all over western Europe, and while Gratian's book never entirely displaced such predecessors as Ivo of Chartres's *Panormia*, it did come to dominate the discipline, and the few would-be

---

[21] Landau, "Gratian," p. 126.

[22] On Ivo of Chartres, see P. Fournier and G. Le Bras, *Histoire des collections canoniques en occident depuis les Fausses Décrétales jusqu'au Décret de Gratien* (Paris: Sirey, 1931–32), II, 55–114; but cf. M. Brett, "Urban II and Collections Attributed to Ivo of Chartres," in *Proceedings of the Eighth International Congress of Medieval Canon Law, San Diego*, ed. S. Chodorow, Monumenta Iuris Canonici, Series C: Subsidia 9 (Vatican City: Biblioteca Apostolica Vaticana, 1992), pp. 27–46.

[23] Landau, "Gratian," p. 127; on the earlier collections, cf. Reynolds, "Law, Canon," pp. 407–12.

[24] The "customary status" of the *Decretum* was ratified by Gregory XIII with the publication of the Roman edition of 1582; cf. text of prefatory letter below, p. 2. On the place and authority of Gratian in medieval canonical thinking, S. Kuttner, "Quelques observations sur l'autorité des collections canoniques dans le droit classique de l'Église," *Actes du Congrès de droit canonique (Paris 22–26 Avril 1947)* (Paris: Letouzey et Ané, 1950), pp. 305–12.

competitors who emerged more often sought to improve on the *Decretum*'s arrangement than to produce anything genuinely new.[25]

The Decretum *and the* Glossa Ordinaria

Medieval scholars' reverence for authority did not entail reluctance to tinker with, add to, comment upon, or criticize others' work. The changes made to Gratian's original plan for the *Decretum*, changes that begin to appear within the first decade of its existence, have already been described. The text also began to attract marginal comments by other scholars, which were copied from manuscript to manuscript. In time, the accumulated material was organized into a running commentary, more like a series of footnotes than a continuous text, which was conventionally copied around the edges of the manuscript page while the text of the *Decretum* occupied the center block.

A commentary of this type is known as a Gloss. (Confusingly enough, so are the individual comments in it; for clarity, the Gloss as a whole text will be referred to with a capital initial, the gloss as an individual comment all in lower case.) When the text of the Gloss for a particular text had become standardized, as was the case not only for the *Decretum* but also for the corpus of Roman law and the Bible, the gloss was referred to as the "Ordinary Gloss" (*Glossa Ordinaria*). The comments of many scholars went into such a Gloss; sometimes the names of the commentators (also referred to as glossators) were preserved, sometimes not. Comments were frequently signed just with initials, some of which scholars are still uncertain about how to interpret (see Translators' Preface and Jurists in the Gloss). But the names of those who did the organizing of the Ordinary Gloss on the *Decretum* are known; the initial compilation was done around 1215–18, by the jurist Johannes Teutonicus, a canon regular of Halberstadt. Approximately 90 percent of the glosses were his work, although many glosses by others were added later. His work was then lightly revised by the legal scholar Bartholomaeus Brixiensis around 1245. Bartholomaeus added references to the Gregorian Decretals (the *Liber Extra*), short passages, and comments but left Johannes's words intact. Other additions were made to the text in the fourteenth century.[26] It was this version which was most often copied, and eventually came to be printed, with minor modifications, in the Roman edition, from which it is translated here.[27]

As befits a series of notes, the Ordinary Gloss is varied and uneven in texture. Some notes provide context for a fact or argument cited in the text. Some define terms or make distinctions. Many provide cross references to related passages in the rest of the *Decretum*, the *Liber Extra*, or *Corpus Iuris Civilis*. Contributors to the Gloss did not hesitate to criticize Gratian himself, to correct his definitions, or even challenge his arguments (cf.

---

[25] An impressive example is the *Compilatio Decretorum* of Cardinal Laborans. The fate of this late twelfth-century work is fairly typical; it never achieved wide circulation and survives in only a handful of manuscripts. Cf. N. Martin, "Die 'Compilatio decretorum' des Kardinals Laborans," *Proceedings of the Sixth International Congress of Medieval Canon Law, Berkeley*, ed. S. Kuttner and K. Pennington, Monumenta Iuris Canonici, Series C: Subsidia 7 (Vatican City: Biblioteca Apostolica Vaticana, 1985), pp. 125–37.

[26] On the composition of the Gloss and its authorship, see the "Prolegomena" to Johannes Teutonicus, *Apparatus Glossarum in Compilationem Tertiam*, ed. K. Pennington, Monumenta Iuris Canonici, Series A: Corpus Glossatorum 3 (Vatican City: Biblioteca Apostolica Vaticana, 1981), especially p. xi.

[27] K. Pennington, "Johannes Teutonicus," *Dictionary of the Middle Ages* 7 (1986); W. Stelzer, "Johannes Teutonicus," *Die deutsche Literatur des Mittelalters Verfasserlexikon* 4 (1982).

gloss g to "long-continued" in D. 1 c. 4, and gloss f to "no dispensation" in *dicta Gratiani ante* D. 13 c. 1). Some argue with earlier commentators.

Certain comments reflect concerns of scholars in the increasingly sophisticated legal world of the late twelfth and early thirteenth centuries, such as how or whether one could use partially tainted testimony (gloss b to "they" in D. 9 c. 7), how to spot a forged document (gloss c to "false" in D. 19 c. 3), or what to make of the example of a revered historical figure (in this case the emperor Justinian) who made, from the canonists' perspective, some shockingly bad rulings (gloss d to "human ordinance" in D. 10 c. 1). In a world of strong, self-confident, and legislatively ambitious monarchs like Henry II of England and the emperor Frederick II, the whole question of the division of jurisdiction between secular and ecclesiastical law was both timely and pointed (gloss e to "bow" in D. 10 c. 3 and glosses j to "divided" and a to "activities" in D. 10 c. 8). And for canonists confronted with the torrent of decretal legislation coming from the papal curia, with the occasional letter having to reverse a previous one because of error or false information, it was only fitting for commentators to observe the fallibility of prelates and official records (gloss e to "rule in" in D. 18 c. 7). In the Ordinary Gloss, study and discussion are reduced to writing, as several generations of canonists worked with Gratian's text, not just as an intellectual exercise, but as a real-world system of law.

The *Decretum* was copied and recopied. Some manuscripts contained the text of Gratian alone, sometimes with large margins left for annotations by students and scholars. In some manuscripts glosses in various hands accumulated in the margins over time, while other manuscripts were copied complete with an apparatus, usually that of Johannes Teutonicus. Manuscripts of the *Decretum* came to follow the standard form for a glossed text: the text of Gratian in the center of the page, usually in double columns, and the apparatus in smaller letters filling the four margins. This layout was imitated by the first printed editions in the fifteenth century.

The Decretum *in Print*

As a standard textbook for the teaching of canon law, the *Decretum* was an obvious early candidate for printing. Legends about it being the next book that Gutenberg printed after the Bible notwithstanding, the first known printed *Decretum* came off a press in Strasbourg, in 1471.[28] For over a century, the text was not standardized; printers worked from versions they had available. Many editions appeared over the next thirty years, sometimes of the *Decretum* alone, sometimes in conjunction with the *Liber Extra* of Gregory IX. The version prepared by Jean Chappuis at Paris in 1501, unremarkable in itself, was significant as part of the first unified edition containing the *Decretum*, the *Liber Extra* (1504), and the *Sextus-Clementinae* (1500). (Chappuis revised the *Sextus* volume in 1507 to include the *Extravagantes Iohannis XXII* and a selection of important later papal legislation, the *Extravagantes Communes*.) Chappuis' edition, although never officially sanctioned, become the model for all subsequent editions of the canon law and was the first to be called, by Pope Gregory XIII, the *Corpus Iuris Canonici*.[29]

---

[28] On this edition, see E. Will, "Decreti Gratiani Incunabula," *Studia Gratiana* 6 (1959), 116. This catalogue lists and describes the various editions of Gratian up to 1500.

[29] On Chappuis' edition, see A. Adversi, "Saggio di un catalogo delle edizioni del 'Decretum Gratiani' posteriori al secolo XV," *Studia Gratiana* 6 (1959), 281–451 at 290–91. This catalogue also lists and describes the other editions of Gratian up to this century.

Renaissance scholarship and reforming zeal began to focus on the *Decretum* only after the conclusion of the Council of Trent. The canon law, particularly the decretals but the *Decretum* as well, had been attacked by Luther, although some of the other reformers, notably Melanchthon, were more positive, especially about the old law which the *Decretum* represented. (In fact, some of the earliest scholarly work on the text and glosses of the *Decretum* was that of a Calvinist, Charles Dumoulin.)[30] Catholic reformers reasserted the value of Gratian's work, but recognized the need for a careful reediting process, both to eliminate errors and textual corruptions and to provide a uniform and authoritative text.

In 1578, Pope Gregory XIII formally appointed a small commission of learned cardinals and other clerics, generally referred to as the *Correctores Romani*, to set about the task of editing the *Decretum*. From the early 1570s at least, scholars working under papal auspices had been preparing the way. They had gone through the Vatican's manuscripts, then sent letters out across Catholic Europe, asking for the loan of, or copies of, manuscripts of Gratian and earlier canonical collections, seeking to collect the best examples local churches could provide. Responses came from curia cardinals, from remote Spanish monasteries, from beleaguered prelates in the Low Countries. The *Correctores* worked their way through the text of the *Decretum*, collating the manuscripts, comparing and discussing variant readings they encountered, and keeping copious notes as they chose the readings they thought most accurate for the new edition. That Roman edition, published in 1582 with Gregory XIII's letter of authorization as its preface, became the standard text within the Catholic world.[31]

The first modern attempts to establish a critical edition of Gratian began in Germany in the mid-eighteenth century and were the work of Lutheran scholars. The first and most important of these editions was that of Just Henning Böhmer, published at Halle in 1747. Böhmer was probably the greatest historical canonist of his time. In his edition he collated the earlier printed editions, including the Roman edition, with four manuscripts of Gratian in Germany that had not been used by the *Correctores*. The next major step toward a modern critical edition was a critical study of the materials used by Gratian, published in 1783 by Carlo Sebastiano Berardi.[32] Half a century later, another distinguished German canonist, Emil Richter, revised Böhmer's work in the light of developments in scholarship. His edition, published at Leipzig in 1833, received extensive exposure as it was reprinted in Jean-Paul Migne's *Patrologia Latina*, volume 187, in 1855.[33]

The most available modern, "working" edition of the *Decretum* is that of Emil Friedberg, published at Leipzig in 1879. For all its elaborate apparatus (massive prefatory

---

[30] Cf. A. Pincherle, "Graziano e Lutero," *Studia Gratiana* 3 (1955), 451–82; J. Heckel, "Das Decretum Gratiani und das evangelische Kirchenrecht," *Studia Gratiana* 3 (1955), 483–538; M. Reulos, "Le Décret de Gratien chez les humanistes, les gallicans, et les réformés français du XVI siècle," *Studia Gratiana* 2 (1954), 677–96, at 682 (for Dumoulin).

[31] On the *Correctores Romani*, see the official guidelines governing their work reprinted in Friedberg's edition, pp. lxxxi–lxxxvii; the correspondence printed in A. Theiner, *Disquistitiones Criticae in Praecipuas Canonum et Decretalium Collectiones* (Rome: Urbanum, 1836), appendix, 11–37; K. Schellhass, "Wissenschaftliche Forschungen unter Gregor XIII für die Neuausgabe des gratianischen Dekrets," *Papsttum und Kaisertum*, Festschrift Paul Kehr (Munich: Brackmann, 1926), pp. 674–90; S. Kuttner, "Some Roman Manuscripts of Canonical Collections," *Bulletin of Medieval Canon Law* 1 (1971), 7–29. The rough notes and correspondence of the commission, as well as the clean MS copy of its findings, are still in the Vatican Library: Vat. lat. 4889, 4891, 4892, 4913, 5399.

[32] C. S. Berardi, *Gratiani Canones Genuini ab Apocryphiis Discreti*, 4 vols. (Venice, 1783).

[33] On these editions, see Adversi, "Saggio di un catologo," pp. 384–94.

materials, two sets of notes, including those of the *Correctores Romani*, and an eyestrain-inducing record of variant readings), Friedberg's text is not a critical edition, and is, in fact, unsatisfactory in many ways. It was based on a small and not particularly representative set of manuscripts. The editor's attempt at completeness in reconstructing the text and in tracing the appearance of sources in earlier collections not only obscures any sense of what Gratian himself actually used and wrote, but also presents a hybrid version of the *Decretum* no medieval commentator or working canonist had ever seen.[34] All such criticisms aside, the Friedberg edition was a considerable accomplishment, and it still serves the needs of many scholars who are interested in the history and development of canon law.

The difficulties involved in producing a critical edition of the *Decretum* are massive, given the layers of development in the text and the sheer number of surviving manuscripts. Computer technology may help surmount some technical obstacles, and the understanding of the manuscript tradition gained in recent decades would make the choice of manuscript witnesses easier, but the task would remain formidable, even for a new team of *Correctores*. Meanwhile, the Roman edition, while not without faults, and also not "critical" by modern standards, remains the edition of choice for serious work on the *Decretum*, and is the basis for the present translation.

How to Read Gratian and the Gloss

The text of this translation of Distinctions 1-20 with the Ordinary Gloss is set up the way medieval manuscripts and early printed copies of the *Decretum* were: Gratian's text appears in the center of the page, with the Gloss arranged around it, in smaller print. Small superscript letters are placed in Gratian's text at each point for which the Gloss contains commentary, which is identified by the same key letter. Superscript numbers refer to the modern notes. (The modern notes appear at the end of the text, for practical reasons. Early printers managed to fit the notes of the *Correctores Romani* in between the individual capitula or on the outer margins of the page.) What medieval scribes accomplished with pen and ink, and early modern printers did by laborious hand typesetting, is now made feasible by computer typesetting and page layout.

This arrangement makes it possible for the modern reader to approach the text as a medieval reader would have done, moving from text to gloss and back to text without flipping pages or juggling two volumes. The Ordinary Gloss is not a freestanding commentary meant to be read on its own; it is a running commentary much like footnotes, meant to be read with the text. Indeed, sometimes it makes very little sense if read in isolation.

In a medieval classroom, the professor of canon law would have read the text aloud, with the appropriate section of gloss, and then explained both, adding his own comments, which students sometimes made a point of writing down.[35] One major hurdle for the

---

[34] T. Lenherr, "Arbeiten mit Gratians Dekret," *Archiv für katholisches Kirchenrecht* 151 (1982), 140–66, demonstrates the limitations of the Friedberg edition. The need for, and difficulties in the way of, a new, critical edition were long ago recognized by S. Kuttner, "De Gratiani Opere Noviter Edendo," *Apollinaris* 21 (1948), 118–28.

[35] On the classroom techniques used in teaching law during the Middle Ages, see M. Bellomo, *L'Europa del diritto comune*, pp. 139–61; or, more generally, J. Baldwin, *The Scholastic Culture of the Middle Ages* (Lexington, Mass.: Heath, 1971).

modern reader is ignorance of the content of the ubiquitous citations in the Gloss to other parts of the *Decretum*, the *Liber Extra*, and the *Corpus Iuris Civilis*. A medieval professor would have looked them up before class if he needed to, just as Professor Gordley did to write his notes on the Gloss. But an experienced lecturer would have had many of them committed to memory. Medieval law students gradually acquired the same facility in the course of their studies, remembering, for example, *Duo sunt quippe* (D. 96 c. 10) as the famous letter of Pope Gelasius I to the emperor Anastasius explaining the relationship between the temporal and spiritual powers, just as modern law students in the United States learn to cite *Brown v. Board of Education* as forbidding school segregation by race, or *Miranda v. Arizona* as establishing certain rights for individuals being arrested. After all, as the modern reader must always remember, this material was not the subject of a merely academic exercise, but the living law of the Christian community of western Europe.

Outline of the Treatise

The summary that follows, more or less in lieu of an index to the contents of the treatise, does not pretend to be exhaustive. Moreover, some of the particular themes discussed, as examples of the methods used by Gratian and the glossators, reflect modern interests as much as medieval ones. Documentation in this section has been kept to a minimum since this material is provided in the backnotes to the treatise and the Gloss.[36]

Distinctions 1–20, the *Treatise on Laws* which opens the *Decretum*, moves from the most general categorizations about law to fairly specific discussion about the underlying premises of law within the Church.

D. 1. Distinction 1, which describes certain basic types of law, introduces some critically important differentiations around which the *Treatise on Laws* is organized. It distinguishes between divine and human law, and among natural law, ordinance or enactment, and usage or custom. Gratian does not explain these concepts by carefully formulated definitions but by showing the reader what others have said that they mean. The series of disorderly and seemingly conflicting ideas he presents are drawn from the seventh-century encyclopedist Isidore of Seville, who took them in turn from heterogeneous sources, including perhaps the *Corpus Iuris Civilis* of Justinian.

There are many apparent discrepancies. Throughout the *Decretum*, "natural law," which is anterior to human law, is contrasted to "ordinance," meaning "written enactment," (c. 3) and to "custom," which is "a sort of law established by usages and recognized as ordinance when ordinance is lacking" (c. 5). "Ordinance" and "usage" are sometimes used more vaguely. For example, in the opening passage of the *Decretum*, a human law consisting of "usages" is contrasted with a natural law contained in "the Law of Moses and the Gospel." In capitulum 1, "divine ordinances . . . determined by nature" are contrasted with "human ordinances" determined by "usages." Throughout the *Decretum*, natural law often seems to be identified with divine law. Yet in capitulum 7, natural law

[36] On the *Treatise on Laws*, see S. Chodorow, *Christian Political Theory and Church Politics in the Mid-Twelfth Century* (Berkeley, Univ. of Calif. Press, 1972), especially chapter 4; but cf. the review of this book by R. Benson in *Speculum* 50 (1975), 97–106.

is said to be based on "natural instinct."[37] In c. 9, this law is distinguished from a "law of nations," which is "used by almost all nations," and governs war, treaties, ambassadors, and the like.

Much of medieval legal theorizing begins with attempts to make sense of such discrepancies. One can see the process underway in the Ordinary Gloss. To avoid identifying natural law and divine law, a gloss to the opening passage "clarifies" the meaning of the word "natural" with the gloss: "that is, divine." To avoid equating natural law with "natural instinct," the gloss to "natural law" in capitulum 7 explains that the phrase may have other meanings as well. It may mean not only a "stimulus or instinct of nature proceeding from physical desire," but an "instinct from nature proceeding from reason" or a "natural precept," such as "do not kill."

DD. 2–4. Distinctions 2 through 4 describe ordinances. Distinction 2 describes the kinds of secular ordinances traditionally recognized by Roman civil law: ordinances, plebiscites, senate resolutions, enactments, the opinions of jurists, tribunitial and consular acts, satiric acts, and the Rhodian laws.[38] Distinction 3 describes different types of ecclesiastical ordinances: canons, the decrees of pontiffs, the statutes of councils, and privileges. The last part of Distinction 3 with Distinction 4 concludes the discussion of ordinances by describing the purpose of an ordinance, the qualities it should have, and some of the conditions necessary for it to be binding. Among these conditions, Gratian recognizes, as do modern lawyers, that an ordinance must be promulgated by competent authority to come into force, and that it may lose its force if people cease to obey it (*dicta Gratiani* §2 *ante* D. 4 c. 4).[39] Unlike modern lawyers, he suggests that, to be binding, an ordinance must be not only promulgated but also "confirmed," i.e. "approved by the usage of those who observe" it (*dicta Gratiani* §1 *ante* D. 4 c. 4). In effect, the community must accept the law; it is not enough for the authorities to impose it, however legitimately.[40]

DD. 5–7. In Distinction 5, as Gratian himself notes, he returns to the topic of natural law. Having identified the natural law with divine command, he asks how the natural law can be immutable, since some divine commands, such as those governing ritual pollution in the Old Testament, are no longer to be observed. Since ritual pollution could be incurred involuntarily, this topic also allows Gratian to discuss a broader question which he continues to examine in Distinction 6: whether an action to which one does not consent can be a sin. He concludes it cannot be, but recognizes that there may be varying degrees of moral responsibility for a sin, and he considers what constitutes consent. Moreover, Gratian's attention to inner meanings, intent, and volition is reflected in his answer to the

---

[37] Cf. Chodorow, *Political Theory*, pp. 98–102, for further discussion of this question.

[38] These legal forms would have been archaic even in Justinian's time, but they appear in the Digest (Dig. 1. 2–3) and were familiar to medieval law students. See B. Nicholas, *An Introduction to Roman Law* (Oxford: Oxford Univ. Press, 1962), pp. 14–45.

[39] Thus there is a longstanding argument among American lawyers as to whether a criminal statute can lose its force if the state fails to prosecute under it for a sufficiently long time. On this, see A. Bickel, *The Least Dangerous Branch* (Indianapolis: Bobbs-Merrill, 1962), pp. 143–54; L. Rogers and W. Rogers, "Desuetude as a Defense," *Iowa Law Review* 52 (1966), 1–30.

[40] On consent to legislation, see B. Tierney, " 'Only Truth Has Authority,' " in *Law, Church, and Society*, ed. K. Pennington and R. Somerville (Philadelphia: Univ. of Penn. Press, 1977), pp. 69–96. See also Chodorow, *Political Theory*, pp. 135–37.

original question about the immutability of natural law. Moral law in itself does not change; expressed in straightforward form such as the Decalogue, it lays down unalterable rules for human behavior. But divine commands are also conveyed in *mystica*, in precepts governing ritual or symbolic actions which express and embody deeper meanings. The outer forms of these *mystica*—such as the specific rules about ritual purity—can and do change, while their underlying significance, as part of the natural law, does not.[41]

In Distinctions 5 through 7, while considering these points, Gratian also presents an historical account of when and how different types of law came into being. In part 1 of Distinction 5, he explains that natural law "began with the appearance of rational creatures." At the end of *dicta Gratiani* §2 *post* D. 6 c. 3, he observes that "customary law began after natural law, when people began to gather as one and live together, possibly at the time when Cain built a city," and that it was almost extinguished at the time of the Flood, but restored at the time of Nimrod. In Distinction 7, he turns to ordinances, describing how they were enacted by Moses, by the rulers of other peoples such as the Egyptians, Athenians, and Lacedaemonians, and finally by the Romans. In part 2 he explains that as "old ordinances became . . . obsolete from age and lack of pertinence" they were replaced by new ones.

DD. 8–9. In Distinctions 8 and 9, Gratian both concludes his discussion of natural law and begins a theme that he will develop until the end of the *Treatise on Laws*: when laws conflict, which of them should prevail?[42] In Distinction 8, he demonstrates that natural law has precedence over custom. Distinction 9, part 1, establishes that natural law should also prevail over the ordinances of princes. In part 2 of Distinction 9, again identifying natural law with divine command, Gratian shows that Scripture has greater authority than the opinions of bishops, scholars, and saints. He is beginning, in this section, to set out a hierarchy of authorities, a topic to which he returns in greater and more systematic detail in Distinction 20.

At the beginning of this discussion of the authority of natural law in Distinction 8, he touches on another problem, the justification of private property, to which he returns elsewhere in the *Decretum* (e.g. D. 47 c. 8; C. 12 q. 1 c. 2). Earlier, natural law was said to entail the "common possession of all things" (D. 1 c. 7), a practice found among the Apostles and recommended by Plato.[43] By customary and enacted law, however, "one thing is called 'mine' and something else 'another's' " (Part 1 of D. 8). Although Gratian does not resolve the problem, for the remainder of the Middle Ages his texts were the starting point for discussion of private property by jurists, theologians, and philosophers.[44]

DD. 10–12. Gratian confronts the potential for conflict between ecclesiastical and secular law in Distinction 10. Ecclesiastical ordinances have greater authority than those of emperors or kings, he insists, although he maintains (in part 2) that secular authorities are to be obeyed within their own sphere. In Distinction 11, he shows that ordinances

---

[41] Cf. Chodorow, *Political Theory*, pp. 102–4, for a discussion of Gratian's distinction between *moralia* and *mystica*, and the comparative normative value of each.

[42] On this, see ibid., pp. 105–9, particularly regarding the question of property.

[43] Cf. Acts 4:32; Plato, *Republic*, III (Jowett tr., pp. 416–18) and V (Jowett tr., p. 465).

[44] E.g. Thomas Aquinas, *Summa Theologiae*, II-II, Q. 66, a. 2. A survey of the effect of canon law on theories of natural law, positive law, and property law may be found in K. Pennington, *The Prince and the Law* (Berkeley: Univ. of Calif. Press, 1993), especially, pp. 119–25.

enacted by those in authority prevail over customary law, though at the end of this distinction, and in Distinction 12, he concludes that customary law is to be obeyed in the absence of an ordinance; custom has its own legitimacy, which is entitled to respect.

DD. 13–14. In Distinctions 13 and 14, he considers the possibility of another kind of conflict: what if the highest law—the natural law—were to be in conflict with itself, so as both to command and to forbid the same action? The sources Gratian cites in Distinction 13 suggest that one confronted with only evil options must choose the lesser. (Gregory I had given such examples as whether or not one could break an oath of confidentiality in order to warn an intended murder victim, or break a promise of obedience to a superior who commanded evil acts, or abandon the responsibilities of an office which one had fraudulently obtained.) The glossators openly disagree with Gratian's choices here, arguing that since sin must be voluntary, it can never be the case that whatever one does will be a sin (cf. gloss f to "no dispensation" in *dicta Gratiani ante* D. 13 c. 1). They explain (citing later sections of the *Decretum* and subsequent laws) that in the examples Gratian relies on, one course of action is not really wrong: e.g. breaking the promise to do a wrongful act (gloss h to "transgression," in D. 13 c. 2 §2). Their argument ultimately turns on the supposition that an individual really ought to realize that one of the available options is, in fact, not sinful.[45] Gratian simply accepts the possibility that one could, in good conscience, at least perceive all options as evil, and he goes on from there. The glossators are technically correct, of course, but Gratian may well reflect a rueful sense of pastoral reality. Such problems have remained among the favorite topics of moral philosophers, medieval and modern; here fine distinctions and speculations are firmly tethered to the practical needs involved in pastoral care.

D. 15. Distinctions 15 through 20 are devoted to the written law of the Church, what Gratian earlier called "ecclesiastical enactments." He uses this term broadly, including therein both doctrinal and disciplinary legislation. In his survey of the sources of ecclesiastical written law, he considers general and regional councils, patristic authorities, diocesan synods, and papal decretal letters. Then, especially in Distinctions 17 and 20, he explains the relationships between these different sources of law.

Distinction 15 first introduces the circumstances and teachings of the first four ecumenical councils: Nicaea I (325), Constantinople I (381), Ephesus (431), and Chalcedon (451). These four councils established orthodox belief concerning Christ and the Trinity, and Gratian, like his earlier medieval predecessors and eastern Christians to this day, gives them a unique status. Mention is also made here of the Fifth Ecumenical Council, Constantinople II (553), but only in passing.

---

[45] It is interesting to notice how much time the glossators spend (gloss f to "no dispensation," in *dicta Gratiani ante* D. 13 c. 1) on an example that Gratian in fact mentions almost in passing (D. 13 c. 2 §3, cf. glosses f to "then" and g to "procreation"): that there may be sin involved in having sexual intercourse even with one's own spouse (e.g., if motivated merely by the desire for physical pleasure). The Gloss carries no sigla for these passages, but they are essentially the work of Johannes Teutonicus, who drew on earlier canonists and commentators. The canonists of the generation or two after Gratian were much concerned with the proper understanding of the physical and spiritual aspects of Christian marriage. Cf. J. Brundage, *Law, Sex and Christian Society in Medieval Europe* (Chicago: Univ. of Chicago Press, 1988); C. N. L. Brooke, *The Medieval Idea of Marriage* (New York: Oxford Univ. Press, 1991).

Attached to D. 15 c. 3 are selections from the document known to historians as the *Decretum Gelasianum*. Bearing the name of a late-fifth-century pope, this document is probably a private compilation produced in Italy during the early sixth century. The sections included in the *Decretum* are lists of approved and condemned writers and books. The earliest manuscripts of Gratian include sections 1 to 17, a basic list of approved patristic writers. Later manuscripts add a greater or smaller part of the remainder, which Friedberg consequently marks as a palea.[46] These sections present an instructive mixture of banned heretical and apocryphal writings, works which, while not condemned, are for one reason or another to be approached with caution and read only privately, and a sequence of approved readings for the yearly cycle of the office (a bit of liturgical legislation unusual in Gratian).

D. 16-17. In Distinction 16, Gratian notes the problematic status of the late fourth-century collection of canons known as the *Canons of the Apostles* (the sources disagree hopelessly; Gratian concludes that the canons are received insofar as they are authentic) and the authority of some later ecumenical councils: Constantinople II (553), Constantinople III (680–81), Nicaea II (787), and Constantinople IV (869–70). He then presents diverging opinions on the Trullan Synod (692), the authority of which was much debated. Although the Latin Church generally rejected its decrees (principally because it elevated Constantinople to near equality with Rome), Gratian and the glossators consider it as supplemental to Constantinople II and III (cf. *dicta Gratiani post* D. 16 c. 6 and gloss b to "same" in D. 16 c. 6). This section concludes with a long list of the general and provincial councils received as authoritative by the Roman Church.

In the course of Distinction 16 it becomes clear that conciliar canons have legal force because of their acceptance or "reception" by the Roman Church. In Distinction 17, Gratian analyzes the relationship between the papacy and councils in a discussion especially important for later papal theory. As understood by the glossators, the authorities cited in this section grant the pope the power to convoke councils and to ratify their decrees. Moreover, decisions on doctrinal matters and major disciplinary legislation are reserved to the Holy See. The distinction concludes with long dicta (adapted from Bishop Ennodius of Pavia, ca. 473–521) upholding papal exemption from both secular jurisdiction and that of councils of bishops, no merely academic concern in the twelfth century, an age of imperially instigated schisms and rebel councils.

D. 18. The strong papalist version of Church authority expounded in Distinction 17 is balanced by Gratian's discussion of episcopal synods in Distinction 18. Although these do not have the power to legislate on doctrine, local synods could issue disciplinary legislation to correct abuses among local clergy (cf. *dicta Gratiani ante* D. 18 c. 1). Gratian here includes a number of texts from early councils and popes requiring that bishops hold synods in their dioceses twice a year. The disciplinary legislation preserved here in the *Decretum* had little effect until it was reconfirmed by canon 12 of Lateran IV, *In singulis*, which obliged bishops to exercise their rights of visitation and correct their clergy.[47] Nevertheless, this distinction provides a powerful array of texts on the frequency and management of such diocesan and provincial synods.

[46] On this text, see notes 192–215, on pp. 99–101 below.

[47] On this, see J. Gilchrist, "Visitation, Canonical, History of," *New Catholic Encyclopedia* 14 (1967).

DD. 19–20. Having explained conciliar enactments and the role of the papacy in their promulgation, Gratian considers the pope as an independent lawgiver in Distinction 19.[48] The principal form of papal legislation by Gratian's time is the decretal letter. Technically, this is a papal letter issued to answer a request for a legal decision, which contains instruction on matters of law or practice involved in the case. For Gratian, decretals are equated with conciliar canons in authority; they not only have supreme legislative force but are binding on everyone. Decretal legislation is of major importance from the second half of the twelfth century onward in the development of canon law, serving, even more than conciliar enactments, as the vehicle for the growth of a responsive, adaptable system of jurisprudence within the Christian community.[49]

Distinction 19, like Distinction 17, expounds a strongly papalist theory of Church government, but this power is not unlimited. The pope has no authority to change defined doctrine or the precepts of the Gospel. Drawing on the medieval legend of the "apostasy" of Pope Anastasius II, Gratian even presents the image of an excommunicated pope who lost his authority by falling into heresy. Although the glossators reject Gratian's interpretation of Anastasius's letter (cf. the Case to D. 19 c. 8), they do leave open the possibility of a pope losing his authority through heresy.[50]

In Distinction 20, Gratian finally evaluates the legal status of the approved patristic authors of Distinction 15 and other learned or holy writers. These are to be favored on account of their learning when interpreting Scripture, he asserts, but they have no independent authority in law.[51] In determining cases, one ought to turn first to Scripture, then to the decrees of popes and councils (as explained above), and finally, when lacking these, to the writings and example of the saints.

The Spirit of the Treatise

Amid all the details of the *Treatise*, several themes recur almost as underlying motifs. One is equity, the idea that sometimes justice is truly served only by not adhering rigidly to the letter of the law but by being attentive to its spirit. Another is the role of personal intention and responsibility, in determining not the objective moral quality of an offense but the actual culpability of the individual. There is a sense of the complexity of human life and human society. Gratian frequently seems to have in mind something like (to use a too-modern expression) a balance of powers among royal statute, papal decretal, ancient precept, and community practice as reflected in local custom, a balance that needs to be recognized and maintained.

Distinctions 1–20, between text and commentary, also include a number of other familiar and significant principles. Realistic distinctions are drawn between what law upholds and what it merely tolerates, between what is legal and what is moral and just. Custom, the written or unwritten enactment of living communities and previous genera-

---

[48] Cf. Chodorow, *Political Theory*, pp. 137–40.

[49] Cf. G. Fransen, *Les Décretales et les collections de décretales*, Typologie des sources du moyen âge occidental 2 (Turnhout: Brepols, 1972/1985); for an illustration of the practical uses and consequences of this form of legislation, see C. Duggan, *Twelfth-Century Decretal Collections and Their Importance in English History*, University of London Historical Studies 12 (London: Athlone, 1963).

[50] See gloss c to "Your Serenity" in D. 19 c. 8. For the attitudes of the canonists on this issue, see B. Tierney, *Origins of Papal Infallibility, 1150–1350* (Leiden: Brill, 1972), pp. 37–39; and Chodorow, *Political Theory*, pp. 138–40.

[51] Chodorow, *Political Theory*, pp. 165–70, focusing on Gratian's understanding of the power of the keys.

tions, is granted a value against the will of an individual legislator, although Gratian and his successors do not endow precedent as such with the force of custom. Finally they subordinate all human lawmaking to the scrutiny of the Gospel and divine law.

The *Treatise* prepares the reader to understand the particular laws of the Church which were expounded in the rest of the *Decretum*, but Gratian (D. 20 c. 3 *in fine*, quoting Mt. 18:20) finishes the *Treatise on Laws* in a spirit of openness to the uncertainties of the future. Cases might well arise, he observes, for which there is neither written law nor precedent. In that case, one should gather the elders of the province and consult with them, "for the Lord, the true guarantor, said, 'If two or three of you gather in my name on earth, whatever they ask in any matter will be done for them by my Father.'"

ACKNOWLEDGMENTS

In the preparation of this translation we have received advice and suggestions from many friends and scholars. We would like to express special thanks to Prof. Kenneth Pennington, the editor of this series, and to Fr. Michael Carragher, O.P., who tested drafts of the translation with his students at the Università Pontificia S. Tommaso in Rome. We would also like to thank Prof. Robert Figuera, and Professors Charles and Anne Duggan, for their suggestions. The copy editors at The Catholic University of America Press, the typesetters at Loyola Graphics, and Dr. Barbara Pike Gordley did much to enhance the readability and appearance of the final text.

A.T.
J.G.
K.C.

THE TREATISE ON LAWS

GREGORY XIII
POPE

To All Christ's Faithful,
Greetings and Apostolic Benediction

The correction of the decrees and texts collected by Gratian had been very advisedly taken up by certain of the Roman pontiffs who preceded us because the text had become exceedingly marred by errors and corrupt readings. Although cardinals of the holy Roman Church had been appointed for this, and the task had been entrusted to the other very learned men who had been recruited, many diverse obstacles have hitherto delayed it. Now that the most ancient codices have been brought from everywhere and collated with the authors whose testimony Gratian used, those passages where anything had been miscopied have been restored, and the correction has been completed with the greatest care and brought to perfection, we order it to be published. Great care has been taken in this project, for this is a work of particular dignity and general utility for those who carry on this discipline. We command, therefore, that whatever has been corrected and reestablished should be preserved with the greatest care, and that nothing be added, changed, or omitted.

SINCE, when new cases arise, new remedies should be sought, I, Bartholomaeus Brixiensis, trusting in the bounty of the Creator, have improved as necessary the apparatus of the *Decretum*, not by removing anything, nor by attributing to myself any glosses I did not write, but simply by remedying any defect where correction seemed necessary, either because decretals had been omitted or shortened, or because new laws had superseded others. I have also added some solutions not included by Ioannes. All this I have done for the honor of Almighty God and the Roman Church, and for the common benefit of all who study canon law. Bar.

D. 1. This distinction is divided into two parts. In the first he proves by four canons that the human race is ruled in two ways, namely, by law and custom. In the second part, which begins, "There is, however. . . ," he gives seven differences among laws. Ioan. de Fan.; Pet.

Dicta Gratiani ante **C. 1. CASE.** The case is as follows. It says here that there are two instruments by which the human race is ruled and governed, namely, natural law and custom or usage. Natural law is what is contained in the Law and the Gospel. By this law each person is commanded to do to others what he wants done to himself and prohibited from inflicting on others what he would not want done to himself. This is proved by the authority of Christ who says, "Whatever. . . ."

ᵃ*human race*—Treating the canon law, Master Gratian begins first with matters simpler according to nature, that is, with natural law, which possesses the greatest antiquity and dignity since it began with rational creatures themselves, as in Instit. 2. 1. 11 [2. 1 (*in medio*)]. He identifies many differences between natural law and other laws until, at D. 15, he reaches his main topic, canon law, and identifies its origin.

ᵇ*two things*—Different ones are given in D. 96 c. 10.⁽¹⁾ But those rule as authorities, these two as instruments. *Dicta Gratiani post* C. 11 q. 1 c. 30.

ᶜ*natural*—that is, divine.

ᵈ*usages*—that is, customary law or written and unwritten human law. C. 25 q. 2 c. 7.

ᵉ*what he wants*—But don't I want another to give me his thing although I don't want to give him my thing? There-

THE HARMONY OF DISCORDANT CANONS

AND FIRST
CONCERNING DIVINE LAW
AND HUMAN ENACTMENTS¹

DISTINCTION ONE

Part 1.

*The human race*ᵃ *is ruled by two things,*ᵇ *namely, natural*ᶜ *law and usages.*ᵈ *Natural law is what is contained in the Law and the Gospel. By it, each person is commanded to do to others what he wants*ᵉ *done to himself and prohibited*ᶠ *from inflicting*ᵍ *on others what he does not want done to himself. So Christ said in the Gospel:*ʰ *"Whatever you want*ⁱ *men to do to you, do so to them. This indeed is*ʲ *the Law and the Prophets."*

*Thus*ᵏ *Isidore says in* Etymologies, *V, II:*²

C. 1. *Divine ordinances are established by nature, human ordinances by usages.*

§1. All ordinances are¹ either divine or human.

fore, interpret "wants" as "ought to want." That interpretation should be given to "Love and do as you will" and to Dig. 46. 3. 1.⁽²⁾ Or interpret "is commanded" as "is counseled." Conversely, the word "ask" sometimes means "command." C. 11 q. 3 c. 25.

ᶠ*prohibited*—We do not find the prohibition in the Law or the Gospel explicitly, but rather as a consequence. Where one of two contraries is commanded, the other is, as a consequence, prohibited. Where something is adjudged mine, it is, as a consequence, adjudged not yours. Dig. 3. 3. 40. 2.

ᵍ*inflicting*—But is it not true that a judge wishes to inflict death on the accused when he does not wish to suffer death himself? You may say that the judge does not inflict death but rather the ordinance, C. 23 q. 5 c. 31; C. 23 q. 5 c. 19. Or you may understand all this to concern the works of mercy that everyone is bound to perform. D. 86 c. 14. Io.

ʰ*the Gospel*—Matthew 7[:12].

ⁱ*want*—that is, should want.

ʲ*This indeed is*—that is, "In this consists." This is the same as with, "Fear God and obey his commandments; this is the whole of man's duty," in Ecclesiastes 12[:13]. *De poen.* D. 2 c. 14.

ᵏ*Thus*—in order to prove the distinction presented above.

C. 1: CASE. This capitulum is divided into three sections. In the first section it says that ordinances are either divine or human. Divine ordinances are determined by nature, human ordinances by usages. Because there is a diversity in human usages according to what ordinances have been established, ordinances vary because some please one people and some another. In the second section, it says that divine ordinance is encompassed by the term "morality" and human ordinance by the term "law." In the third section, it says that to pass through another's field is moral, that is, permitted by divine law, but not legal, that is, not permitted by human law. The second section begins, "Morality is. . . ." The third section begins, "To pass through. . . ."

¹**All ordinances are**—that is, each ordinance is. The plural is used for the singular. If you show that there are two ordinances, one divine and the other human, it cannot truly

be said that both ordinances are either human or divine. This interpretation sometimes holds for rescripts. It is sometimes written "if these are true" when what is meant is "if either is true." X 2.28.48 (*in fine*); X 3.5.18; X 1.3.2; C.2 q.1 c.7; Dig. 35.1.33; Dig. 1.5.3.

[a]**vary**—Nevertheless, they are not contrary. Divine ordinance permits one to pass through another's field and human ordinance prohibits it. But prohibition and permission are not contraries, for the Lord permits an unfaithful wife to be dismissed, and the Apostle prohibits it. C.28 q.1 c.8.

[b]**different**—D.12 c.11; D.32 c.13.[3]

[c]**another's**—But is it not true that all things are common by natural law, as in c.7 below and in D.8 c.1? Therefore, no field is "another's." So interpret "another's" to mean "in some way another's."

[d]**is moral**—that is, it is equitable when there is a reason and the passing through does not disturb another. C.23 q.2 c.3. Again, by divine law it is permissible to eat grapes in another's field but not to take them away. It is permissible to break off ears of grain and eat them. C.6 q.3 c.1. But it is not permitted to use a sickle. *De cons.* D.5 c.26. Although it is equitable by divine law, it is not legal, that is, law does not give a civil action. When something benefits me and does not injure you, it is equitable that you not forbid me to do it although the law fails to require this. Dig. 39.3.2.

5. Nevertheless, there are cases where one is allowed to pass through another's field: if there is a servitude, Cod. 3.34.11; if one wants to dig up one's own treasure, Dig. 10.4.15 (*in fine*); if one's fruit fell into another's field, Dig. 43.28.1 [43.27.1]; when one is looking for a fugitive, Dig. 11.4.3 [11.4.4]; C.23 q.2 c.3; and when a public road has been destroyed, Dig. 8.6.14.1. Io.

Dicta Gratiani post **C.1. CASE.** Gratian concludes from the preceding capitulum that there is a difference between

Divine ordinances are determined by nature, human ordinances by usages; and thus the latter vary[a] since different things please different[b] people.

§2. Morality is divine ordinance. Law is human ordinance.

§3. To pass through another's[c] field is moral,[d] but it is not legal.

From the text of this authority one can understand clearly how divine and human ordinances differ, since whatever is moral is included in the term "divine or natural ordinances," while by the term "human ordinances" we understand the usages drawn up in writing and passed on as law. Law is a general term, containing many species.

Thus Isidore says in Etymologies, V, III:[3]

C.2. *Ordinance is a species.*[4]

Law [*ius*][e] is a general term; ordinance is a species of law. Law is so called because it is just [*justum*]. Law consists of ordinances and usages.

[*Isidore,* Etymologies, V, III:][5]

C.3. *What ordinance is.*

Ordinance[f] is written enactment.

[*Isidore,* Etymologies, V, III; II, X:][6]

C.4. *What usage is.*

Usage is[7] long-continued[g] custom, derived to

divine ordinance and human ordinance, for all that is moral may be understood by the term "divine or natural ordinance," and usages that are written down and passed on may be understood by the term "human ordinances." At the end, he says "law" is a general term that contains many species, which he proves in what follows.

CC.2–4. CASE. The case of the three following capitula is clear, as you will see yourself.

[e]**Law [*ius*]**—so called because it is just [*iustum*], as no one is said to be a judge [*iudex*] unless he is just. C.23 q.2 c.1. But sometimes something is lawful that is not equitable or just. For example, one whose wife is adulterous may not be promoted, D.34 c.11, which I understand to mean that he may not if he has relations with her afterwards, for he should not be punished without a fault of his own. C.16 q.7 c.38. Again, it is equitable and just that no one become richer through another's loss. X 5.37.9; Dig. 12.6.14. Nevertheless, usucaption and prescription have been instituted contrary to this equity. Again, it is iniquitous that one be punished in place of another, for a punishment should not go further than putting right the wrong. X 3.11.2. But many laws speak against this equity: *dicta Gratiani* §4 *post* C.1 q.4 c.11; *dicta Gratiani post* C.6 q.1 c.11; X 4.1.11. But you may say that in all of these cases a rigor contrary to natural equity has been instituted for a purpose and for the sake of peace or society. But sometimes a rigor contrary to equity has been instituted without a purpose, and then the only reason for it is that the law was written that way. Dig. 40.9.12.

[f]**ordinance**—commanding what is just and prohibiting the contrary. C.23 q.4 c.42 (*in fine*). It is called an ordinance [*lex*] because it orders [*ligat*] one by law. *De cons.* D.2 c.21. Archi.

[g]**long-continued**—What custom would you consider long, or how many repetitions would you say introduce a custom? What is done twice? C.25 q.2 c.25. Or what is done three

times? X 1. 6. 34 (*in fine*). Or what is done more than three times? X 2. 12. 3. Or what is done ten times, as prescription is called "long" when it has lasted ten years? Cod. 7. 33. Or what has been done from beyond memory? C. 3 q. 6 c. 10; Dig. 43. 20. 3. 4 [43. 19. 3]. You may say that in criminal cases two instances usually introduce a custom, but in other cases three are not enough. Cod. 1. 4. 4 [1. 7. 4] (*in fine*). Io. You may take it as certain that, according to canon law, a custom is not valid unless requisite time has passed and it is reasonable. X 1. 4. 11. Here it would seem that a fourth repetition will introduce a custom. Cod. 3. 34. 14. Bar. Brix.

ᵃ**from usages**—This definition seems inadequate in two ways: the term to be defined is used in the definition, and the same term is used for both species and genus. But you may say that the terms "usage," "usages," and "custom" are used in different ways. "Usage" is used for unwritten law; "custom" is used generally for law whether written or unwritten, as in the next capitulum; and "usages" is used for frequently performed human actions. Ioan.

a certain extent from usages.ᵃ

[*Isidore*, Etymologies, *V, III; II, X:*]⁸

C. 5. *What custom is.*

§1. Custom is a sort of law establishedᵇ by usages and recognized as ordinance when ordinance is lacking.ᶜ

§2. It does not matter whether it is confirmed by writing or by reason, since reason also supports ordinances.

§3. Furthermore, if ordinance is determined by reason,ᵈ then ordinance will be all that reason has already confirmed—all, at least, that is congruent with religion,ᵉ consistent with discipline,ᶠ and helpful for salvation.ᵍ Custom is so called

with custom. X 2. 15. 3; D. 12 c. 11; D. 32 c. 13. Many other things are also required for something to be called a custom, as we observe below at D. 8 c. 7.

ᶜ**is lacking**—Here it seems recourse is made to custom only when ordinance is lacking. And so it may be argued that one is never to judge according to custom if law prescribes the contrary. D. 11 c. 4; D. 11 c. 2; D. 8 c. 5; D. 8 c. 8; X 2. 27. 8; X 2. 2. 9. It may be answered that one is not to judge according to custom but according to the laws. Dig. 47. 12. 3. 5. But much can be found that is against this position. D. 32 c. 13; X 2. 15. 3; X 4. 11. 3; X 1. 43. 4; X 1. 4. 2; X 3. 26. 8. In all these texts you find that custom has force against written law. We will solve the question of when custom may detract from law below at D. 8 c. 7. Ioan. You may hold that rational and long-standing custom detracts from written law. It so appears to me from X 1. 4. 11, even if the other elements mentioned by Ioan at D. 8 c. 7 are not present. B. But to which custom does one

C. 5. CASE. This capitulum is divided into three sections. In the first section the definition of custom is presented, that is "Custom. . . ." In the second section, which begins, "It does not matter. . . ," it says that it does not matter whether custom is in writing or by reason alone, that is, determined without writing, since reason also supports ordinances. In the third section, which begins, "Furthermore. . . ," it says that as an ordinance will be a rule when it is rational, so custom will be an ordinance, that is, will be obeyed like an ordinance, as long as it is rational, congruent with religion, consistent with discipline, and helpful to salvation. It is called custom because it is in common use.

ᵇ**established**—It is evident that many repetitions are not sufficient for something to become a custom unless it has been done so that a custom be established. For something is often permitted as a favor or through tolerance. X 5. 40. 25; C. 10 q. 3 c. 6. Accordingly, granted that something is done often, unless it is done with the intention that it be done thereafter, this use, however lawful, is not called a "use." Dig. 43. 19. 1. 6 [43. 18. 1. 6];⁽⁴⁾ Dig. 43. 19. 7 [43. 18. 7]. Moreover, another reason may be seen why repetition alone does not introduce a custom: even though a matter has been adjudged a certain way several times, it need not be judged the same way thereafter, for one must judge not in accord with past cases but in accord with ordinances, Cod. 7. 45. 13, although one certainly does judge in accord

have recourse? To the custom of the region, or to Roman custom, or to that of the place where a contract was made, or that of the neighboring provinces? It would seem that one has recourse to Roman custom. D. 11 c. 11; Instit. 4. 11. 7. On the contrary, it would seem that one has recourse to the custom of the place. D. 12 c. 11; Cod. 8. 10, and the laws cited earlier lead to this conclusion. To this I say that a judge delegate ought first to judge according to the canons, and, if these are lacking, according to [civil] ordinances. X 5. 32. 1; D. 10 c. 7. If all law is lacking, he should turn to general custom, or even to particular custom if general custom is lacking. But some say that one should then have recourse to the custom of Rome. If both law and custom are lacking, one must proceed by analogy from similar cases. D. 20 c. 3; Dig. 1. 3. 12 [1. 3. 11]. If all else is lacking, one should turn to the custom of Rome, Dig. 1. 3. 32 pr. [1. 3. 31 pr.], although it may be argued that one should turn to the custom of neighboring provinces. X 3. 39. 22.

ᵈ**reason**—So it may be argued that when law or canon is lacking one may proceed in accord with reason. D. 19 c. 1; D. 8 c. 7.

ᵉ**congruent with religion**—Many things contrary to reason are nevertheless congruent with religion such as that the Virgin give birth.⁽⁵⁾

ᶠ**consistent with discipline**—Since, although for cause, a prelate may coerce a delinquent subject, nevertheless he must coerce him in a disciplined manner so as to help him to salvation. D. 45 c. 8.

ᵍ**helpful for salvation**—Although reason says to attack an enemy, this, nevertheless, is not helpful for salvation.⁽⁶⁾

***Dicta Gratiani post* c. 5. CASE.** He infers from c. 5 above, which says that it does not matter whether custom is written or unwritten, that some custom is passed on in writing and some is preserved in the usages of those who follow it. What is written is called "enactment" or "law." What is not written is called "custom." He says there is another distinction among laws, and, on this point, he presents the next capitulum, giving some examples for each branch of the distinction.

CC. 6–7. CASE. These capitula are divided into three sections. In the first, Isidore draws a threefold distinction as to law: natural law, civil law, and the law of nations. In the second section, which begins "Natural law. . . ," he says that natural law is common to all nations as it proceeds from an instinct of nature and not from any enactment. In the third section, which begins "For example: the union. . . ," he presents eight things, such as the union of men and women, that proceed from natural law, for these and things like them proceed from natural law.

ᵃ**Natural law**—To understand this, note that the word "nature" is used in many ways. Sometimes nature means a force residing in things so that like propagates like. Second, sometimes nature means the stimulus or instinct of nature proceeding from physical desire in respect to appetite, procreation, and child-rearing. C. 32 q. 5 c. 17; Dig. 25. 4. 1; Instit. 1. 2. pr. Third, nature means an instinct of nature proceeding from reason; law proceeding from nature in this sense is called natural equity. According to this law of nature, all things are called common, that is, to be shared in time of necessity. D. 47 c. 8. Fourth, the law of nature means natural precepts such as "do not kill," "do not commit adultery." C. 32 q. 7 c. 16;⁽⁷⁾ Instit. 4. 1 pr. All divine law is said to be natural law, and according to this law, too, all things are called common, that is, to be shared. Things may also belong to a particular person by divine law. For it was said to Adam himself [Gen. 3:19], "In the sweat of your brow

because it is in common use.

So, when it says, "it does not matter whether custom is confirmed by writing or by reason," this shows that, in part, custom has been collected in writing, and, in part, it is preserved only in the usages of its followers. What is put in writing is called enactment or law,[9] *while what is not collected in writing is called by the general term "custom."*

Part 2.
There is, however, another division of law, as Isidore attests in Etymologies, *V, IV, when he says:*[10]

C. 6. *What the species of law are.*
§ 1. Law is either natural, civil, or that of nations.

[*Isidore,* Etymologies, *V, IV:*][11]

C. 7. *What natural law is.*
§ 2. Natural law[a] is common to all nations because it exists everywhere through natural instinct, not because of any enactment.
§ 3. For example: the union[b] of men and women, the succession[c] and rearing[d] of children,[12] the common possession[e] of all things, the identical liberty of all, or the acquisition of things that are taken[f] from the heavens, earth, or sea, as well as the return of a thing deposited[g] or of

you shall eat your bread," and elsewhere [Exod. 20:17], "Do not covet what is your neighbor's." D. 47 c. 6. Similarly "civil law" has various meanings. Sometimes "civil law" means the law that is neither natural law nor the law of nations. When, as here, civil law is used in that sense, canon law may be called civil law. Second, "civil law" means all law that is not canon law. Third, "civil law" means the Laws of the XII Tables. Dig. 1. 2. 2. 3. Fourth, something is "civil law" in contrast to praetorian law. Ioan.

ᵇ**the union**—If you understand the text to mean the union of their bodies, then this is the natural law that proceeds from physical desire. If you understand it to mean the union of their souls, this is the natural law that proceeds from reason. X 1. 21. 5.

ᶜ**succession** — Do not understand the text to mean the succession through inheritance, since that is not natural, but rather the succession propagated through the flesh. Or you may understand it to mean the succession by which children succeed parents according to the law of nature. Dig. 38. 6. 1 [38. 7. 1]; Dig. 38. 6. 7. 1 [38. 7. 6].

ᵈ**rearing**—since fathers lay up treasures for their sons, not sons for their parents. C. 16 q. 1 c. 64 [cf. 2 Cor. 12:14]. But if a father is in need, his son is similarly compelled to support him. C. 22 q. 4 c. 22; Cod. 5. 25. 1; Cod. 5. 25. 2. So also in certain cases a son must support his mother, and a freedman his patron. Dig. 25. 3. 5. 3; Dig. 25. 3. 5. 18.

ᵉ**common possession**— that is, nothing belongs to a person by divine law. Or you may say that "common" means to be shared in time of necessity. D. 47 c. 8. Indeed, according to the Rhodian Law, food in particular is common in time of peril. Dig. 14. 2. 2. 2; C. 12 q. 1 c. 2.

ᶠ**taken**—these and other goods belonging to no one go to the one who first possesses them. Instit. 2. 1. 12.

ᵍ**deposited**—This rule does not apply in two cases. One is described in C. 22 q. 2 c. 14.⁽⁸⁾ The other is a case in which the owner and the person who made the deposit both ask for the thing, and then it is better to return it to the owner. Dig. 16. 3. 31.

ᵃ**entrusted**—entrusting is the same as depositing. Dig. 16. 3. 27.

ᵇ**by force**—which anyone may do. Dig. 1. 1. 3 (*in fine*); X 5. 39. 3 (*in fine* at *Si vero*). As to this, see the comment at C. 23 q. 1 c. 7.⁽⁹⁾ Ioan.

C. 8. CASE. It says here that civil law is what a people or commonwealth establishes for itself for divine or human reasons.

ᶜ**commonwealth**—So each church may make law for itself. D. 11 c. 8; *De cons.* D. 3 c. 1.

ᵈ**divine or human**—that is, with respect to God, *De cons* D. 3 c. 3, or to men, Dig. 2. 12. 1.

C. 9. CASE. Here eleven [*sic*] things are enumerated that arise from the law of nations, for example, occupation of habitations, and so forth. This law is called the law of nations because almost all nations make use of it without distinction.

ᵉ**habitations**—that is, those of enemies, as in C. 23 q. 7 c. 2; C. 23 q. 5 c. 25; Instit. 2. 1. 17; Dig. 41. 1. 5. 7. Or you may say that it means vacant habitations, which belong to those who occupy them. Instit. 2. 1. 12. Otherwise, if someone seizes his own thing by his own authority, he loses ownership, as in C. 16 q. 6 c. 1; Dig. 4. 2. 13; Cod. 8. 4. 7, unless he cannot seek the return of the thing from a judge. C. 23 q. 2 c. 1; C. 23 q. 2 c. 2; Dig. 42. 8. 10. 16 [42. 9. 10]. Ioan.

ᶠ**servitude**—Elsewhere it says that servitude was introduced through drunkenness. D. 35 c. 8. Elsewhere it says that it was introduced by the rule about the seven-year period as I will explain at *dicta Gratiani ante* D. 7 c. 1, in the gloss which begins, "That is, with the judgments" on the word "prescriptions." It is said to have been introduced by the law of nations, not

money entrusted ᵃ to one, and the repelling of violence by force.ᵇ This, and anything similar, is never regarded as unjust but is held to be natural and equitable.

[*Isidore*, Etymologies, *V, V:*]¹³

C. 8. *What civil law is.*

Civil law is what each people and each commonwealthᶜ establishes as its own law for divine or humanᵈ reasons.

[*Isidore*, Etymologies, *V, VI:*]¹⁴

C. 9. *What the law of nations is.*

The law of nations deals with the occupation of habitations,ᵉ with building, fortification, war, captivity, servitude,ᶠ postliminy,ᵍ treaties, armistices,¹⁵ truces, the obligation of not harming ambassadors,ʰ and the prohibition of marriage with aliens.ⁱ This law is called the law of nations because almost all nations make use of it.

[*Isidore*, Etymologies, *V, VII:*]¹⁶

C. 10. *What military law is.*

Military law deals with the formalities of declaring war, the obligations involved in making a treaty,ʲ advance against the enemy on signal, commitment to combat,¹⁷ and withdrawal, again on signal, military punishment of shameful acts such as deserting ᵏ one's post, the payment of stipends,ˡ the order of ranksᵐ and conferring of honors such as a wreathⁿ or a chain,ᵒ the distribution of booty, its just division according to the status and the exertions of different persons, and the prince's share.ᵖ

because the law of nations first invented it, but because that law accepts it. Therefore, if a war is just, one captured becomes the slave of his captor. C. 23 q. 5 c. 25. And accordingly, such a captive sins if he escapes from his master. C. 17 q. 4 c. 37. But if the war is not just, then it is permitted for captives to flee if they can. Dig. 49. 15. 26 [49. 15. 25]. Ioan.

ᵍ**postliminy**—Postliminy is the law by which something lost on account of captivity is restored to someone, C. 16 q. 3 c. 13; C. 34 q. 1 c. 1, with the exception of his weapons which are not returned when he has lost them shamefully. Dig. 49. 15. 2.

ʰ**ambassadors**—If anyone impedes the ambassador of an ally or enemy, he is excommunicated according to the canons. D. 94 c. 2; C. 24 q. 3 c. 4. According to [civil] ordinance, he is handed over to the enemy to become their slave. Dig. 50. 7. 18 [50. 7. 17]. Joannes Theutonicus.

ⁱ**aliens**—As in C. 28 q. 1 cc. 15, 16, 17.⁽¹⁰⁾

c. **10. CASE.** Here Isidore shows what pertains to military law, that is to say, the formalities of declaring war, obligations involved in making a treaty, and so forth.

ʲ**a treaty**—that is, for making peace.

ᵏ**deserting**—According to the canons, he who flees during a war is degraded. C. 6 q. 1 c. 17. According to [civil] ordinance, he is executed. Dig. 49. 16. 6. 3. Ioannes Theutonicus.

ˡ**stipends**—See C. 12 q. 2 c. 25; C. 16 q. 7 c. 1; C. 16 q. 7 c. 29.⁽¹¹⁾

ᵐ**order of ranks**—that is, who is worthier or superior to another.

ⁿ**a wreath** — that is, a higher honor.

ᵒ**a chain**—that is, a lesser honor.

ᵖ**prince's share**—Not everything captured in battle goes to the prince. But contrary to this is C. 23 q. 5 c. 25, which says that everything belongs to the king. But you may say that all things belong to the prince as to their custody, and he is bound to divide them according to the deserts of individuals. C. 12 q. 2 c. 25; C. 12 q. 2 c. 26.

C. 11. CASE. Public law concerns sacred things, priests, and magistrates. This is because, if anyone commits an offense against these or other public persons, it is a matter of public law. He acts against the commonwealth because responsibility for the state belongs to these persons.
[a]**Public law**—So whoever harms a priest or some sacred thing may be charged by anyone with a public crime. Argument from C. 2 q. 1 c. 7.

C. 12. CASE. This capitulum is divided into two sections. In the first it says that the law of the Quirites is that law proper to the Romans and that it applies only to the Romans and those subject to them. In the second section it says that Roman law deals with legal inheritance, cretion, guardianship, and usucaption, because all these matters pertain to the Romans alone. The second section begins at the words, "This law deals. . . ."
[b]**Quirites**—From Quirinus, that is, from Romulus.
[c]**none**—To the contrary is Cod. 1. 9. 8 [1. 12. 7] where it says that the Jews are subject to Roman law. But in that text, all subject to the Roman Empire are called Romans. So, it might be said that, just as it is peculiar to the Romans for a child to be under his father's power, so also the nations are under the Roman Empire because the emperor is prince of the entire world. C. 7 q. 1 c. 41. But various kings have been established under him in the different provinces. C. 6 q. 3 c. 2; Dig. 14. 2. 8; Dig. 14. 2. 9. So whoever refuses to be subject to the Roman Empire may not have his inheritance or anything else listed here according to the Roman law. Argument from D. 8 c. 1.
[d]**inheritance**—Either as an intestate or by a formal will. Inheritance is succession to all rights that the deceased had at the time of his death, or to what remains after deducting what is owed to others.
[e]**usucaption**—Usucaption is acquisition of ownership by continued possession for a period of time defined by ordinance. Dig. 41. 3. 3.

D. 2. This distinction is divided into two parts. In the first part he describes five different types of secular laws. The second part begins "Certain acts. . . ." Ioan. de Fantu.

CC. 1–4. CASE. In the previous distinction, mention was made of the law of the Quirites. Therefore, Gratian added a second distinction where he shows that the law of the Quirites consists of ordinances, plebiscites, senate resolutions, enactments of princes, edicts of the senate, and the opinions of jurists. Then he speaks of certain ordinances that are named from the individuals who enacted them, such as consular or tribunitial ones, and so forth. He gives examples of each. These four capitula are clear, as you will see for yourself.
[f]**The law**—The second distinction treats the parts or species of Roman law. It also treats why consular ordinances, tribunitial ordinances, and other ordinances are so called.
[g]**people**—At one time the people made ordinances, but today they do not because they transferred this power to the emperor. Instit. 1. 2. 6. Or, it may be said that today the people may still do so, and that in that text "transferred" means "conceded."
[h]**greater by birth**—They are called greater by birth on account of their greater nobility, age, dignity, or knowledge. C. 2 q. 7 c. 18; C. 2 q. 7 c. 52.

[*Isidore,* Etymologies, *V, VIII:*][18]

C. 11.   *What public law is.*
Public law[a] treats sacred things, priests, and magistrates.

[*Isidore,* Etymologies, *V, IX:*][19]

C. 12.   *What the law of the Quirites is.*
§1. The law of the Quirites[b] is that peculiar to the Romans, and it binds none[c] save the Quirites, that is, the Romans.
§2. This law deals with legal inheritance,[d] cretion,[20] guardianships, and usucaption.[e] These laws are met with among no other people, but are particular to the Romans and laid down for them alone.

DISTINCTION TWO

Part 1.
The law[f] of the Quirites consists of ordinances, plebiscites, senate resolutions, imperial enactments and edicts, and jurists' opinions.[21]

[*Isidore,* Etymologies, *V, X; II, X:*][22]

C. 1.   *What an ordinance is.*
An ordinance is an enactment of the people,[g] by which the plebeians together with those greater by birth[h] have established something.

^a**Plebiscites**—Plebiscites were first held because discord existed between the nobles and plebeians. Dig. 1. 2. 2. 20.

^b**enactment or edict**—Properly speaking, enactments are made by the prince and edicts by praetors. One may also speak of the edict of a judge as in C. 24 q. 3 c. 6; D. 19. 42. 1. 53.

[*Isidore*, Etymologies, *V, XI:*]²³

C. 2. *What a plebiscite is.*

Plebiscites^a are what the plebeians have established by themselves. They are called plebiscites because the plebeians decreed them, or because the plebeians deliberated on them and requested them.

[*Isidore*, Etymologies, *V, XII:*]²⁴

C. 3. *What a senate resolution is.*

A senate resolution is what the senators, acting by themselves, decree in regard to the people.

[*Isidore*, Etymologies, *V, XIII:*]²⁵

C. 4. *What an enactment or edict is.*

An enactment or edict^b is what a king or emperor enacts or decrees.

[*Isidore*, Etymologies, *V, XIV:*]²⁶

C. 5. *What jurists' opinions are.*

Jurists' opinions^c are what legal experts give to those who consult them; thus the statements of Paulus are called opinions. There were certain jurists and arbiters of equity who produced handbooks of civil law for settling^d suits and disputes of contending parties.

[*Isidore*, Etymologies, *V, XV:*]²⁷

Part 2.

C. 6. *What tribunitial and consular acts are.*

Certain acts take their names from those who issued them, for example, consular acts, tribunitial acts, the Julian acts, and the Cornelian acts. So the consuls Papius and Poppaeus,²⁸ who were chosen under Octavian Caesar, drew up the Papian-Poppeian Act, which was named for them and which contained rewards^e for fathers who rear children. Under the same emperor, Falcidius, the tribune of the plebeians, drew up an act that forbade leaving so much to outsiders through legacies that a fourth part would not remain for one's heirs.²⁹ This was named the Falcidian Act after him.

C. 5. CASE. Here it says that opinions, such as the opinions of Paulus, are what jurists give when they are asked. Certain prudent men chosen as arbiters of equity

have collected their opinions in writing, and these were used in lawsuits to resolve differences.

^c**opinions**—A person could once pass on his entire estate to another, but Falcidius enacted that a fourth part of the estate must be given to the legal heir. The Falcidian Act has three parts. One concerns what belongs to the legal heir in accord with natural law. Another concerns what may legally be claimed by an instituted heir according to the rights of institution when the entire estate is exhausted. Io. A son who has been instituted heir may today have the benefit of both parts. X 3. 26. 18. That put an end to the opinions given by the authorities. Cod. 6. 50. 10 [6. 49. 10]. B. The third part is called the "Trebellian Quarter" and concerns an instituted heir called upon to pass the estate on to another. X 3. 26. 16. Ioannes.⁽¹²⁾

^d**settling**—A judge may not deviate from these opinions. Instit. 1. 2. 8.

Part 2. The second part of the distinction discusses certain ordinances named for the individuals who enacted them. Io. de Fan.

CC. 6–8. CASE. Here seven laws are enumerated that take their names from those who enacted them. Of these, four lived before Octavian Caesar. Three lived under Octavian Caesar: namely, Papius and Poppaeus, who enacted laws giving rewards for child-bearing (that is, for the rearing of children), and Falcidius, the tribune of the plebeians, who permitted parents to dispose of their wealth and leave it to outsiders, excepting the one quarter of their estate that they were bound by the law of nature to leave to their immediate heirs. In the remaining two capitula the case is clear enough, and you may state it yourself.

^e**rewards**—One reward was that, if a man in Rome had three children, a man in Italy had four, or a man in the provinces had five, he could not be required to assume the

burden of legal guardianship. Instit. 1. 25 pr. It also established that a man less than twenty-five years old was excluded from office, but if he were twenty years old and had five children, the number of children would make up for the number of years. Dig. 50. 4. 8; Dig. 4. 4. 2.

^a**satiric**—We find nothing on the satiric law, but it is mentioned in Cod. 7. 6. 1 pr.; Dig. Const. *Omnem* 1 [Proem. II, 1 (*in fine*)].

^b**Rhodian**—This was a very wicked ordinance: those who suffered shipwreck lost everything to the inhabitants. Dig. 14. 2. 9.[(13)] But today this law has been corrected. Auth. *Navigia* post Cod. 6. 2. 18; X 1. 4. 11. Indeed, such persons are automatically excommunicated. X 5. 17. 3.

D. 3. This distinction is divided into three parts. In the first he shows what a canon is. The second part begins, "Moreover, some. . . ." The third part begins, "The function. . . ." Ioan. de Fan.

Dicta Gratiani ante c. 1. CASE. Beginning with D. 1. c. 6, he identified the kinds of secular ordinances. Since an enactment is either civil (so-called from the civil law or civil forum) or ecclesiastical (which he principally intends to treat), he accordingly adds this third distinction in which he shows by what name an ecclesiastical ordinance is called. He says that it is called a "canon." Then he discusses what a privilege is and what the function of ordinances is. The case of the next capitulum is clear by itself.

^c**All**—But because he treated the types of secular ordinances above, now he wants to treat ecclesiastical enactments. They are called by different names. Sometimes they are called canons, sometimes decrees, and sometimes decretal letters. Canons are those that are laid down at a general council. [D. 23 c. 6.][(14)] Decrees are those that the pope lays down, in consultation with his cardinals but without having been consulted by anyone. Decretal letters are those

which the pope lays down, either alone or with his cardinals when he is consulted by someone. D. 59 c. 3; D. 19 c. 1. Again, we find other canonical enactments, such as dogmas, mandates, interdicts, and sanctions. C. 25 q. 2 c. 18. A dogma is a teaching of the Christian faith. D. 23 c. 2. A mandate is a teaching on conduct. D. 23 c. 3. It is an interdict if no penalty is added. D. 32 c. 16. It is a sanction if a penalty is added. D. 36 c. 2.

[*Isidore,* Etymologies, *V, XVI:*][30]

C. 7. *What a satiric act is.*

Now a satiric^a [31] act is one that says many things at the same time. It is so called from its abundance of subjects and, so to speak, from its satiety. Thus, to write satire is to compose diverse poems, like those of Horace, Juvenal, and Persius.

[*Isidore,* Etymologies, *V, XVII:*][32]

C. 8. *What the Rhodian Laws are.*

The Rhodian^b Laws are those of seaborne commerce and take their name from the island of Rhodes. In them is the practice of the merchants of antiquity.

DISTINCTION THREE

Part 1.

All^c the preceding are species of secular ordinance. But, as an enactment is either civil or ecclesiastical, and that of the civil forum or civil law is a civil enactment, let us now examine what an ecclesiastical enactment is. An ecclesiastical enactment is called a canon.

Isidore tells us what a canon is in Etymologies, *VI, XVI, saying:*[33]

C. 1. *What a canon is.*

"Canon"^d is Greek for what is called a "rule" in Latin.

[*Isidore,* Etymologies, *VI, XVI:*][34]

C. 2. *Why it is called a rule.*

It is called a rule because it leads one aright and never takes one astray.^e But others say that it is called a rule because it rules, presents a norm for living rightly, or sets aright what is twisted or bent.

^d**Canon**—Canons may be of four types. C. 25 q. 2 c. 18.[(15)]

C. 2. CASE. A rule is so called because it leads one aright and does not lead us astray from rectitude. Others have said it is a rule because it rules, presents a norm for living, or sets aright what is bent.

^e**astray**—If a rule never leads one astray, then every rule is law. So Dig. 50. 17. 1 speaks badly when it defines a rule in this way: a rule briefly expounds something but not in

such a way that a law may be drawn from the explanation. Dig. 50. 17. 1. You may reply that, if by rule, you mean whatever lays down something generally without adding any exceptions, then law may not be derived from it. The ordinance cited speaks in this way. But if by rule you mean what includes in itself its exceptions, then such a rule never fails. This is the way it is taken here.

Part 2.

§ 1. *Moreover, some canons are decrees of pontiffs, others are statutes of councils. Some councils are universal, others provincial. Some provincial councils are held by the authority of the Roman pontiff, that is to say with a legate*[a] *of the holy Roman Church present, others by the authority of the patriarchs, primates, or metropolitans of the same province. What has been said concerns general rules.*

§ 2. *On the other hand, there are also certain private ecclesiastical and secular ordinances that are called "privileges."*

Concerning these, Isidore says in Etymologies, V, XVIII:[35]

C. 3. *What a privilege is.*

Privileges[36] are ordinances for private[b] individuals, private ordinances as it were. Now, a privilege is so called because it concerns a private matter.[c]

Part 3.

The function of secular or ecclesiastical ordinances is to command what must be done, to prohibit what is evil, and to permit what is licit (such as seeking a prize) or even illicit (such as giving a bill of divorce) lest worse things happen.

So, in Etymologies, VI, XIX, *Isidore writes:*[37]

C. 4. *What the function of an ordinance is.*

Each ordinance either permits[d] something, for example, "let a strong man seek the prize," or it prohibits something, for example, "no one may

jurisdiction may not hold a council. Dig. 1. 21. 2. But may not a metropolitan make canons in his councils? It would seem not. D. 17 c. 4; D. 17 c. 5. The contrary may be argued from D. 11 c. 8; *De cons.* D. 3 c. 1. You may say that he may make canons in small matters and in what concerns duties, but he may not in large matters. D. 17 c. 5; C. 24 q. 1 c. 12.

ADDITION. On this, see D. 18 (at the beginning), where it is followed word for word. Ioan.

[b]**for private** — Properly speaking, private individuals are those on whom no position has been conferred. C. 24 q. 1 c. 32. But here private refers to all exempted from the common law, whether associations or particular persons. C. 7 q. 1 c. 17. Thus one can see why the words of a privilege are to be taken in a causal, not conditional, sense. When it says "as you justly possess," if this expression is contained in a privilege, "as" is to be interpreted to mean "so that." The reason is that, since a privilege is an ordinance, and an ordinance ought to be certain, D. 4 c. 2, the words of a privilege ought to be certain. This explanation is given by Innocent IV to X 5. 40. 25 (at *Praeteriti temporis moram*).[(16)]

[c]**private matter** — that is, private individuals.

Part 3. This is the third part, in which he says what the function of ordinances is. Ioan. de Fan.[(17)]

Part 2. This is the second part of the distinction, in which he distinguishes provincial councils, general councils, and privileges. Ioan. de Fan.

***Dicta Gratiani post* c. 2. CASE.** Here Gratian draws a distinction. Some canons are decrees of pontiffs, others are statutes of universal councils, and others are statutes of provincial councils, which are sometimes held by the authority of the pope or of patriarchs or of archbishops. These are called general rules. There are also private ordinances called privileges. As to them, he presents the following capitulum, the case of which is clear.

[a]*a legate*—specially commissioned for this. Although someone is a general legate, he may not hold a general or even a provincial council, for what is conceded by the pope particularly is not transferred by a grant of general jurisdiction. X 1. 30. 4. One who receives a grant of general

***Dicta Gratiani post* c. 3. CASE.** It says that the function of ordinances is to command what must be done, to prohibit what is evil, to permit what is licit, and sometimes to permit what is illicit lest worse things happen.

C. 4. CASE. It says here that the function of ordinances is fourfold. An ordinance permits something, as that a strong man seek the prize, or it prohibits something, as to marry a nun, or it punishes, as when one who commits murder is to be beheaded, or it commands, as in, "You shall love the Lord your God."

[d]**permits**—Something may be permitted in three ways. First, when it is not prohibited by any law, as to contract a second marriage. C. 31 q. 1 c. 9. Second, when it is allowed although it is against human enactments, as to contract

marriage within the fifth degree. C. 35 q. 3 c. 20. This is true permission and is called absolute permission. Third, when something illicit is permitted in order to avoid what is more illicit, such as feasting on Sunday. D. 4 c. 6. Or, as adultery is permitted to prevent homicide. C. 33 q. 2 c. 9. So too it is permitted that a subdeacon have one woman so that he does not sin with many. X 4. 6. This is called relative permission, but it would be better called toleration than permission. The canons use permission in this sense to mean that we permit what we do not approve. C. 31 q. 1 c. 9. A decretal says, speaking of this permission, that we tolerate much that would be forbidden if we were to judge it. X 3. 5. 18.

[a]**commits**—*Dicta Gratiani post De poen.* D. 1 c. 9.[(18)]

[b]**murder**—But may an ecclesiastical judge pronounce such a decision in a case of blood since he may not be involved in cases of blood? C. 23 q. 8 c. 30. But you may say that an ecclesiastical judge may state the law if he is asked, but he may not command or counsel. C. 5 q. 6 c. 5. Ioan. But today this seems to have been corrected. X 5. 31. 10. B.

[c]**with**—"by."

[d]**its**—that is, ordinance's.

[e]**rewards**—that is, permissions.

[f]**commands** — this pertains to higher things.

D. 4. This distinction is divided into four parts. In the first it is asked why ordinances are made. The second part begins, "Furthermore. . . ." The third part begins, "When ordinances. . . ." The fourth part begins, "Although these ordinances. . . ." Io. de Fan.

***Dicta Gratiani ante* c. 1. CASE.** He explained above what the function of ordinances is. In this fourth distinction he shows why ordinances are instituted, what is contained in them, when they are instituted, and that some capitula have been abrogated.

[g]***The purpose***—Here begins the fourth distinction, in which he shows how ordinances are made. Secondly, he shows what matters are to be considered in enacting ordinances. Finally he shows that some ordinances have been abrogated by contrary customs.

C. 1. CASE. Isidore was asked why laws are made and instituted. He answered that they are made for three reasons. The first is that human temerity can be controlled through fear of them. The second is that the innocent be protected in the midst of wicked people. The third is that by punishing one person, others' capacity to harm can be restrained.

[h]**controlled**—because ordinances do not force one to do good, but prohibit one from doing evil. C. 23 q. 5 c. 33.

[i]**protected**—that is, so that the good can live among the wicked in peace. C. 23 q. 5 c. 18. Ioan.

Part 2. This is the second part of the distinction, in which he presents eight points to be observed in the promulgation of laws. Ioan. de Fan.

***Dicta Gratiani post* c. 1. CASE.** Now Gratian says what should be considered about an ordinance when it is enacted. On this matter he presents the next capitulum.

C. 2. CASE. In this capitulum Isidore lists the ten qualities that an ordinance should have. Here, that it be suitable to the country, the place, and the time is counted as a single attribute, like proper, just, possible, and so forth.

[j]**proper**—because in law propriety is even more desirable than justice. C. 35 q. 3 c. 22.

marry consecrated virgins"; or it punishes, for example, "the one who commits[a] murder[b] shall be beheaded." For human life is tempered with[c] its[d] rewards[e] and punishments. Divine ordinance simply commands:[f] for example [Deut. 6:5], "Love the Lord your God."

DISTINCTION FOUR

Part 1.

The purpose[g] of legal enactments is to check human temerity and the capacity to harm, as Isidore attests in Etymologies, V, XX, saying:[38]

C. 1. *Why ordinances were made.*

Ordinances were made so that, by fear of them, human temerity can be controlled,[h] innocence can be protected[i] in the midst of wicked people, and the capacity of the wicked to harm others can be restrained by fear of punishment.

Part 2.

Furthermore, in the enactment of ordinances, particular attention should be given to the character of the enactment, to insure its nobility, justice, practicality, suitability, and the other things that Isidore enumerates in Etymologies, V, saying:[39]

C. 2. *What an ordinance should be like.*

A ordinance, then, shall be proper,[j] just,[k] possible,[l] in accord with nature,[m] in accord with the the custom of the country,[n] suitable to the

[k]**just**—for it is only a law [*ius*] when it is just [*iustum*]. D. 1 c. 2.

[l]**possible**—for if someone transgresses an impossible ordinance, it is vain to punish him. C. 15 q. 1 c. 10; C. 23 q. 4 c. 22; Dig. 49. 4. 1. 7.

[m]**nature**—that is, natural reason. D. 1 c. 5. Ioan.

[n]**country**—because what is against the custom of the inhabitants is abrogated through their contrary custom. *Dicta Gratiani ante* D. 4 c. 4; D. 4 c. 4. Again, because ordinanc-

es are interpreted according to custom. X 5. 40. 25; Dig. 1. 3. 34 [1. 3. 33]; Dig. 1. 3. 37 [1. 3. 36].

^a**place**—because some things are laid down in some places that are not received elsewhere. D. 31 c. 1; D. 31 c. 14. Again, in enacting law, consideration must be given to nearness and remoteness of place. D. 63 c. 25.

^b**time**—All things, indeed, ought to be appropriate to their time. C. 23 q. 4 c. 42; C. 2 q. 1 c. 19.

^c**necessary**—because law should be laid down only when there is a present necessity. D. 29 c. 2.

^d**useful** — because the useless should be rejected. D. 68 c. 5; D. 12 c. 12.

^e**clear**—C. 4 q. 3 c. 3 § 27.[19]

^f**deception**—so that no one can interpret it deceptively, or so that no snare can be contrived for anyone through it. C. 27 q. 1 c. 42. Ioan.

^g**private**—because then it would be a privilege.

Part 3. This is the third part of the distinction, in which he explains that ordinances may be abrogated by desuetude or confirmed through custom. This is shown by four authorities. Ioan.

Dicta Gratiani ante **c. 3. CASE.** Gratian says that these matters are to be considered in laying down ordinances because after they have been instituted one may not judge them; rather, after they have been instituted, lesser judges may not judge them but must judge according to them. On this matter he presents the following capitulum.

C. 3. CASE. Augustine says that when laws are being instituted one may judge them, but after they have been instituted lesser judges are not allowed to judge them but instead must judge according to them.

^h**past judgment**—Therefore, when the pope wants to make a canon, the bishops may contradict him and say that the

place^a and time,^b necessary,^c useful,^d clear^e enough so that it contain no hidden deception,^f[40] and not accommodated to some private^g individual, but composed for the common utility of the citizens.

Part 3.

When ordinances are enacted these characteristics should be considered, because after they have been instituted, one will no longer be free to pass judgment on them; rather, one must pass judgment according to them.

Augustine says in On True Religion, *XXXI:*[41]

C. 3. *Judgment is to be passed on ordinances when they are being enacted, not afterward.*

In the case of temporal ordinances, although men pass judgment^h on them when they are being instituted, a judge may notⁱ pass judgment on them after they are instituted and confirmed, but only according to them.

§1. *Ordinances are instituted when they are promulgated; they are confirmed when they have been approved by the usage of those who observe them.*

§2. *Some ordinances have now been abrogated^j by the usage of those acting contrary to them because ordinances are confirmed by the usages of those who observe them. Thus, one is not guilty of transgression for acting contrary to the ordinance of Pope Telesphorus in which he decreed that all clerics should*[42] *abstain from meat and delicacies from Quinquagesima Sunday because it was not approved by the usages of those following it.*

canon is not in accord with the customs of our regions. D. 4 c. 2. But which is more to be adhered to, the apostolic decision or that of all the bishops? It would seem that of all the bishops because the world is greater than the capital city. D. 93 c. 24. It may be argued from C. 35 q. 9 c. 5 that the decision of the pope prevails for even the error of a prince makes law. Dig. 33. 10. 3 (*in fine*). You may say that the decision of the pope prevails against all others, C. 9 q. 3 c. 13; C. 9 q. 3 c. 17, unless he speaks against the faith. C. 25 q. 1 c. 6.[20]

ⁱ**may not**—So it may be argued that what has been adopted may not thenceforth be rejected. C. 8 q. 2 c. 2; C. 8 q. 1 c. 15; C. 32 q. 5 c. 17. Ioan. Unless there is some new reason to do so. X 1. 29. 25.

Dicta Gratiani post **c. 3. CASE.** This passage is divided into two sections. In the first section it says that ordinances are instituted when they are promulgated and that they are confirmed when they have been approved by the usages of those who observe them. In the second section, which begins, "Some ordinances. . .," it says that, just as ordinances are confirmed by the usages of those who observe them, so some ordinances are abrogated by desuetude. In this way an ordinance of Telesphorus, which proposed that clerics fast from Quinquagesima Sunday, was abrogated. On this point he presents the next capitulum.

^j**abrogated** — To abrogate is to cancel an ordinance entirely. To derogate is to cancel a part. Dig. 50. 16. 102. But how may the people abrogate a canon when they may not make a canon? Especially since all power was transferred to the prince. Dig. 1. 4. 1. But you may say that the people may not abrogate it without the express consent of the pope. X 3. 5. 18. Some say, however, that the mere knowledge of the pope is sufficient. Io. But I believe that rational and long-

standing custom cancels an ordinance. X 1.4.11. This is so even without the prince's knowledge. Note that it would be difficult for him to know all the customs that are observed. B.

C. 4. CASE. This capitulum is divided into two sections. In the first it says that clerics should begin fasting from Quinquagesima Sunday so that the clerical way of life may be distinguished from that of laymen. In the second section, which begins, "Therefore. . . ," it says that, while they fast during the seven weeks before Easter, the clergy ought to participate day and night in hymns, vigils, and prayers.

[a]**We**—On these two capitula, see *De cons.* D. 3 c. 6, where it is commanded that forty days of Lent be observed. But you may say that this capitulum is not binding because today a fifty-day Lent is not observed although fifty days are celebrated after Easter. Io.

[b]**We establish**—that is, "we abrogate" or "we establish" means "we advise."

[c]**clerics**—lest they be thought unworthy. C. 1. q. 1 c. 45.

C. 5. CASE. This capitulum is clear in itself. These two capitula have been abrogated, along with the next capitulum's beginning. Gratian says this in the next section, which begins, "What St. Gregory writes. . . ."

C. 6. CASE. This capitulum is divided into five sections. In the first section Augustine asked Gregory whether clerics should begin to fast from Quinquagesima Sunday. He answers yes, for as their rank excels that of laymen, so should their religious observance. In the second section, which begins, "Concerning that same Sunday . . . ," it is asked whether laymen who are accustomed to celebrate such Sundays by feasting ought to be prevented from observing this custom. He answers no, so as not to provoke something worse, and he proves this by the authority of Solomon who said that too much pressure draws blood. In the third section which begins, "It is appropriate. . . ," he asks whether during the period of fasting one should abstain from eggs, cheese, and milk. Gregory responds yes, because, as one should

abstain from meat, so one should abstain from all things which take their origin from the sowing of the flesh. In the fourth section, which begins, "On the other hand. . . ," it is asked whether fish may be eaten during Lent. He answers yes, as sustenance for infirmity but not for pleasure, and not big fish but small ones. In the fifth section, at the end of the capitulum, he is asked whether wine may be used, and he answers yes, provided we avoid drunkenness.

Telesphorus, bishop[43] *of the city of Rome, to all the bishops,* Letter *1:*[44]

C. 4. *Let Clerics abstain from meat and delicacies for the seven weeks before Easter.*

§1. We[a] establish[b] that all clerics called to the Lord's work fast from meat[45] for seven full weeks before Easter because, just as the life of clerics[c] ought to be different from the habits of lay people, so there ought to be a distinction in the way they fast.

§2. *And further on:* Therefore, for these seven weeks, let all clerics fast from meat and delicacies, and let them strive to take part day and night in hymns, vigils, and prayers to the Lord.[46]

Also, Ambrose says in his Book of Sermons:[47]

C. 5. *Telesphorus added a seventh week to Lent.*

Lent has six weeks, to which Pope Telesphorus added a seventh week, and this period is called Quinquagesima.

What St. Gregory writes to Augustine, bishop of the English, is to be understood in a like manner:[48]

C. 6. *Let those who have been honored with the dignity of church office adopt the practice of fasting from Quinquagesima Sunday.*

§1. Finally, let priests, deacons and all others graced with the dignity[d] of ecclesiastical rank adopt the practice of fasting from Quinquagesima Sunday. And let them add other things to the burden[e] of their sacred practices so that they excel laymen in their religious observance as they do in their rank.[f]

§2. Concerning that same Sunday,[g] we hesitate[h] over what to say. On that day all laymen and seculars[i] crave meat more acutely than they

[d]**dignity**—Here you find that every ecclesiastical order is called a dignity or honor. C. 1 q. 1 c. 7. Sometimes secular powers are called dignities. C. 23 q. 5 c. 26. Sometimes firm men are said to have dignity, and accordingly slaves are said to have dignity. Dig. 7. 1. 15. 1 [7. 1. 18]. It also appears from this that clerics are not private persons since only those who do not have a dignity are called private persons. C. 24 q. 1 c. 32.

[e]**burden**—that is, the quantity, so that they be two groups.

[f]**their rank**—that is, their dignity. So it may be argued that one who excels another in dignity ought to excel him in other things. C. 1 q. 1 c. 45. Io.

[g]**Sunday**—"Meatfare" Sunday.

[h]**hesitate**—not as to what the law is but about what should be ordered so that scandal does not arise. Cod. 6. 23. 19; C. 1 q. 2 c. 2.

[i]**and seculars**—"and" means "that is."

^a**custom**—So it may be argued that custom is an excuse for a wrongful act, as here and in C. 32 q. 4 c. 7; X 1. 11. 2. On the contrary, custom does not diminish a sin but augments it. C. 24 q. 1 c. 34; C. 32 q. 7 c. 13; X 5. 3. 8. Indeed, custom may make a venial sin to be mortal. *Dicta Gratiani* § 4 *post* D. 25 c. 3. The solution is that custom excuses one from temporal punishments but not from those of hell.

scandal. Indeed, crimes are to be endured on account of scandal or schism, C. 23 q. 4 c. 32, and by reason of their number, D. 50 c. 25. Today this is not tolerated. X 3. 1. 14.

^c**worse**—This is relative permission.

^d**blood**—So one offends who corrects excessively. D. 45 c. 8. Elsewhere it says that one should not be just to excess. *De poen.* D. 1 c. 47; *dicta Gratiani* pr. *post* C. 2 q. 7 c. 27.⁽²¹⁾

normally do on other days and, unless they stuff themselves with gusto until midnight, they do not think they have fittingly observed this sacred time. These act from appetite rather than reason, or, better, in a kind of mental blindness, and they cannot be weaned away from this custom.^a So, out of mercy,^b they should be left to their own devices, lest perhaps they become even worse^c if they are prevented from following their usual custom. As Solomon [cf. Prov. 30:30] said, "Too much pressure draws blood." ^d

§3. *And a little further on:* It is appropriate^e that, on the days we abstain from meat, we also fast from all^f things whose origin is in the sowing^g of the flesh, that is, from milk, cheese, and eggs.

§4. *And a little further on:* On the other hand, a Christian is permitted food made from fish to sustain his infirmity but not to prick his appetite. For this reason, he who abstains from meat should never prepare sumptuous^h banquets of seafood.

§5. And the drinking of wine is permitted but only if drunkenness is completely avoided. In other matters,ⁱ let us deal likewise with whatever pleases the body.

Part 4.

*Although these ordinances were enacted, nevertheless, because they were not approved by common use, those who do not observe them are not guilty of transgression; otherwise, those who disobey them would be deprived of their rank, since those who disobey the canons immediately forfeit any office they have received.*⁴⁹ *Or perhaps one might say that these canons were composed as exhortations,^j not laid down as commandments. For a decree imposes a necessity but an exhortation appeals to free will.*

DISTINCTION FIVE

Part 1.

What^k has been written above about privileges and other matters applies to secular as well as ecclesiastical ordinances. Now, let us return

^e**appropriate**—that is, equitable and just.

^f**all**—that is, because flesh is prohibited, so also are all things that come from the flesh.

^g**sowing**—that is, seed.

^h**sumptuous**—But one may eat small fish. D. 82 c. 5.

ⁱ**other matters**—So it may be argued that when one thing is conceded, all similar things are therefore understood to be conceded. D. 5 c. 4; D. 27 c. 6; C. 22 q. 2 c. 19.

Part 4. This is the fourth part of the distinction, in which he solves the difficulty mentioned above. Archid.

Dicta Gratiani post c. 6. CASE. Gratian says that the three capitula presented above have been abrogated, and therefore those who do not observe them are not called transgressors. If they have not been abrogated, those disobeying them should be deprived of their rank, unless these capitula may be said to give a counsel, not a precept.

^j*exhortations*—for one does not obey a command when one has merely been exhorted. Dig. 3. 2. 20.

^b**mercy**—Why, then, is it said elsewhere that mercy is never given to the impenitent? C. 24 q. 2 c. 2. So you must understand this to concern mercy as to punishment, not mercy as to fault. Therefore, Gregory tolerates such a crime because of the danger of schism and scandal. So it should not be said that he overlooks them, although he does not punish them on account of their number or on account of

D. 5. This distinction is divided into two parts. In the first he proves that natural law does not change. The second part begins, "But, since. . . ."

Dicta Gratiani ante c. 1. CASE. The master continues the topic he has been treating from [continued on next page]

^k*What*—In this fifth distinction he begins to identify the difference between natural law and other laws. It should be

noted, therefore, that natural law differs from other laws in four ways: in origin, dignity, scope, and the force of its decisions. It differs in origin because it began with the appearance of rational creatures. *Instit.* 2. 1. 11 [2. 1 (*in medio*)]. But other laws arise from human invention. D. 6 c. 3. It differs in dignity because natural law does not change. *Instit.* 1. 2. 11. For what is contrary to natural law is iniquitous. D. 1 c. 7 (*in fine*). The same is true as to scope since by natural law all things are common, but this is not the case by other law. The same is true as to the force of its decisions because there may be no dispensation from natural law, although there often is from other laws.

Dicta Gratiani ante **c. 1.** **CASE.** (continued) D. 3 c. 3 until now. He has been explaining everything that pertains to both secular and ecclesiastical ordinances. Now in this fifth distinction he returns to natural law and identifies the differences between natural law and other laws. Natural law receives first place among other laws because of its age and dignity. It does so because of its age since it began with the appearance of rational creatures and because of its dignity since it does not change. But since it says above that natural law is contained in the Law and the Gospel, and certain things are now conceded contrary to these, it appears that the natural law is mutable and changes. This is shown by the example of women who may now enter a church immediately after giving birth and during menstruation although the Law says otherwise; and by the example of a child who may be baptized immediately after birth. On this matter he presents the following capitula.

[a]began—as to its understanding, not as to its essence. Indeed, it would be more correct to say that it then began as to its use because natural law in the sense of natural equity existed from eternity, unless you wish to understand this of divine law, which existed before it was reduced to writing.

[b]immutable—as to its precepts and prohibitions. *Dicta Gratiani post* D. 6 c. 3.

Part 2. This is the second part of the distinction, in which an objection is raised against the statement that natural law does not change. It is shown in the following three capitula that this law does change. The solution is given below at *dicta Gratiani* pr. [§ 1] *post* D. 6 c. 3. The master's objection is that women after childbirth and during menstruation were at one time prohibited from entering a church but today are not so prohibited, and that this prohibition came from the

to the difference[50] *between natural law and other laws. Natural law receives first place among all others because of its age and dignity. For it began[a] with the appearance of rational creatures and does not change over time, but remains immutable.[b]*

Part 2.

But, since, as said above, natural law is that contained in the Law and the Gospel, and since we find certain things are now conceded which are contrary to what is prescribed in the Law, it seems that natural law is not immutable. For in the Law [cf. Lev. 12:2–5] it was commanded that a woman not enter the temple for forty[c] days if she had given birth to a male child, and for eighty days in the case of a female. In contrast, a woman is not now prohibited from entering a church immediately after giving birth. Again, a woman undergoing menstruation was considered unclean according to the Law [Lev. 15:19]. Now, however, she is not prohibited from entering a church immediately[51] or from receiving the sacrament of holy communion; nor is it prohibited that a mother or her child be baptized immediately after the birth.

So, Gregory writes to the same Augustine, bishop of the English:[52]

[PALEA C. 1.

[You have learned from the precepts of the Old Testament [Lev. 12:2–5] how many days after she has given birth a woman may enter the church. She ought to abstain for thirty-three days in the case of a male, and sixty-six days in the case of a female, but, be it understood, this is to be taken symbolically.]

natural law. Therefore, it follows that natural law has changed.

[c]forty—because this is the number of days that the male embryo is not alive before the infusion of the soul, whereas the corresponding period of the female fetus is eighty days.[(22)] But then it would seem that the prohibition ought to apply to the time following conception. It is otherwise on account of uncertainty: because the time of conception is unknown and it is also unknown whether a male or female will be born. Io.

C. 2. CASE. A woman may enter a church immediately after giving birth because there is no burden of sin in this, for there is fault in the delight of the flesh, not in pain. Otherwise we would turn the pain of childbirth into a fault.

^a**If a woman**—Some codices place c. 1 here, prefixed to this. That text is a palea.

^b**burden of sin**—But is it not true that one can read in a

---

[Gregory in the same place:][53]

C. 2. *A woman incurs no burden of sin if she enters a church to give thanks in the very hour she has given birth.*

If a woman,^a in the very hour she gives birth, enters a church to give thanks, she incurs no burden of sin^b for there is fault in fleshly delight, not in pain. So, while in fleshly intercourse there is pleasure, in giving birth to children there is only pain and sorrow. So it was said at first to the mother of all[54] [Gen. 3:16], "In pain you shall bring forth children." So then, if we were to forbid a woman who has given birth from entering a church, we would be classing her very punishment^c as a fault.

Also, to the same:[55]

C. 3. *Nothing prohibits the baptism of a woman or her child in the very hour of the birth.*

When there is danger of death, it is in no way forbidden[56] to baptize either a woman who has given birth or her child, even in the very hour when she has given birth or the child been born, because, although the grace of the holy mystery should be granted with great care to the living and those understanding it, in the case of one near death, it should be given without any delay, lest, at the very time someone seeks to be granted the mystery of redemption, that one not be redeemed on account of some short delay.^d

Also:[57]

C. 4. *Before a child has been weaned and the mother purified, her husband should not initiate sexual relations.*

§1. A husband ought not initiate sexual relations until the newborn has been weaned.^e Nevertheless,[58] among married couples the depraved

there is a necessity or not. X 3. 47. 1. Nevertheless, custom is to the contrary. Io.

^c**punishment**—Indeed, affliction ought not to be added to those already afflicted. C. 7 q. 1 c. 2. Nevertheless, there is a contrary instance, for a woman corrupted by violence may not become a consecrated virgin. D. 26 c. 2; C. 32 q. 5 c. 14. Again, one who has his members mutilated is not promoted [to higher ecclesiastical rank]. D. 55.

C. 3. CASE. A woman and the child just born to her may be baptized when they are in danger of death, lest a short delay endanger their redemption.

^d**delay**—So it may be argued that delay is to be avoided when there is fear of danger. D. 28 c. 13; *De cons.* D. 4 c. 98. The contrary argument may be made from Dig. 5. 1. 21; Dig. 46. 3. 105. The solution is that the latter texts apply to contracts and the former ones to dangers to the soul. Io.

C. 4. CASE. Three points are made in the present capitulum. First, a man ought not to sleep with his wife during the time of purification before her child is weaned. Nor should the child be given to another to nurse on account of incontinence. The second section, which begins, "And so women . . . ," says that a menstruating woman may enter a church because the excrescence ought not to be accounted a fault. The third section, which begins, "Reception. . . ," says that a woman at the time of childbirth is not to be pre-

---

brocard on the *Penitential of Theodore*⁽²³⁾ that a woman ought to wait thirty-three days after the birth of a male before entering a church and forty-six days after the birth of a female? If she enters before that time she shall do penance on bread and water for as many days as should have elapsed before she entered the church. Also, one who had sexual relations during these days shall do penance for ten days on bread and water. This custom is contrary to what Gregory says in this capitulum. You may understand Theodore to be speaking of a woman who does not enter the church out of devotion, or of one who enters without necessity. But I believe it to be more correct that she may enter whether

vented from approaching the Body of Christ. Nevertheless if she abstains out of devotion it is praiseworthy.

^e**weaned**—Here the time of weaning means the time after birth when the woman is filled with too much milk and unless it is drawn off by the child she will become sick. Therefore, she is prohibited during this time from sexual relations with her husband because sickness and leprosy can result from that union. What if the woman asks what is owed her from her husband during the time of menstruation or the time of purification? I say he should not render the debt to her unless he is afraid she will fornicate. D. 13 c. 1. Again, if the man asks the woman for the debt during the

time of menstruation, the woman should refuse and explain the reason to him. Dig. 46. 3. 105.

[a]**prevented**—that is, they should be dissuaded by a prohibition. That is how some explain this text.

[b]**unwillingly**—As a rule, what one suffers against his will does not prejudice him, as one can see here and in D. 50 c. 32; Cod. 6. 25. 1; Cod. 5. 31. 8; Cod. 7. 62. 5. The opposite may be argued from D. 55 c. 13; D. 49 c. 2; Cod. 6. 46. 4. Again it may be argued that what is done to people against their will and contrary to their wishes ought not to be imputed to them. *De cons.* D. 5 c. 26; C. 15 q. 1 c. 5; C. 15 q. 6 c. 1; C. 31 q. 2 c. 4. Io. The solution is that if anyone is forced by an absolute constraint to do something against God, it is not imputed to him with respect to God. It is otherwise if the constraint is relative. X 1. 40. 5; D. 50 c. 32. In contracts, if someone is coerced by a fear that ought to shake a constant man, it is not imputed to him, as is seen in the same texts and X 1. 40. 4, unless this fear arises through his own fault, as in Dig. 4. 2. 21. It is otherwise in religious orders, for if a person is mutilated by force he may not be promoted. X 1. 20. 6. Also, a woman who has been corrupted by force may not be a consecrated virgin. C. 32 q. 5 c. 14. This is out of reverence for the sacraments and the harm it does to the symbolism. So it seems to me, Bart. Brix., that it is to be briefly explained.

[c]**person**—So it may be argued that what is conceded to one is conceded to others. D. 4 c. 6. This is true if something is conceded according to the common law. A privilege is different. C. 16 q. 1 c. 39; C. 7 q. 1 c. 17.

[d]**acknowledge**—The contrary may be argued from C. 22 q. 2 c. 9. You may say that anyone may call himself a sinner

as long as he does not believe the opposite. *De poen.* D. 3 c. 32.[(24)]

[e]**without fault**—So it may be argued that guilt should not always be imputed where there is prior fault. C. 15 q. 1 c. 7.

D. 6. CASE. Gratian asks whether, after nocturnal pollution or emission, one may receive the Body of Christ or a priest may celebrate the Mass. The law as to this is set forth in

custom has grown up of women refusing to nurse their own babies and handing them over to other women to nurse. The only reason, apparently, is their incontinence, for they refuse to nurse their newborns to avoid practicing continence.

§2. And so women following this depraved custom, who hand their children over to others to nurse, should not have relations with their husbands before their purification has been completed [Lev. 15:24]. So too, even when they have not given birth, they should certainly be prevented[a] from having relations with their husbands when they are undergoing their usual flow of menstruation. For the sacred law [Lev. 20:18] inflicted death on a man who approached a menstruating woman.

Nevertheless, a woman undergoing the usual period of menstruation should not be prohibited from entering a church since fault ought not to be imputed to an excrescence of nature. Thus, it is unjust that, on account of what is suffered unwillingly,[b] they be deprived of entrance into a church. For we know that the woman who suffered from the issue of blood, coming up[59] behind the Lord, touched the hem of his garment and was immediately freed from her infirmity [Matt. 9:20–23]. Therefore, if it was praiseworthy for her with the issue of blood to touch the garment of the Lord, why should a woman suffering menstrual bleeding not be allowed to enter the Lord's[60] church? *And later:* If, then, it was proper that the woman presumed to touch the Lord's garment in her illness, why should what was granted to one infirm person[c] not be conceded to all women who endure a similar infirmity due to a natural debility?

§3. Reception of the sacrament of holy communion should not be prohibited during the same period. If a woman, on account of her great reverence, does not presume to receive, that is to be commended; but if she receives she is not to be judged. Even when they have no fault good people will sometimes acknowledge[d] one. This is because things that happen without fault often occur on account of a fault. For example, we eat, which is without fault,[e] when we are hungry, but it is because of the first man's sin that we become hungry.

DISTINCTION SIX

Now,[f] since mention has been made of an excrescence of nature, it is to be determined whether, after the emission that sometimes happens

the following chapters.

[f]**Now**—Here begins the sixth distinction, in which, because he has made mention of an excrescence of nature, he

digresses from his main point to speak of nocturnal pollution. Accordingly, he shows on the authority of Gregory how and why it happens, and when it is a sin, and when not. Afterwards, he responds to objections concerning what has been said in the section that begins, "Here is our solution. . . ." Note that according to some, nocturnal pollution and emission are not even a venial sin when they arise from infirmity, especially when there is sorrow, as in the follow-

polluted in sleep, did he sin or not? It would seem that he did. One could answer that although he was contrite, nevertheless vestiges and remnants remain, just as in a freed man vestiges of servitude remain and therefore his master has rights of succession. Instit. 3. 7. 3 [3. 8]. So, the marriage of a madman continues on account of what remains of his previous will. Dig. 1. 6. 8. Therefore, the act would be imputed to me in any event, if I had impure thoughts initially.

during dreams, one may receive the Body of the Lord, or, if one is a priest, celebrate the sacred mysteries.

Concerning these issues, St. Gregory writes to Augustine, bishop of the English (Reply 9):[61]

C. 1. *Concerning the different sorts of emissions.*

§1. The Testament[a] of the Old Law calls such a man[b] polluted before the Lord[62] and, unless he has been washed with water, he is not allowed to enter the assembly until the evening.

§2. Spiritual people, however, consider a man who is tempted to impurity[c] through a dream and then defiled in his imagination through actual[63] fantasizing[d] to be polluted. He is "to be washed with water," [e] that is, guilty thoughts are to be cleansed away by tears; and, until the fires of temptation have subsided, he should count himself guilty until evening,[f] as it were.

C. 1. CASE. This capitulum is divided into three sections. In the first section it says that if someone has been polluted by nocturnal pollution, he is not permitted to enter a church until evening, unless he has washed with water. In the second section, which begins, "Spiritual people. . . ," Gregory says that this may be understood spiritually, that is, of one polluted in his mind by impure thoughts, who is to be washed with the water of penitence and who is to consider himself guilty until evening unless the fires of temptation have previously subsided. In the third section, which begins, "But a distinction. . . ," it says that pollution occurs in three ways. Sometimes, be it noted, it occurs because of a superfluity of nature or illness, sometimes from overeating, and sometimes from earlier impure thoughts. When it arises from natural superfluity or infirmity, pollution is not to be imputed to anyone, for it is more an affliction than a sin. When however, it proceeds from overeating, such pollution involves some guilt, but, nevertheless, in case of necessity, a priest is not prohibited on this account from celebrating Mass, although he ought not to celebrate if other priests are present. But he is not prohibited from taking the Body of Christ, especially if the pollution in sleep was not brought on by impure fantasies. When, however, it proceeds from previous impure thoughts, then he ought to abstain from both for his mind appears to have been at fault because he experienced unconsciously what he thought of consciously.

ing capitulum where it says that this pollution or emission "is in no way to be feared since a mind. . . ." That which proceeds from overeating is a venial sin, as in the following capitulum where it says the mind is thus partially at fault. Similarly, that which proceeds from earlier thoughts is a sin, but a distinction must be drawn because the pollution arising from them is a venial sin when these thoughts did not proceed to consent. If they did proceed to consent, then the sin is mortal. According to the opinion of some people, someone can, without knowing it, sin mortally or venially, or do what is good and merit eternal life, for when the body is sleeping the soul is on watch. Thus it is written [Cant. 5:2], "My heart watches for you, O God." They say the same as to a madman, that fault arises in his madness, as may be argued from C. 15 q. 1 c. 13 (*in fine*). Indeed, one can sin without knowing it. C. 23 q. 7 c. 4. The contrary may be argued from Dig. 44. 7. 5 pr. [44. 7. 4], where it says that one does not sin without knowing it. Others say that sleeping people do not sin. C. 15 q. 1 c. 8; C. 15 q. 1 c. 5. Sleeping people, be it noted, are compared to madmen, Dig. 41. 2. 1. 2, and so do not sin. If, therefore, a man did not arrive at consent, he does not sin at all in nocturnal pollution. If he did, however, according to these people, he sins mortally, unless, perhaps, he imagined himself with his own wife, and then he would not sin mortally because his affection would be directed toward his wife. This opinion is favored by H. and proven from D. 6 c. 3 (at "Indeed, lustful imaginings [*Luxuriae*]"). But it is not true because he in no way sins. D. 6 c. 1; C. 15 q. 1 c. 5. But it may be objected against the previous opinion that if he had impure thoughts, but repented immediately before he slept, and then was

have previously subsided. In the third section, which begins, "But a distinction. . . ," it says that pollution occurs in three ways. Sometimes, be it noted, it occurs because of a superfluity of nature or illness, sometimes from overeating, and sometimes from earlier impure thoughts. When it arises from natural superfluity or infirmity, pollution is not to be imputed to anyone, for it is more an affliction than a sin. When however, it proceeds from overeating, such pollution involves some guilt, but, nevertheless, in case of necessity, a priest is not prohibited on this account from celebrating Mass, although he ought not to celebrate if other priests are present. But he is not prohibited from taking the Body of Christ, especially if the pollution in sleep was not brought on by impure fantasies. When, however, it proceeds from previous impure thoughts, then he ought to abstain from both for his mind appears to have been at fault because he experienced unconsciously what he thought of consciously.

[a]**Testament**—It is written in Leviticus [15:16] that the Lord said that if a man is polluted nocturnally by semen, he must leave the camp and not return until he washes before evening. After the sun goes down he may return to camp. Gregory expounds this text and refers it to those who have been mentally polluted.

[b]**such a man**—The custom in question is observed by the Romans. C. 33 q. 4 c. 7.

[c]**impurity**—that is, impure thoughts.

[d]**fantasizing**—that he sees a woman and takes pleasure in her.

[e]**water**—that is, penitence.

[f]**evening**—that is, until the fire of temptation has subsided. ADDITION. Wrongful thought is to be explained in this

way: the guilt lasts as long as the thinking, but when the sin passes into action, the guilt then remains. C. 32 q. 7 c. 5;[25] *De cons.* D. 4 c. 146. Or you may say that "until evening" means "until penitence," for evening means the end of the sin. Hu. is of the same view.

[a]**suffered**—since he is understood to have suffered something rather than to have done something.

[b]**fault**—that is, it is venial sin, and one is not prohibited from taking the Eucharist, but one is prohibited and should not confect it except in cases of necessity.

[c]**necessity**—for necessity knows no law. *De cons.* D. 1. c. 11.

[d]**humbly**—Therefore, this is a matter of counsel. Note that he may indeed celebrate if he wishes for a priest need not abstain from the celebration of Mass on account of slight faults, but he must abstain on account of those for which he could be excommunicated. *De cons.* D. 2 c. 15. Nevertheless, for any mortal sin he is personally suspended, X 3. 2. 10, unless he does penitence. X 1. 11. 17. Hu.

[e]**however**—that is, especially.

[f]**the emission**—the pollution itself.

[g]**not guilty**—as though to say that the mind is not guilty in sleep, nor guilty after sleep, when it has free will. But then it is guilty if he falls into gluttony. Thus it seems clear enough that a man does not sin in sleep.

[h]**free**—add, "though he sinned earlier."

[i]**source**—that is, the evil thoughts.

§3. But a distinction must be made concerning the emission itself, and what caused it in the sleeper's mind should be carefully examined. Sometimes pollution occurs because of overeating, sometimes because of a mere superfluity of nature or infirmity, and sometimes because of thoughts. Certainly, the kind of emission that comes from a superfluity of nature or infirmity is in no way to be feared, since a mind that has unconsciously suffered[a] something is more to be pitied than one that has done something. Also, when a gluttonous appetite gets caught up in excessive eating and the reservoirs of the humors are overburdened from this, then the mind is partially at fault,[b] but not, however, to such an extent as to justify prohibition from participation in the sacred mysteries or even the celebration of Mass, if a feast day requires it or necessity[c] compels one to perform the mystery because there is no other priest in the vicinity.[64] If there are others who can perform the mystery,[65] an emission caused by overeating should not prevent one from participating in the sacred mystery (although, in my opinion, one should humbly[d] abstain from offering the sacred mystery). This, however,[e] is only true when the emission[f] did not come upon the sleeper because of impure thoughts. There are some in whom emission usually happens in such a way that, the mind, overcome by bodily sleep, is not defiled by the impure emission.[66]

In this matter, one thing is clear: the mind itself is not guilty[g] then, yet[67] it was completely free[h] in its act of willing, because it recalls falling into gluttony while awake, even though it does not remember what happened while the body was asleep. But, it seems, if the emission occurred in the sleeper's mind because of impure thoughts while awake, his mind is guilty. For that was the source[i] of the pollution, because what he thought about consciously, he then experienced unconsciously. On account of such pollution, it is fitting to abstain from the sacred mystery.[68]

[**PALEA**[69] **C. 2.** *Sin is not said to be committed by thought alone but by delight and consent.*

[It should be considered whether thoughts happened as a suggestion, or with delight, or (what is the worst) with consent to sin. A sin is constituted by three things, suggestion, delight, and consent. The suggestion is certainly by the Devil, delight by the flesh, and consent by the spirit. In this way the serpent first suggested the sin, then Eve (the flesh as it were) delighted in it, and Adam (the spirit as it were) consented.

[Much discernment between suggestion, delight, and consent is necessary for the mind to act as its own judge.[70] For, although an evil spirit might suggest a sin to the mind, if no delight in the sin follows, sin is in no way committed because sin comes to birth only when the flesh begins to delight in sin. If consent arises after deliberation, then the sin is complete. Therefore, in suggestion is the seed of sin, in delight its nurture, in consent its completion.

[It often happens that the flesh delights in what an evil spirit has sown in thought but the mind does not consent to the delight. And, because the flesh cannot delight without the soul, the mind, while struggling against the delights of the flesh, becomes bound up in them unwillingly. Thus, through reason the soul repudiates the delight and does not consent to it. Nevertheless it is both bound up in the delight and at the same time acutely distressed to be so bound. And thus the most valiant soldier of the celestial army lamented and said [Rom. 7:23], "I see another law in my members fighting against the law of my mind and leading me captive in the law of sin that is in my members." But[71] if he was a captive, he was not fighting; nevertheless he both was captive and did fight. If, however, he fought, he was not a captive. Thus there was a law in his members fighting against the law of his mind. If the mind fought, then it was not captive. So you see that the man (as I have said) is both captive and free, free by the justice that he loves, captive by the delight that he bears unwillingly.]

Also, Isidore, in Opinions on the Supreme Good, *III, VI:*[72]

C. 3. *When there is sin in pollution during dreams.*

There is no sin when one is polluted unwillingly during a dream. It is a sin if impure desire preceded pollution. Indeed, lustful imaginings of things we have actually experienced often enter sleepers' minds, but this is harmless if it happens without desire.[a]

The one who is polluted by nocturnal emission, even without memory of impure thoughts, nevertheless feels himself defiled; in this case, then, let him ascribe his being tempted to his own fault and immediately wash the uncleanness away with tears.

§1. Here is our solution to this:[b] *Natural law is contained in the Law and the Gospel, but it can be shown that not everything contained in the Law and the Gospel pertains to natural law. For certain things in the Law are moral precepts such as* [Exod. 20:13; Deut. 5:17.] *"You shall not kill"; others are symbolic such as, for example, the precepts concerning sacrifice, and other similar things, like the lamb.*[73] *Moral commandments pertain to natural law and so they are seen to be unchangeable. Nevertheless, the symbolic precepts conjoined with the natural law, in so far as they deal with observances, may be seen to be different from natural law and, although their observances seem to undergo change, their moral significance does not change. Thus, as said above, natural law, which began with the appearance of rational creatures, remains unchanged.*

Dicta Gratiani post **c. 3. CASE.** This passage is divided into two sections. In the first section Gratian resolves the question that he raised above at *dicta Gratiani ante* D. 5 c. 1 concerning the mutability and variation of the natural law. He said that natural law is contained in the Law and the Gospel. But, nevertheless, not everything in the Law and the Gospel belongs to natural law insofar as its literal forms are concerned. There are in the Law, be it noted, certain moral precepts such as you shall not kill, and so forth. These do not change, nor does natural law in them. There are some symbolic precepts such as the sacrificing of a lamb, and similar things. These change as to their literal forms but not as to their moral meaning, and, as to this meaning, natural law is unchanged and remains as it has been since the appearance of rational creatures. In the second section, which begins, "Customary law. . .," it says that customary law began after natural ordinance when men began to live together, which is believed to have happened at the time when it is written that Cain built a city. This law, after it was almost extinguished on account of the flood, was either restored by Nimrod or, more probably, continued unchanged because he began to oppress men. This is proven by the authority of Genesis [10:8].

[b]*to this*—Here the master presents a solution to the objections that were raised in the previous distinction. Following him, we accordingly can distinguish even more completely. Of the things contained in the Law, some are moral, some symbolic. Those that are moral shape our conduct. Consequently, they are understood according to their literal meaning: for example, you shall

C. 3. CASE. Isidore asks whether man sins through nocturnal pollution when he is sleeping. He answers no, unless desire is present, for he sins when he incites lust while awake. Nevertheless, however pollution occurred, he ought to account it a fault.

[a]**desire**—that is, without the ardor of his earlier lust.

love God; you shall not kill; honor your father. This is discussed in C. 32 q. 7 c. 16. Symbolic things should be taken as types signifying something beyond the literal sense. Of these, some are sacramental, others ritual. For sacramentals, one can give some explanation for the literal expression given to the prescriptions: for example, circumcision and the observance of the sabbath. X 3. 42. 3; X 1. 2. 3. No explanation can be given for the literal expression given to ritual commandments: for example, you shall not plow with an ox and an ass together, C. 16 q. 7 c. 22; you shall not make clothing of wool and linen mixed; you shall not sow a field with different seeds. Therefore, the moral law does not change, but the literal form of sacramentals and rituals does. One may not say on that account that natural law changes for natural law is not found in the literal form, which is changeable, but in the symbolic meaning, which does not change. Therefore, the law does not change. C. 1 q. 1 c. 64.

ªCustomary law—Here he shows when customary law and enactments began. He says that customary law began at the time of Cain, the first to build a city, which he named Enoch after his son, and that the law of enactments began with Moses. Io.

ᵇalmost extinct—The law, therefore, did not end—that is, it did not end with those seven people, just as it could not begin with those seven, because at least ten are needed to form a community. C. 10 q. 3 c. 3.

ᶜbefore the Lord—that is, "of those who were the Lord's"; or "with the Lord's permission" because everything happens according to God's will. C. 26 q. 5 c. 14.

D. 7. This distinction is divided into two parts. The second begins, "After a while. . . ."

Dicta Gratiani ante c. 1. CASE. It was shown above when natural law and customary law began. Now he shows in this seventh distinction when enacted law began. Gratian says that it began first with Moses and later with others, as it says in the following capitulum.

ᵈThe enactment—In this seventh distinction he shows when and by whom human enactments, both ecclesiastical and secular, were begun. Ecclesiastical enactments were be-

gun in Moses' time by Moses. Secular ordinances began with different people at different times, as appears in the following capitulum.

ᵉprescriptions—that is, with judgments. It is written in Exodus [21:1–6] that the Lord said to the children of Israel through Moses: If you buy a Hebrew slave, that is, one who was not a slave before, he shall serve you six years, unless the Jubilee Year intervenes, and in the seventh he shall go

§2. *Customary law* ª *began after natural law, when people began to gather as one and live together. It is believed that this happened at the time when Cain built a city [Gen. 4:17]. But with the flood [Gen. 7], this law seems to have become almost extinct* ᵇ *because of the scarcity of people. Afterwards, at the time of Nimrod, it was restored, or more probably continued unchanged, since he, along with some others, began to oppress other people. Others, out of weakness, also became subject to their power, as is read of him in Genesis*[74] *[10:9], "Nimrod became a great hunter before the Lord,"* ᶜ *that is, a great oppressor and killer of the men he had gathered to build the tower.*[75]

DISTINCTION SEVEN

Part 1.

The enactment ᵈ *of law began with the prescriptions* ᵉ *that* ᶠ *the Lord gave to Moses, when he said [Exod. 21:1]: "If you buy a Hebrew slave. . . ."*

So, Isidore in Etymologies, *V, 1, says:*[76]

C. 1. *Concerning lawgivers.*

§1. Among the Hebrew people, Moses was the first of all those who set

free without charge, with such clothes as he had when he arrived. If he earlier had a wife and children, he will leave with the wife and children. If his master gave him a wife, the woman and children will stay with the master. But if the slave chooses to remain with his master for love of the master or of his wife and children, his master will bring him to "the gods," that is, to the priests, and take him to the door of the tabernacle; his ear will be pierced with an awl as a sign of perpetual servitude; and he will be a slave as long as he lives, or until the next Jubilee Year. Moses began his judgments with this enactment as is said in Exodus [21:1]. Ioan.

ᶠthat—for one equipped with the divine Scriptures has acquired the beginning of all science. *Dicta Gratiani* pr. *post* D. 37 c. 7.

C. 1. CASE. In the first section of this capitulum, seven people are enumerated who compiled the first laws for others: Moses, Phoroneus, Mercury, and so forth. In the second section, which begins, "Then, because. . . ," it says that the Roman people commissioned ten men to translate the books of Solon into the Latin language onto ten tables and that they later added two tables explaining them.

Trismegistus—so called because of his three powers, namely, eloquence, knowledge, and virtue, as you will find in D. 37 c. 14; C. 16 q. 1 c. 26; Cod. 10. 53. 7 [10. 52. 7].

first—Romulus gave laws earlier but only a few. Dig. 1. 2. 2. Because they were few, it says here that this person was the first to compile them.

forth the divine ordinances in the sacred Scriptures. King Phoroneus was the first to issue ordinances and decisions.[77] Mercury Trismegistus[a] was the first to propound ordinances for the Egyptians. Solon was the first to give ordinances to the Athenians. Lycurgus was the first to make laws by the authority of Apollo for the Lacedaemonians. Numa Pompilius, who succeeded Romulus in the kingship, was the first[b] to decree ordinances for the Romans.

§2. Then, because the people could not put up with their conniving magistrates, they created the Decemvirs[c] to write down their ordinances. These arranged the ordinances, which were translated into Latin from the books of Solon, on twelve tables.

[*Isidore,* Etymologies, *V, I:*][78]

C. 2. *The names of those who arranged the Laws of the XII Tables.*[79]

§1. Appius Claudius, T. Genutius, P. Sestius, Sp. Veturius, C. Julius, A. Manlius, Ser. Sulpicius, P. Curatius, T. Romilius, and Sp. Postumius were chosen as Decemvirs for compiling the ordinances. The consul Pompeius was the first who wanted to arrange the ordinances in books, but he did not succeed for fear[d] of detractors. Later, Caesar began to do it, but he was killed before he could finish.

Part 2.

§2. After a while, the old ordinances became so obsolete from age and lack of pertinence that some were completely worthless. Now, although these are no longer in use, an acquaintance with them seems necessary.[e]

§3. New ordinances began with the Caesar Constantine and his successors but were confused and disordered. Later, the Augustus Theodosius II drew up, after the model of the Gregorian and Hermogenian Codes, a collection of enactments beginning with the time of Constantine, under titles belonging to each emperor.[80] This he called,[f] from his own name, the Theodosian Code.

wanting in the ten tables, added an additional two tables. These laws were called the Laws of the XII Tables. Then Isidore immediately indicates in the next capitulum who these ten men were.

C. 2. CASE. This capitulum is divided into three sections. In the first section, the names of the ten men who first translated the laws are given. It says that the consuls Pompeius and Caesar first wanted to arrange the laws, but they were not able to complete the task. In the second section, it says that the laws fell into disuse on account of their age. Knowledge of them is necessary even if they are not in use. In the third section, it says that the new laws began with Constantine and his successors, but because they were confused and disordered Theodosius II drew up a code on the model of the Gregorian and Hermogenian codes from the enactments of the emperors, which he called the Theodosian Code. The second section begins, "After a while. . . ." The third section begins, "New ordinances. . . ."

fear—So it may be argued that fear of words is an excuse. C. 23 q. 8 c. 21 § 1. The same may be argued from Dig. 29. 2. 6 (*in fine*). The opposite may be argued from X 1. 40. 5.

necessary—But if the use of them has vanished why should they use up parchment? D. 19 c. 1. But knowledge of them is necessary in order to know why they vanished. Cod. 6. 51. 1. The pope himself argues from abro-

Decemvirs—As the laws had fallen into disuse for thirty years on account of strife between the plebeians and nobles, ten men were appointed who translated the laws collected from the Greek cities into Latin and wrote them on tablets of ivory. Later the same ten men, having received power to correct and interpret the laws, and seeing that much was

gated law, as in X 2. 1. 13. Or it is necessary not so that they be approved but so that what is badly expressed be rejected. D. 37 c. 7; D. 37 c. 11.

called—Later Justinian changed this and made a single code out of the three. Cod. Proem. I pr. [Cod. 1. 1 pr.] Ioan. Theutonicus.

D. 8. This distinction is divided into two parts. In the first, he shows that by natural law all things are common. The second part begins, "Now natural law. . . ."

***Dicta Gratiani ante* C. 1. CASE.** Earlier, in D. 5, what makes natural law different from other laws was identified. Now he explains how natural law is different from other laws as to scope, for by this law all things are common, but not by the other laws. He repeats what was said about its dignity. Accordingly, in this section, it says that the natural law differs from custom and enactment, for by natural law all things are common. This is shown by the authority of the New Testament and of Plato. By the law of custom, however, this is called "mine" and that "yours." On this matter, he presents the following capitulum.

ᵃ***natural law***—In this eighth distinction, the master shows how natural law excels other laws in its scope for according to this law all things are common.

ᵇ***those***—that is, the Apostles. C. 12 q. 1 c. 2.

ᶜ***his own***—As Plato imagined a republic in which all things are common, each person loved the other as himself.

C. 1. CASE. Certain heretics complained that they had been unjustly despoiled of the things they possessed in the name of the Church. Augustine attacked them saying that they could not complain, because they either possessed them by divine law or by human law. By divine law all things are common, so by it they could not possess the Church's goods. But by human law, human law being the ordinances of the emperors, heretics may possess nothing in the name of the Church. If they renounce the laws of the emperors, they must also renounce their possessions, whether they claim to possess them in the name of the Church or in their own name, because the Apostle commanded that kings be honored.

ᵈ**defend**—that is, claim, or defend retaining.

ᵉ**law**—So it appears that something is possessed not by divine law but by human law alone. To the contrary is C. 23 q. 7 c. 1, where it says that something is possessed by divine law. But this is not contrary because it says there that all

things are common by divine law among the just. So it certainly may be that something is proper to someone by divine law. Accordingly, it says there that possessions are possessed by human law because human law treats possessions most comprehensively, whereas canon law principally treats tithes and first fruits. Or you may say that there, divine law is taken narrowly as meaning canon law. Here, canon law is included in human law so that the defence of

DISTINCTION EIGHT

Part 1.

Natural law ᵃ *differs from custom and enactment. By natural law all things are common to all people, a practice found not only among those* ᵇ *of whom it was said* [Acts 4:32], *"The multitude of believers were of one heart and one mind. . . ," but also found in earlier times in the teachings of philosophers. So Plato lays out the order for a very just commonwealth where no one considers anything his own.* ᶜ *In contrast, by customary and enacted law, one thing is called "mine" and something else "another's."*

So, Augustine says on John 1 in Tracts [on John], *VI:*⁸¹

C. 1. *By divine law all things are common to all; by the enacted law, this is mine and that another's.*

By what law do you defendᵈ the Church's⁸² estates, divine or human? We find the divine law in the Scriptures, human law in the ordinances of kings. By which does each one possess what he possesses? Is it not by human law? For according to divine lawᵉ [Ps. 23:1], "The earth is the Lord's and the fullness thereof." God made poor and rich from the same clay and he nourishes poor and the rich by the same earth. In contrast, human law says, "This estate is mine, this house is mine, this slave is mine." ᶠ Now, human laws are the emperors' laws.⁸³ Why? Because God apportioned human laws to the human race through the emperors and kings of this world.

heresy may be raised against a claim for restitution. Note that it is not licit for a heretic to possess anything. C. 23 q. 5 c. 35; C. 23 q. 7 c. 1; C. 23 q. 7 c. 2. Also, it may be argued from this text that when there is a claim for restitution, we must ask by what law the claim is made: by an interdict or by the authority of the court.⁽²⁶⁾ Also, a claimant is obliged to explain the basis of his claim and what action is brought under canon law. X 2. 1. 15; X 2. 3. 3,⁽²⁷⁾ notwithstanding X 2. 1. 6.⁽²⁸⁾ The solution, I believe, is that the basis and the kind of action must be given so that the judge can make a decision according to the kind of action. X 5. 3. 31. Nevertheless, one is not compelled to specify an action, for according to [civil] ordinance the basis alone is sufficient. Cod. 6. 33. 3. Bar.

ᶠ**mine**—The words "mine" and "yours" pertain to ownership, not to good faith possession. Dig. 11. 7. 2. 1.

^a**benefit**—either through retaining possessions or recovering them.

^b**ordinances**—Enactments of the emperors as to ecclesiastical things would not have been valid had they not been subsequently confirmed by the Church. D. 96 c. 1.

^c**possess anything**—The canons commanded this. C. 23 q. 7 c. 1; C. 23 q. 7 c. 2.

^d**say**—So it may be argued that whoever says one thing says everything that follows from it. C. 11 q. 3 c. 84; C. 11 q. 3 c. 85; X 3. 24. 6;⁽²⁹⁾ Dig. 4. 2. 1. Again, it may be argued that the law as to one of several connected things is the same as the law as to the remainder. C. 1 q. 3 c. 7; C. 3 q. 6 c. 10. Again, it may be argued that whoever renounces one thing renounces everything that follows from it or is connected with it. D. 81 c. 17; C. 1 q. 1 c. 8; C. 9 q. 2 c. 3.

Also, in the same place, a little way down: Destroy⁸⁴ the laws of the emperors, and who would dare say that estate is mine, or that slave is mine, or this house is mine? If then, in order to possess these things, people follow the laws of kings, do you want us to overlook these laws for your benefit?^a

Also, in the same place, after a few intervening passages: Let those ordinances^b be examined where the emperors expressly command that those outside the communion of the Catholic Church, who usurp the name of Christian and refuse to worship in peace the author of peace, should not dare to possess anything^c in the name of the Church.⁸⁵ But what has the emperor to do with you? I have already said this concerns human law. Nevertheless, one of the Apostles wanted kings to be served and honored, and he said [1 Pet. 2:17], "Reverence kings." Do not say^d then, "What does this have to do with the king and me?" What then has it to do with your possessions and you? It is by the laws of kings that possessions are possessed. You say, "What does this have to do with the king and me?" Do not call those possessions yours since you possess those possessions by the very human laws you renounce.

Part 2.

Now^e *natural law similarly prevails by dignity over custom and enactments. So whatever has been either received in usages or set down in writing is to be held null and void if it is contrary to natural law.*

So, Augustine says in Confessions, *III, VIII:*⁸⁶

C. 2. *No one is permitted to act contrary to natural law.*

Acts against human usages^f are offenses^g to be avoided on account of the diversity^h of customs. No one, whether citizen or foreigner,ⁱ may, to suit his own pleasure, violate a people's agreement among themselves, whether established by the custom of the society or by law. For any part clashing with the whole is a disgrace.

But, if God commands anyone to do something contrary to custom or agreement, it must be done even if it has never been done there before. If it is a practice which has been discontinued, it must be resumed; if it was not previously instituted, it must be instituted. In the commonwealth he governs, a king has the right to order things that neither he nor any other has ever ordered before. Obedience to his orders is not against the

Part 2. He shows that natural law differs from others in dignity, for an enactment or custom contrary to it is void. He proves this in the following capitula.

^e**Now**—This is the beginning of the second part of the distinction, in which he shows why natural law is of greater dignity than other laws. Any enactment or custom contrary to it is void. On this matter, he presents all the following capitula.

C. 2. CASE. It says in this capitulum that offenses against human conventions are to be avoided so that the agreement of the people and the customs of the society be observed and not violated by anyone but enjoy perpetual validity. If, however, God commands something contrary to agreement or custom, then he should be obeyed. For if a king is to be obeyed in his kingdom or city, much more is the king of all creatures to be obeyed.

^f**usages**—good ones.

^g**offenses**—that is, like offenses. C. 32 q. 7 c. 13.

^h**diversity**—that is, opposition. Io.

ⁱ**foreigner**—Are travelers and scholars, then, bound to obey the customs of those among whom they sojourn? It may be argued that they are from this text and D. 12 c. 11; D. 41 c. 1. It may be argued to the contrary that travelers are not subject at random to the forum of the places they pass through. Dig. 5. 1. 19. 2. It may also be argued that only permanent inhabitants are bound by civic laws. Dig. 20. 1. 32.

^a**rather**—which is to say that it is not against the agreement of human society to obey him. Rather it is in accordance with that agreement for in every agreement it is always understood that there is an exception for acts of a higher authority. X 2. 24. 19.

^b**generally**—that is, by general ordinance.

^c**So**—This bears out his point because what God commands, as it belongs to natural law, stands ahead of customs or enactments.

^d**greater authority** — Therefore, a monk should obey his bishop more than his abbot, which is false. D. 58 c. 1;   D. 58 c. 2. But you may answer as noted in C. 11 q. 3 c. 97.⁽³⁰⁾

C. 3.   CASE. An evil custom had grown up in the archdiocese of Rheims. Accordingly, the pope commanded Hincmar, the archbishop of Rheims, to abolish the custom, for unless that custom were pulled up by its roots it would be adopted as law by impious people, and infractions would begin to be respected as ordinances.

^e**An evil**—The next seven capitula deal with bad customs.

^f**evil custom**—So it may be argued that something unlawful does not become lawful by reason of custom. The contrary may be argued from D. 4 c. 6. To the contrary, X 1. 4. 11. It is less reasonable that a custom create law. X 1. 41. 8. Again, it may be argued from this text that a good custom may create a privilege. C. 9 q. 3 c. 8; D. 82 c. 3.

C. 4. CASE. The following capitulum is clear and speaks for itself.

^g**truth**—It may be argued that truth prevails over opinion from this text and from D. 81 c. 5; X 1. 21. 4; X 4. 17. 12; X 5. 35. 2; X 4. 15. 6. The contrary may be argued from *Dicta Gratiani post* C. 3 q. 7 c. 1; X 3. 38. 19; Cod. 4. 20. 1.

^h**become manifest**—through teaching and revelation.

ⁱ**doubt**—Nevertheless, sometimes custom prevails over ordinance. X 1. 4. 11.

C. 5.   CASE. A certain bishop had a certain evil custom. Gregory wrote to him and ordered him to abolish it. That he ought to do so is proven by the authority of Christ who said [John 14:6], "I am the Truth," and did not say, "I am custom." It is also proven by the statement of Cyprian who said that a custom, no matter how ancient, is to be abolished when it is contrary to truth.

^j**says**—So it may be argued that one should stick closely

---

common interest of the community;   rather^a it is against the common interest when they are not obeyed. (Indeed, human society has generally^b agreed to obey its kings.) How much more then is God, the ruler of all his creation, to be obeyed without demur in what he has commanded? So,^c as in the government of human society, the greater authority^d is to be obeyed over the lesser, God is over everything.

Also, Pope Nicholas wrote to Hincmar, archbishop of Rheims:[87]

C. 3. *Dangerous custom is to be torn up by its roots.*

An evil^e custom^f is no more to be tolerated than a dangerous[88] infection because, unless the custom is quickly torn up by its roots, it will be adopted by wicked men as entitling them to a privilege. And then unchecked deviations and various[89] infractions will soon be revered as lawful and honored as immemorial privileges.

Also, Augustine, in On One Baptism [against the Donatists], *III, VI:*[90]

C. 4. *Custom is to be set aside in favor of truth and reason.*

"When the truth^g has becomes manifest,^h let custom yield to the truth."[91] So, respond plainly: who would doubtⁱ that custom should yield to manifest truth?   *Also:* "Let no one prefer custom to reason or truth because reason and truth always void custom." [92]

Also, Gregory wrote to Guitmund, bishop of Aversa:[93]

C. 5. *Every custom ought to be subordinate to truth.*

If you happen to oppose any custom, keep in mind that the Lord says^j [John 14:6], "I am the truth and the life." He did not say, "I am custom," but rather "I am the truth." And certainly (as we follow the opinion of St. Cyprian) every custom, no matter how ancient,^k no matter how widespread, is always to be subordinate to the truth; and usage that is contrary to the truth is to be abolished.

to the words. X 3. 30. 12.

^k**ancient**—C. 1 q. 3 c. 15. The contrary may be argued from Dig. 1. 3. 32. 1 [1. 3. 31]; Dig. 8. 4. 13. 1 [8. 4. 14]; X 1. 4. 8; X 3. 38. 11. So on account of a long passage of time what is less reasonable is upheld. You may say that what is ancient should be followed if it can be done without scandal. To the contrary, D. 4 c. 6.

C. 6. CASE. Some people were following custom in
contempt of the truth. Augustine says that they are acting
against their brethren and against God who said, "I am the
truth," and did not say, "I am custom." This is proven by
the example of Peter who yielded to Paul, the preacher of
truth. Thus reason and truth void custom.

ªcircumcision—and he made distinctions as to food
because of which Paul defied him to his face [Gal. 2:11]. C.

Also, Augustine in On [One] Baptism against the Donatists, *III, v:*[94]

C. 6. *When the truth has been revealed, custom should yield to it.*

Let the truth be shown to whoever in contempt of the truth presumes
to follow custom or is hateful and ill-disposed against the brethren. If
one is ungrateful toward God, let that one's church be set in order by his
inspiration. *And below:* The Lord said in the Gospel [John 14:6], "I am
the Truth." He did not say, "I am custom." And so, when truth has
become manifest, let custom yield to truth.[95] *And below:* Since the truth
has been revealed, let custom yield to truth, just as Peter, who had earlier
practiced circumcision,ª yielded to Paul, the preacher of truth. *And below:* Christ is the truth, we ought to follow truth rather than custom, because[96] reason and truth always void custom.

Also, in On [One] Baptism against the Donatists, *IV, III:*[97]

C. 7. *Custom opposes reason in vain.*

"In vain," he says, "do those defeated by reason advance customᵇ
against us, as if custom were greater than truth, and as if something that
the Holy Spirit has revealed to be better in spiritual affairs should not be
done." It is clearly true that reason and truth are to be preferred to
custom. But, when truth supports custom, nothing should be embraced
more firmly.

Also, Cyprian to Pompey in the letter against Stephen:[98]

C. 8. *Custom ought not stand in the way of reason.*

§1. Customᶜ that has crept into certain circles should not prevent truth
from prevailing and conquering. Since custom without truth is old error,

some are forced to elect those of another church. X 1. 4. 8
(*in fine*). Again, on account of custom a bishop may be
elected as provost. X 3. 8. 6. Again, on account of custom
a minor church may be chosen as the cathedral. X 2. 12. 13;
X 3. 8. 6; X 3. 8. 9. Again, by reason of custom, the abbot
collects stipends alone without the consent of his brothers.
X 3. 10. 6. Again, custom prevails in holy baptism. *De cons.*
D. 4 c. 80. Again, custom is respected in marriage. X 4. 11.
3. Again, in the case of clerical incontinence. D.
84 c. 4. Also in other cases which are noted in D. 1
c. 5. You should know, therefore, that for custom
to prevail against law, one requirement is that it gain
force through the passage of time. X 2. 12. 3; X 1.
4. 11. Again, that it be maintained by a contrary
popular judgment. X 5. 40. 25; Dig. 1. 3. 34. A-
gain, that it be done in the belief that they are acting
rightfully and with the in- tention of acting the same
way in the future. Other- wise, such a practice is
not to be called a practice, as Dig. 43. 19. 1. 6 [43. 18.
1]⁽³¹⁾ correctly says. A- gain, the matter must be
one where rights may change with the passage
of time. D. 93 c. 22. Again, one must be able
to say it is ancient and approved. X 1. 5. 4 (*circa
fine*). Again, it must con- tain natural equity. X 2.
14. 1; X 1. 4. 10. Again, it must be introduced with
the knowledge of the prince and not merely tolerated. X 3. 5. 18. Again it must not be introduced
through error. Dig. 1. 3. [continued on next page]

2 q. 7 c. 33.

C. 7. CASE. Some people put custom before truth, contrary
to the sacraments and other spiritual things. Accordingly,
Augustine was asked what the law is. Augustine answered
that it is vain to urge custom against the truth. If, nevertheless, truth supports a custom, nothing should be embraced
more firmly.

ᵇcustom—It would seem from all of these capitula that
law always prevails over custom. So now we will see when
custom prevails over law. We find in elections that custom
prevails over law, for one otherwise ineligible is eligible on
account of custom. D. 12 c. 8. Again, on account of custom

C. 8. CASE. This capitulum is divided into two sections.
In the first section it says that a bad custom which has crept
into certain circles ought not to prevail against truth and
reason. This is proven by the example of [3] Ezra [4:38]
saying that the truth prevails and holds firm. In the second
section, which begins, "One who is. . . ," it says something
may and should be overlooked in someone who acted in
ignorance. This is proven by the example of Paul saying [1
Tim. 1:13], "I obtained mercy because I acted in ignorance."
But whoever acts knowingly does not deserve indulgence.

ᶜCustom—You may understand this case in the same way
as *De cons.* D. 3 c. 2; D. 3 c. 3.⁽³²⁾

bCustom—(continued) 39; D. 8 c. 8. Again, the greater part of the people must be accustomed to the use of this custom because, as a minority of the people may not introduce a law, neither may they introduce a custom. Nevertheless, some say that for a custom to prevail over law, it must be immemorial. Such a custom, be it noted, has the status of an enactment. Dig. 43. 20. 3. 4 [43. 19. 3]; C. 3 q. 6 c. 10. Ioan. Briefly, you may take it that it suffices according to the canons that custom be reasonable and have gained force through passage of time. X 1. 4. 11. Bar. Brix.

aEzra—when he prohibited the Jews from marrying foreign women unless they were descended from their own tribe, and some married foreign women from the children of the Canaanites. Dicta Gratiani ante C. 28 q. 1 c. 1. Or it refers to how the Bible and Psalter, destroyed by the Babylonians, were restored by Ezra. Or, otherwise, when asked what has the greatest strength, and some responded woman, others the king, others man, and others the truth. Ezra approved the last answer.
bin ignorance—So it may be argued that ignorance of the law is an excuse, as here and in C. 30 q. 1 c. 6; dicta Gratiani pr. post C. 2 q. 3 c. 8; C. 24 q. 1 c. 41; D. 28 c. 16.

C. 9. CASE. Cyprian says in this capitulum that not every custom is to be imitated but only the truth of Christ and what he who is before all others did. This is proven by the authority of Isaiah attacking the Jews who did not follow truth.
calone—that is, no one contrary to him. C. 8 q. 1 c. 10.
dmen—Therefore, it would seem that the Jews were governed by human enactments. So this text is contrary to D. 12 c. 12, where it says that the Jews were ruled by divine enactments alone. But the truth is that at one time they were ruled by human enactments, namely, those of the Scribes and the Pharisees, as it says here. But today they are not, as it says there.

D. 9. This distinction is divided into two parts. In the first

it is proven that a custom contrary to God is not valid. In the second, which begins, "Do not treat. . . ," it is shown by nine capitula that the expositions of the saints do not prevail over the New and Old Testaments. Io. de Fan.

Dicta Gratiani ante c. 1. CASE. It was shown in the previous distinctions that natural law prevails over custom. In this ninth distinction it is shown that natural law prevails

we ought to follow truth and abandon error, recognizing with Ezraa that truth conquers, as it is written [3 Esdras 4:38], "The truth remains and will prevail unto eternity, it lives and holds firm for ever and ever."

§2. Also:[99] One who is simply in error may be forgiven,[100] as the Apostle Paul said of himself [1 Tim. 1:13], "I, who before was a blasphemer, a persecutor, and a reviler, obtained mercy since I acted in ignorance." b After inspiration and revelation, however, he who continues in his error sins with deliberation and knowledge, without the excuse of ignorance; having been conquered by reason, he now asserts himself out of presumption and obstinacy.

Also, to Caecilian, in Letters, *II, III:*[101]

C. 9. *One should follow the truth of God rather than human custom.*

If Christ alonec is to be heard, we should pay no heed to what those before us thought should be done, but rather to what Christ, who is before all others, did first. One should not follow human custom, but rather the truth of God for God spoke through the prophet Isaiah and said [Isa. 29:12], "They worship me to no purpose, teaching the commandments and precepts of men." d

Thus it is obvious that custom is subordinate to natural law.

DISTINCTION NINE

Part 1.

That enactmentse also yield to natural law is proved by many authorities.

For Augustine says to Count Boniface, in Letter *L:*[102]

over enactments. This is proven in the following capitula and should be understood of natural law consisting of precepts and prohibitions.
eThat enactments—Earlier, in D. 8, he showed how natural law prevails over custom. In this ninth distinction he shows how natural law overturns and prevails over human enactment. Throughout this distinction, the expression "natural law" is used for the divine law, which is contained in the Law and the Gospels. Also, throughout this distinction, the Old and New Testaments are called "the canonical Scriptures."

[**PALEA C. 1.** *The ordinances of princes should not prevail over natural law.*

[§ 1. When emperors establish evil ordinances that favor falsehood over truth, true believers are tested and the steadfast earn their crowns. When, on the other hand, they ordain good ordinances that defend truth against falsehood, evildoers are intimidated and the discerning corrected.]

§ 2. Therefore,[a] whoever refuses to obey imperial ordinances[b] laid down in favor of God's truth receives abundant punishment. But, whoever refuses to obey imperial ordinances made contrary to God's truth[103] receives abundant reward.[104]

[For, in the times of the prophets, all the kings among the people of God who did not prohibit and overturn everything instituted contrary to God's precepts are blamed; while those who prohibited and overturned them have their merits praised over those of others. King Nebuchadnezzar, when he was a slave of idols, established a sacrilegious ordinance that images be adored. Those who refused to obey his impious enactment did so piously and faithfully [Dan. 3]. The same king, when he had been corrected by a divine miracle, established a pious and praiseworthy ordinance in favor of the truth, that whoever spoke blasphemy against the God[105] of Shadrach, Meshach, and Abednego would immediately die, along with his whole house.]

Also, from a passage in Isidore's Opinions on the Supreme Good, *III, III:*[106]

C. 2. *Princes are bound to live according to their own ordinances.*

It is just that the prince be restrained by his own ordinances. For then, when he himself shows them respect, he shows that ordinances should be respected by all. That princes are to be bound by their own enactments in itself prohibits them from infringing the ordinances they have imposed on their own subjects. So, the authority of their pronouncements is just if they do not allow to themselves what they prohibit to their people.

Also, Augustine in the prologue of On the Trinity, *III:*[107]

Part 2.
C. 3. *Treatises are subject to the canonical Scriptures.*

Do not treat my writings as if they were the canonical[c] Scriptures. When you find something you did not believe in the latter, believe it without hesitation; in the former,[d] do not take as fixed what you did not think to be certain[108] unless you know it is certain.

Also, to Vincent Victor, in On the Soul and Its Origin, *IV, 1:*[109]

C. 4. *In the works of scholars are found many things that must be corrected.*

I cannot and ought not deny[e] that, just as in the writings of our predecessors, so in many of mine, there is much that sound judgment may condemn without hesitation.

C. 1. CASE. It says in this capitulum that one who disobeys good ordinances laid down in accord with truth should be punished but one who disobeys bad ordinances laid down against the will of God should be rewarded.

[a]**Therefore**—The capitulum begins here. The rest is a palea. The same appears in C. 23 q. 4 c. 41.

[b]**ordinances**—Note that a conclusion is drawn here from its contrary, as in C. 15 q. 3 c. 1; C. 24 q. 1 c. 6; C. 24 q. 2 c. 3; D. 25 c. 4; or more clearly, in Dig. 1. 21. 1; C. 11 q. 3 c. 98.

C. 3. CASE. Some people asked Augustine if they should place the same faith in his works as in the canonical Scriptures of the New and Old Testaments. He answered no. What is found in the canonical Scriptures is to be believed without hesitation. What is found in the works of Augustine is not to be taken as established unless it is shown to be certain.

[c]**canonical**—because we are not to argue whether the canonical Scriptures are right or not. D. 9 c. 8.

[d]**former**—This is said of that time when, as yet, the [continued on next page]

C. 4. CASE. Vincent criticized the works of Augustine, saying there was much falsehood in them. Augustine replied that it would be no wonder if his works were blameworthy, since the works of previous generations were also.

[e]**deny**—using right judgment. Thus Augustine later retracted many of his works. C. 23 q. 6 c. 3; C. 12 q. 1 c. 18; C. 26 q. 4 c. 3.

^d**former**—(continued) works of Augustine and the other holy fathers were not authoritative. Today, however, we are commanded to embrace them entirely, down to the last iota. D. 15 c. 13. Or he says this to show that the authority of the Old Testament is greater than that of the holy fathers, as in D. 19 c. 6.

C. 5. CASE. Jerome asked Augustine whether he believed the authors of the Old and New Testaments had erred in writing them. Augustine answered no, rather, if anything in these writings seems false, it must be said that the text is corrupt, or that the translator did not correctly put them into Latin from Greek, or that I do not understand what is written. Other authors are not to be believed even if they are holy unless what they wrote may be proven from canonical authorities.

^a**writings** — that is, "writers."

^b**errors**—It is iniquitous to say that the Scriptures lie. C. 23 q. 5 c. 6. On the contrary, we ought to defend what is said in them even to shedding our blood. C. 25 q. 1 c. 6.

^c**however much**—So it may be argued that it does not matter by whom something is said. D. 19 c. 8. So it is argued concerning the testimony of witnesses that greater credence is not to be given to more honorable people, because the truth is to be preferred, no matter who speaks it. C. 2 q. 7 c. 36; D. 9 c. 10; Dig. 33. 10. 7. Note that those who have greater expertise are more to be believed. *Dicta Gratiani ante* C. 4 q. 3 c. 3. Nor does the sanctity of a person help him to be believed more readily. D. 50 c. 27, and it may be argued, C. 1 q. 1 c. 56; C. 6 q. 2 c. 3; C. 3 q. 9 c. 21. The contrary may be argued from C. 11 q. 1 c. 35; D. 97 c. 3; C. 8 q. 3 c. 1; D. 41 c. 1; C. 11 q. 3 c. 14.

^d**probable**—So it may be argued that reason has the force of a canon, as above, D. 1 c. 5; D. 9 c. 11. Ioan.

C. 6. CASE. It says in this capitulum that, as one is to have recourse to the Hebrew texts if doubt arises as to the Old Testament, so one is to have recourse to the Greek versions if there is doubt as to the New Testament.

^e**Old**—that is, the Old Testament.

^f**Greek**—Jerome states the contrary in the second prologue to the Bible, saying that corrections are to be made from the Latin text rather than the Greek, and the Greek rather than the Hebrew. But Augustine was speaking of the primitive

Church when the Greek and Hebrew texts had not been corrupted. In the time that followed, however, as the Christian people increased greatly and many heresies arose among the Greeks, the Jews and Greeks corrupted their texts out of envy of the Christians. So it happened that, when Jerome was speaking, their texts had become more corrupt than the Latin. Or he is speaking of the Latin text as rendered by faithful translators, and Augustine of the Latin text

Also, to Jerome, in Letter *XIX:*[110]

C. 5. *No falsehood is found in the canonical Scriptures.*

I learned that such respect and honor are alone to be rendered to the writings^a now called canonical, that I dare not impute any errors^b of composition to them.[111] And so, if anything in them offends me because it seems contrary to truth, I have no doubt that either the text is corrupt, the translator has not properly construed the text, or I have totally misunderstood it. But when I read other authors, however much^c they abound in sanctity and wisdom, I do not for that reason take something as true simply because they thought it so, but only when they have been able to persuade me from other authors, canonical Scriptures, or probable^d arguments that they have not departed from the truth.[112]

Also:[113]

C. 6. *The authoritative meaning of the books in the Old Testament is taken from the Hebrew version, that of the New, from the Greek.*

As the meaning of the books of the Old^e is to be determined from the Hebrew texts, so the understanding of the New is sought from the Greek^f version.^g

as rendered by false and unfaithful translators, in which case, he says, one should turn to the originals if some falsity appears. Or you may say that, in this matter, Jerome is more to be believed than Augustine because among these three, Augustine, Jerome, and Gregory, Augustine is more to be believed as to disputed questions, Jerome as to history and translations, and Gregory as to morals. Not everyone is to be believed in everything but certain people in certain things. Cod. 1. 17. 1 [1. 20. 1]. It may also be argued from this text that, however authentic an instrument may be, if there are two copies of it, the one is to be produced from which the other takes its origin. D. 76 c. 7 pr.; C. 25 q. 2 c. 16; and most of all, X 2. 27. 13. This is contrary to Master Albericus, who says that if one public document takes its origin from another, it is not necessary to produce the original. Argument from Nov. 127. 4 [Coll. IX. 7]. It is otherwise with private documents. Nov. 119. 3 [Coll. IX. 2]. An argument for that position may be made from D. 19 c. 1. On the law as to this matter, see D. 100 c. 8.⁽³³⁾

^g**version**—All of the New Testament was written in Greek except the Gospel of Matthew and the Epistle of Paul to the Romans, which was written in Latin. Ioan.

C. 7: CASE. Augustine says that if there were any false-hoods in Scripture, even an harmless one, no authority would be left to it, nor could a judgment rest on it.

ª**harmless**—"harmless" means what is innocent, hurts no one, and helps someone. Thus a testament is called harmful when it is against one's responsibility to the family. Dig. 5. 2. 3.

Also, Augustine to Jerome, in Letter *IX:*[114]

C. 7. *Any falsehood in the canonical Scriptures would rob them of all authority.*

If one falsehood, however harmless,ª were contained in the sacred Scriptures, what authority would theyᵇ possess? What opinion could be supported by the Scriptures, if the deceit of an indisputable falsehood detracted from their weight?ᶜ

Also, in On [One] Baptism against the Donatists, *II,* III:[115]

C. 8. *Sacred Scripture is placed above the letters of all the bishops.*

Who does not know that the holy canonical Scriptures of the Old as well as the New Testament are contained within certain limitsᵈ and rank so far above all later letters of bishops that no one may possibly doubt or differ over ᵉ whether anything written in them is true or correct? On the other hand, if there is any deviation from the truth in the letters which bishops have written or will write since the establishment of the canon, may they not be rejected in favor of a wiser expert's opinion on the matter, or of another bishop's learned prudence and greater authority, or of a council?

Also, to Vincent against the Donatists, in Letter *XLVIII:*[116]

C. 9. *Let not the words of any bishop be advanced as a subterfuge against the divine commandments.*

Brother, do not seek, against such abundant, clear, and unquestionable divine testimony, to marshal any subterfugeᶠ using the writings of our bishops, such as Hilary, or of those of the united Church (before the faction of Donatus ᵍ separated), such as Cyprian or Agrippinus.[117] First, because the authority of their letters must be distinguished from that of the canon. They are not to be treated as though they could provide a testimony from which none may dissent when they have a meaning contrary to truth. For we certainly count ourselves among those proud to make our own the saying of the Apostle [Phil. 3:5], "And if in any-thing you are otherwise minded, this also God has revealed[118] to you."

43. 5; X 3. 5. 19; Cod. 2. 4. 42. The solution is that, if several points are interconnected or if one is accessory to another, then when one is destroyed those interconnected or accessory are destroyed as well. It is otherwise when they are diverse and separate. Dig. 4. 4. 45. 1 [4. 4. 47]; Dig. 3. 5. 16 [3. 5. 18]; *dicta Gratiani* §§ 2, 19 (*circa fine*) *post* C. 2 q. 6 c. 41. Or one may distinguish as in X 2. 22. 3. Ioan. I say that if any falsity is found in an instrument, the whole is rendered suspect and is not to be believed. Dig. 22. 4. 2 (*in fine*). I so noted in my *Quaestiones Dominicales et Veneriales.* Bart. Brixien.

ᶜ**weight**—that is, author-ity.

C. 8. CASE. It says in this capitulum that every-one should know that the Scriptures of the Old and New Testaments are to be placed above the writings of bishops. No one should doubt whether what is contained in them is true or correct. Other writings, however, may be criti-cized by those who are more careful, more expert, or of greater authority.

ᵈ**limits**—that is, books.

ᵉ**differ over**—so that what is established might be thrown into doubt. It is permitted, however, to argue about it so as to un-derstand it but not so as to reject it. D. 96 c. 7.

C. 9. CASE. Vincent the Donatist criticized the Old and New Testaments be-cause he found things to be criticized in the writ-ings of some bishops. Augustine criticized him because, while the former may not be criticized, the latter may be criticized since they do not have the authority of the canon. And so they should be criticized when they are written contrary to truth. This is proven by the au-thority of Paul in Philippians 3:5.

ᵇ**they**—So it may be argued that if an instrument or testimony is found to be false in part, the whole may be rejected. D. 16 c. 1; C. 3 q. 9 c. 17; *De cons.* D. 3 c. 7; Dig. 21. 1. 34. The contrary may be argued from D. 37 c. 11; C. 12 q. 2 c. 33; *De cons.* D. 4 c. 72; C. 17 q. 4 c. 41; X 1.

ᶠ**subterfuge**—The words of the law are not to be evaded by subterfuge. D. 37 c. 14; Dig. 10. 4. 19.

ᵍ**Donatus**—Donatus was first a Catholic and later fell into heresy. Cyprian and Agrippinus also fell into this heresy.

C. 10. CASE. Augustine criticized what had been said by certain experts, and Fortunatian criticized him for doing so. Now he writes back, saying that he does not embrace these writings with the same faith as he does the canon. Although he grants them due honor, he would correct them if he found they needed correction. He wants his own writings to be treated the same way.

ᵃ**arguments**—that is, expositions. Note that another's reputation is not harmed by the mere fact that his testimony is rejected. X 2. 25. 1.

ᵇ**their writings** — So it may be argued that what the law lays down for one, it lays down for others. C. 2 q. 6 c. 14; C. 22 q. 5 c. 18; Dig. 2. 2. 1; X 1. 2. 6.

C. 11. CASE. Augustine was asked whether an argument from natural law should prevail over example. He answered yes, but not over one that already accords with reason.

ᶜ**sure** — elsewhere, "surely."

ᵈ**harmonize** — sometimes.

ᵉ**it**—that is, the reasoning.

ᶠ**something**—namely, an example. He says this because example should not always be imitated. Cod. 7. 45. 13. But the example of the pope should be followed. C. 16 q. 3 c. 5; X 2. 27. 19.

ᵍ**more excellent**—which was not so with the example of Lucretia.⁽³⁴⁾ C. 32 q. 5 c. 4 § 1.

ʰ**in religion**—So it may be argued that compassion should be sought in judges. D. 45 c. 4; C. 26 q. 7 c. 12; D. 50 c. 14; C. 1 q. 7 c. 16; C. 1 q. 7 c. 18; D. 86 c. 14; C. 35 q. 9 c. 5; De poen. D. 1 c. 73. The contrary may be argued from D. 50 c. 26; C. 23 q. 4 c. 33; C. 35 q. 9 c. 2. To the contrary, D. 45 c. 17; X 5. 21. 2.

ⁱ**Since**—He draws an inference from what has been said and makes a transition to what follows in this way: As in natural law nothing is commanded or prohibited unless [continued on next page]

D. 10. This distinction is divided into two parts, of which the first proves in five capitula that the ordinances of princes may not prevail over canons. The second part begins, "See, then. . . ." Ioann. de Fan.

***Dicta Gratiani ante* c. 1. CASE.** It was shown above that natural law prevails over custom and enactment, whether ecclesiastical or secular. In this tenth distinction it is shown

Also, to Fortunatian, in Letter *CXII:*¹¹⁹

C. 10. *Equal authority should not be ascribed to the canonical Scriptures and commentaries on them.*

Nor ought we to hold to any arguments,ᵃ no matter how Catholic and praiseworthy their authors, as if they were sacred Scripture. Nor are we forbidden, on account of the honor we owe such men, from condemning or rejecting anything in their writings,ᵇ if perchance we find them to have a sense contrary to the truth as we or others have understood it with divine help. As I treat others' writings, so I want interpreters to treat mine.

Also, to Marcellinus, in The City of God, I, XXIII:¹²⁰

C. 11. *Sure reasoning is preferred to examples.*

Sureᶜ reasoning is to be preferred to example. An example may harmonizeᵈ with it,ᵉ but somethingᶠ is more worthy of imitation if it is more excellentᵍ in religion.ʰ

*Since,*ⁱ *therefore, nothing is ordered by natural law unless God wishes it, and nothing is forbidden unless God forbids it, and since everything in the canonical Scriptures is divine ordinance, divine ordinance is indeed consonant with nature. Clearly, then, whatever is contrary to the divine will or canonical Scriptures is also contrary to natural law. Whence, if it is shown that something is subordinate to the divine will, canonical Scriptures, or divine ordinances, then it is subordinate to natural law too. So, both ecclesiastical and secular enactments are to be rejected entirely if they are contrary to natural law.*

DISTINCTION TEN

Part 1.

*Enactments*ʲ *of princes do not stand above ecclesiastical enactments, but rather are subordinate to them. So Pope Nicholas wrote to the bishops gathered in council at Convicinum:*¹²¹

that ecclesiastical enactment prevails over secular ordinance. The following capitula are presented on this point.

ʲ**Enactments**—In this tenth distinction, the master shows that secular enactment gives way to ecclesiastical because imperial ordinance conforms to the sacred canons. *Dicta Gratiani post* C. 2 q. 3 c. 7; X 2. 1. 8.

ᶦ*Since*—(continued) God wishes it to be or not be done, and as there is nothing in the canonical Scriptures that is not divine ordinance, divine ordinance is consonant with nature. Clearly, then, whatever is contrary to divine or canonical ordinance is also contrary to natural law and must be subordinate to natural law. Here he relates natural law to canonical Scripture and divine ordinance.

C. 1. *Imperial ordinance may not abrogate ecclesiastical laws.*

§1. Imperial ordinances are not to be followed in any ecclesiastical dispute, especially since they sometimes contradict an evangelical or canonical sanction.

§2.[122] *Also:* Imperial ordinances are not above the ordinance of God, but below it. Ecclesiastical laws may not be abrogated by an imperial judgment. The two following testimonies of Innocent and Gregory are sufficient to show this.[123]

St. Innocent in his decretal letter to Bishop Alexander of Antioch said, "You wish to know whether two metropolitan sees should be established and two metropolitan bishops named when a province is divided in two by an imperial decree.ᵃ It does not seem that God's Churchᵇ should be conformed to unstable worldly needs or adjust itself to offices and divisionsᶜ that the emperor has established to suit his own needs."

Now, St. Gregory, writing to the noble lady Theoctista, said among other things, "If he says that marriages should be dissolved on account of religion, it should be observed that what human ordinanceᵈ allows may still be forbidden by divine ordinance." So you see that ecclesiastical laws may not be abrogated in any way by an imperial decree. And you see that things human ordinance has allowed, divine ordinance has prohibited.

§3. We do not say that imperial ordinances (which the Church often invokes against hereticsᵉ and tyrants, and which defend it against evil-doers) should be completely rejected, but we do affirm that they may not be applied to the prejudice of evangelical, apostolic, or canonical decrees (to which they should be subordinate).

C. 1. CASE. This capitulum is divided into three sections. In the first section, Nicholas is asked whether imperial ordinances may be applied in all ecclesiastical controversies. He answers that they may not when they depart from the canons. In the second section which begins, "Imperial ordinances are not above. . . ," it asks whether an ordinance of the emperor takes precedence over a divine one, so that ecclesiastical laws lose force because of it. He answers no, and proves this by two authorities, namely, Innocent and Gregory. Innocent says that there may only be one metropolitan in a province, as the Church has so ruled, but, although the emperor divides a province in two, there will not then be two metropolitans. Again, the Church has ruled, as Gregory says, that after carnal intercourse one spouse may not enter religious life without the other's consent. But a secular ordinance provides for the contrary. The law of the Church nevertheless prevails when human ordinance permits something but divine ordinance prohibits it. In the third

section which begins, "We do not say. . . ," it says toward the end that we may apply secular ordinances when they do not contradict the canons.

ᵃ**decree**—The emperor divides provinces. Dig. 1. 22. 3. The pope divides bishoprics and unites episcopal churches. X 5. 31. 8. The law as to uniting and dividing is described at C. 16 q. 1 c. 49; C. 16 q. 1 c. 48. Although the emperor divides one province into two, there are not, therefore, two metropolitans, as is shown here and in D. 101 c. 1. It may be argued from this text that if the prince makes something lawful in temporal matters it is not for that reason lawful in spiritual matters, X 4. 17. 13, except where the prince rehabilitates someone who is degraded for the crime of a parent. *Dicta Gratiani post* C. 6 q. 1 c. 11.

ᵇ**Church**—The Church is not bound by worldly ordinances. C. 33 q. 2 c. 6. Nor may the emperor make ordinances concerning ecclesiastical matters, D. 96 c. 1, unless he requests it of the Church, *Dicta Gratiani ante* D. 17 c. 7, or unless he provides some privilege for the Church. C. 16 q. 1 c. 40; C. 16 q. 3 c. 17. Io.

ᶜ**divisions**—It may be argued that the bishop may not divide a parish against the will of the people. Nor may the pope divide a bishopric against the will of the bishop. C. 16 q. 1 c. 51. For what is one may not be divided. C. 24 q. 1 c. 18; C. 24 q. 1 c. 34. Ioan. But I believe that the pope or even a bishop may do this for cause. X 5. 31. 8. Bart.

ᵈ**human ordinance**—as you will find in C. 27 q. 2 c. 19. But, as Justinian was a truly Catholic emperor, it is amazing that he made rulings against the ordinance of the Lord, for the Lord said that a wife may be separated from her husband only on account of fornication [Matt. 5:32]. C. 33 q. 2 c. 18. But you may say, and some do say, that he allowed this out of ignorance and therefore deserves indulgence. D. 8 c. 8. Or he erred like Jerome in D. 26 c. 1. Or he permitted this in order to avoid greater evils, as usury may be permitted in order to avoid robbery or divorce may be permitted to prevent wife-killing. C. 33 q. 2 c. 9.

ᵉ**heretics**—And so I use in favor of myself what I do not use against myself, D. 37 c. 13; C. 2 q. 7 c. 26, and thus it is contrary to D. 19 c. 1 (*in fine*); *dicta Gratiani* § 42 *post* C. 4 q. 3 c. 3.

C. 2. You may state the case of this capitulum for yourself.

[a]**Neither**—So an argument may be made against those ordinances that permit usury to be exacted. C. 11 q. 1 c. 35; D. 9 c. 1 § 1 [§ 2]; D. 96 c. 1; C. 11 q. 3 c. 95; C. 25 q. 1 c. 8; C. 25 q. 1 c. 4; C. 25 q. 1 c. 11; C. 23 q. 8 c. 21. The contrary may be argued from D. 63 c. 22.

C. 3. CASE. The emperor wanted to control ecclesiastical affairs. He refused to obey the prelates of the Church. What is more, he wanted to dominate them and to impose laws on them. Pope Felix teaches him that he ought to bow his head to the Church and not to try to dominate its priests. If he does the contrary he will be in contempt of the Creator.

[b]**It is certain**—This capitulum treats much the same subject as D. 10 c. 6 and D. 10 c. 8.

[c]**affairs** — that is, precepts.

[d]**whose** — that is, the Church's.

[e]**bow**—The emperor, be it noted, is a son of the Church, not its bishop. D. 96 c. 11. He is to bow his head to bishops. D. 63 c. 3. He may be excommunicated by a bishop. D. 18 c. 7; D. 96 c. 10.

[f]**bounds** — that is, "the emperor exceeding the bounds."

[g]**Enactments**—Is it then true that canons always deprive ordinances of force? This is so only in spiritual cases, as is said in *De cons.* D. 3 c. 22. The nature of secular cases is different from that of divine ones as may be argued from D. 10 c. 1. Each of them is constituted in its own way according to its own nature, and each way is different, as may be argued from D. 10 c. 3. Nor may the pope abrogate ordinances except in his own sphere. The empire and priesthood are said to proceed from the same principle. Nov. 6 [Coll. I. 6] pr.; argument from D. 10 c. 8. But I do not believe that. X 2. 26. 20.

[h]**morals**—Nor is an oath binding when it is against good morals. X 2. 24. 25; Dig. 30. 1. 112. 4 [30. 1. 115]

[i]**administration**—His power is distinguished from pontifical power. D. 10 c. 8; D. 96 c. 6. If he otherwise usurps their offices, he is struck with leprosy like Uzziah [2 Chron. 26:16–20]. *Dicta Gratiani* § 2 *ante* C. 2 q. 7 c. 42. Nevertheless it can be found that kings may confer a deanship. X 1.

Also, Pope Symmachus at the Sixth Roman Synod, in the time of King Theodoric:[124]

C. 2. *The emperor is not allowed to do anything opposed to evangelical norms.*

Neither[a] the emperor, nor any protector of piety, may in any way encroach on divine commandments or do anything opposed to evangelical, prophetic, or apostolic norms.

Also, Pope Felix [III]*:*[125]

C. 3. *In ecclesiastical affairs the royal will is to be subordinate to priests.*

It is certain[b] that, in your affairs, salvation demands that, when dealing with the affairs of God, you take care to make the royal will subordinate, not superior, to the priests of Christ and to learn sacred affairs[c] from the bishops rather than teach these to them. It requires that you follow ecclesiastical form, neither placing the following of human ordinances above it nor refusing to be subject to the sanctions of her to whose[d] clemency God commands you to bow[e] your head in pious devotion. Otherwise, by exceeding the bounds[f] of heavenly dispositions, insult will be offered to him who established them.

Also:[126]

C. 4. *Enactments may not contradict good morals and the decrees of the Roman pontiffs.*

Enactments[g] contrary to the canons and decrees of the Roman bishops, or against good morals,[h] are of no account.

Also, Pope Nicholas I in the letter to the emperor Michael [III] *that begins, "We had established. . . :"*[127]

C. 5. *What pertains to priests may not be usurped by kings.*

Your imperial rule ought to be content with the daily administration[i] of public affairs and not usurp what pertains to God's priests alone.

Also, Gregory of Nazianzus in his address to the outraged citizens of Nazianzus and their angry magistrates:[128]

4. 5 (*in parte decisa*). Ioan.

C. 6. CASE. The emperors at Constantinople placed their enactments ahead of those of the Church. Gregory of Nazianzus attacked them, saying that Christ gave a greater and more perfect dominion to the Church's bishops than to the emperors themselves. Therefore, if they accept the ordinance of Jesus Christ, they ought to be subject to the power of the Church just as the spirit is to placed above the flesh and divine ordinance above human law.

^a**Do you not accept**—that is, "You ought to accept."

^b**word**—that is, the message of preaching.

C. 6. *The tribunals of kings are subject to the priestly power.*

Do you not accept^a the freedom of the word?^b Do you not freely admit that the law of Christ puts you under the priestly power and subjects you to its tribunals? For it has both given us power and granted us a dominion far more perfect^c than your dominion. So, would you ever think it just if the spirit^d yielded to the flesh?^e If heavenly things were overcome by earthly ones? Or if the human were set above the divine?

Part 2.

See, then, that the enactments of princes are subordinate to ecclesiastical ordinances. But whenever these are not opposed to evangelical and canonical decrees, they are worthy of all reverence.

So Augustine says in his dialogue, that is, in Against the Letters of Petilian, *II, LVIII:*¹²⁹

C. 7. *Ordinances of the emperors in favor of the Church may be accepted.*¹³⁰

If you think that the ordinances of the earthly empire should be accepted when they help^f you, we do not blame you. Paul [Acts 22: 25–29] accepted them when he declared to those attacking him that he was a Roman citizen.^g

Also, Pope Nicholas I to the emperor Michael [III], in Letter *VII:*¹³¹

C. 8. *Kings need pontiffs in eternal matters, and pontiffs need kings in temporal ones.*

Because^h the mediator of God and men,ⁱ the man Christ Jesus, desiring that human hearts be raised up by the medicine of humility¹³² and not thrown down into hell by human pride, divided^j the proper offices of

^c**perfect**—D. 96 c. 10.⁽³⁵⁾
^d**spirit**—that is, ecclesiastical enactment.
^e**flesh**—that is, secular enactment.

Part 2. This is the second part of the distinction, in which it is shown in seven capitula that when ordinances do not contradict the canons they are to be accepted. Archid.

***Dicta Gratiani post* c. 6. CASE.** This section is clear by itself. To demonstrate what is proposed in this passage, Gratian presents the following capitula.

C. 7. CASE. Petilian used ordinances to defend himself against Augustine and other Catholics. Augustine did not

blame him for this because Paul did the same when he said he was a Roman citizen.

^f**help**—This is said because ordinances are not to be invoked except in the absence of a canon. X 5. 32. 1.

^g**citizen**—He called himself a Roman citizen because his father became a confederate of the Romans as a sign of which he was given a Roman surname.

C. 8. CASE. The emperor Julian⁽³⁶⁾ claimed for himself both the empire and the pontificate as had been the case in the Old Testament. But Cyprian says that after the coming of Christ the powers of the two offices were divided. The emperor presides over worldly matters and the pontiff over heavenly ones, lest, prideful on account of his double power, a man be thrown down into hell. Rather the work of each power is to support the other. The case is the same as D. 96 c. 6.

^h**Because**—This capitulum appears as part of D. 96 c. 6.

ⁱ**God and men**—that is, between the divine and human natures. *De cons.* D. 2 c. 82.

^j**divided**—As, therefore, these powers are distinct, it may be argued that the empire is not held from the pope and that the pope does not possess both swords. For the army makes the emperor. D. 93 c. 24. And the empire is held only of God. C. 23 q. 4 c. 45. Otherwise, if it were held of the pope, one could appeal to him in temporal matters, something prohibited by Alexander III, who says that such matters do not belong to his jurisdiction. X 2. 28. 7; X 4. 17. 7; X 4. 17. 5. Again, the Church pays tribute to the emperor. C. 11 q. 1 c. 28. But, to the contrary, rights as to both the celestial and the worldly empire are conceded to the pope. D. 22 c. 1. Again, the emperor swears an oath to the pope. D. 63 c. 33. The pope deposes the emperor. C. 15 q. 6 c. 3. Again, the pope transferred the empire from the East to the West. X. 1. 6. 34. I believe that these powers are distinct, although the pope may sometimes assume both powers, as when he confers legitimacy on children in both spiritual and temporal matters. X 4. 17. 13. But this was at the request of a king who could have done it himself, as is said there. Nor is it an

objection that there may be an appeal from a secular judge to the pope. This occurs in the absence of a secular judge, as it said in X 2. 2. 10, and it is done at the request of the king. For, indeed, when the imperial throne is vacant, the pope may fill the vacancy. X. 2. 2. 10.

ᵃ**activities**—that is, their offices. Some things, be it noted, were done by Christ as emperor, as when he drove the buyers and sellers from the temple with a whip. C. 1 q. 3 c. 9; C. 1 q. 3 c. 10. Others were done as priest, as when he offered his own body to his disciples saying, "This is my body." De cons. D. 2 c. 89. But the contrary is shown by this authority, namely, that God did not wish these powers to be divided, as he exercised both of them himself. In response, it may be said that he did this in order to show that both powers proceed from the same source, not that one person should exercise or administer both offices. That these two gifts, the empire and the priesthood, are from the same source is shown by Nov. 6 [Coll. I. 6] pr.

ᵇ**affairs**—So it may be argued that imperial laws are not to be applied in matrimony and other spiritual cases. To the contrary, see C. 35 q. 5 c. 2. You may say, therefore, that "exclusively" refers to "temporal affairs," not to "follow," and so, just as spiritual cases do not pertain to the secular judge, so cases involving shedding of blood do not pertain to the Church. C. 23 q. 8 c. 29; C. 23 q. 8 c. 30.

ᵉ**voided**—C. 25 q. 2 c. 13.[37] This rule is completed by another rule, according to which, when the principal thing is voided, accessories and all that follows from it are voided. X 2. 22. 6 (in fine). But this rule has many exceptions. It is against ordinance to contract marriage after simple vows; nevertheless, the marriage is valid. C. 27 q. 1 c. 41. Again, it is prohibited to give a judicial decision subject to a condition; nevertheless, the decision is valid if so given. C. 2

both powers according to their proper activitiesᵃ and distinct dignities, Christian emperors need the pontiffs for eternal life, and pontiffs follow imperial ordinances exclusively in temporal affairs.ᵇ Thus, spiritual activity is kept free from fleshly incursions, and as [2 Tim. 2:4] "the soldier of God does not enmesh himself at all in secular matters," likewise, one enmeshed in secular matters is not seen to preside over divine matters.

Also, Leo IV to the Augustus Lothar:[133]

C. 9. *The ordinances of emperors should be obeyed.*

Since the capitularies and imperial orders of you and of your predecessor pontiffsᶜ should unquestionably be obeyed and preserved, we profess that we will, insofar as we were able and are able with Christ's favor, obey all of them both now and forever. And, if perchance someone has told you or will tell you otherwise, you can know for certain that he is a liar.ᵈ

Also, John VIII to the emperor Louis:[134]

C. 10. *The authority of an ordinance voids what is contrary to it.*

You see, my dearest son, that what is accepted contrary to an ordinance deserves to be voidedᵉ through the ordinance.

Also, Gelasius to Bishops Rufinus and Aprilis:[135]

C. 11. *Ordinances of princes or rules of the fathers are not to be held in contempt.*

Who would declare contemptible,ᶠ then, the ordinances of princes, the rules of the fathers, or paternal admonitions, except the one who thinks that in his case an act committed should go unpunished?

C. 9. CASE. Lothar heard that Pope Leo had refused to obey the imperial laws, and therefore he asked the pope whether this was true. Accordingly, Leo writes to him and says that he unquestionably obeys these laws and that whoever says otherwise is a liar.

ᶜ**pontiffs**—Note that emperors were at one time called pontiffs. D. 21 c. 1.

ᵈ**liar**—He speaks here out of his great humility, as elsewhere. C. 2 q. 7 c. 41.

CC. 10–11. CASE. That of the two following capitula is clear.

q. 6 c. 29 (circa pr.). Again, it is prohibited for a bishop to consecrate another's church, but, nevertheless, if he consecrates it, the consecration is valid. C. 7 q. 1 c. 28. But you may say that this rule applies to matters where there is a perpetual cause for the prohibition. For example, that a son may not contract marriage with his mother. Or you may say that, although such actions deserve to be voided, they are tolerated where there is an enactment. To the contrary is D. 45 c. 5, but that provision was established for the advantage of the faith. Dig. 11. 7. 43.

ᶠ**contemptible**—Whoever holds ordinances in contempt sins, but not everyone sins who does not obey ordinances given as counsels. C. 14 q. 1 c. 3. So contempt is one thing and disobedience another. Ioan.

C. 12. CASE. Some people refused to obey ordinances in clerical affairs, although they did so in lay affairs. Concerning this, the pope wrote to King Theodoric that, if ordinances are to be obeyed in lay affairs, they are even more to be obeyed in clerical affairs.

Also, to King Theodoric:[136]

C. 12. *All must obey ordinances of the Roman princes.*

It is certain that Your Magnificence, for his greater felicity, wants the ordinances of the Roman princes, which you ordered[a] to be followed in human affairs,[b] to be even more carefully observed in what concerns the reverence due St. Peter.

Also, Leo IV to the emperor Lothar:[137]

C. 13. *The Roman law ought not be broken through anyone's impudence.*

We implore Your Clemency that the Roman law, inasmuch as it was previously in force despite all adversities and remembered[c] to have been suspended for no human person,[d] now enjoy its proper strength and force.[138]

DISTINCTION ELEVEN

Part 1.
Custom[e] yields to ordinances according to Isidore in Synonyms, *II:*[139]

C. 1. *Evil practice is overturned by reason and ordinance.*

Let practice[f] yield to authority;[g] let ordinance and reason vanquish[h] bad practice.

Also, Pope Nicholas I to the emperor Michael [III]:[140]

C. 2. *No one's custom may oppose pontifical statutes.*

It follows[i] that what is sanctioned with full[j] authority by the rectors of

Dicta Gratiani ante **c. 1. CASE.** It was said earlier in D. 8 that custom yields to natural law. Now he says that custom yields to divine and human enactment. On this point, he presents the following capitula, of which the first is clear. You are to understand that the capitula up to Part 2 refer to bad custom, and the rest, until the end, to good.

[e]*Custom*—Here begins the eleventh distinction, in which it says that bad custom yields to both ecclesiastical and secular ordinance. But note that some customs are general and some special. On special customs, see D. 11 c. 8; D. 12 c. 11. General customs are those that are approved universally by the consent of all and that bind all. They are to be observed like a canon or ordinance. D. 11 c. 5; D. 11 c. 11. Special or local customs are those that bind the men of a particular place. They have the force of ordinance in that place, D. 11 c. 8, unless they are onerous, D. 12 c. 12; D. 68 c. 5, or give occasion for evil; then they are to be rejected. This may be argued from D. 12 c. 8. At one time, the Donatists were easily received back into the Church, and, by custom, they were promoted to be primates. That was abolished because heretical depravity became less to be feared. Custom has the force of ordinance, moreover, unless it is contrary to enactment, D. 11 c. 2; D. 11 c. 3; unless it arose from certain causes, as in D. 29 c. 1; unless the prince consents; or unless it concerns indifferent matters, as in D. 12 c. 11. Hug. But it is better to analyze this as I did at D. 8 c. 7. Io.

[f]**practice**—bad practice.
[g]**authority**—written authority.
[h]**vanquish**—D. 8 c. 4. Io.

C. 2. CASE. Ignatius, the patriarch of Constantinople, was unjustly deposed by his suffragans as a favor to the emperor Michael and by his authority. Pope Nicholas reprehended them for excusing themselves on account of custom. Therefore, Nicholas says in this capitulum that no custom may be an impediment to what the pope has established to be inviolately observed.

[i]**It follows**—that is, "It is right."
[j]**full**—Papal authority is plenary. That of other bishops is partial because they are called to a share in responsibility,

---

[a]**which you ordered**—that is, "because you ordered them."
[b]**human affairs**—This means that, because ordinances should be obeyed in lay affairs, they should be obeyed even more in clerical affairs, unless they infringe upon established canons.

C. 13. CASE. Some people disobeyed the ordinances in order to more freely harm other people. Therefore, the pope wrote to Lothar and asked that he cause the ordinances to be obeyed as they had been previously.

[c]**remembered**—in passive voice.
[d]**for no human person**—for that which has been instituted generally may be overlooked for no one. D. 61 c. 5.

D. 11. This distinction is divided into two parts. In the first Gratian proves that custom yields to ordinance. The second begins, "Now, when. . . ." Io. de Fant.

not the plenitude of power. C. 2 q. 6 c. 11; C. 2 q. 6 c. 12.

ᵃ**custom**—Unless it is a custom that may override the law, as noted at D. 8 c. 7. Io.

C. 3. CASE. Some bishops, deviating from the rule of the Roman Church, were led astray by various truly alien doctrines and customs. Pope Julian rebukes them, saying that they ought to follow the rule they had seen followed and taught by the See of St. Peter, and so receive their authority from where the Lord placed the primacy.

ᵇ**taught** — It appears from this that we need not always follow the custom of the Roman Church unless it requires the custom to be followed. D. 11 c. 11. The Roman Church observes many things that others do not. D. 31 c. 14; *De cons.* D. 4 c. 80; *De cons.* D. 1 c. 54.

C. 4. CASE. This ordinance says that the authority of custom is great and not insignificant. Nevertheless, it is not of such authority that it prevails everywhere against reason and ordinance, but it does prevail where it is observed. Some, however, understand the first part to pertain to good customs and the second to pertain to evil ones, which I do not believe to be right.

ᶜ**prevail over**—It may be argued that custom never prevails over ordinance. D. 1 c. 5. But it is objected that this law must speak either of good customs or of evil ones. If it speaks of good customs, then reason will never prevail against them. If it speaks of bad, then it cannot be said that their authority is "not insignificant." On this point, some say that the beginning speaks of good custom and the end of bad custom. This interpretation is inappropriate, however, because it separates the tail from the head, which is not permitted. X 3. 42. 3. Almost all others expound the text, when it says that custom does not prevail over ordinance, to mean that custom does not do so everywhere but may prevail in the city where it is obeyed.

But as to this matter, surely no one ever doubts that local custom may not prevail against ordinance everywhere else. Therefore, it should be understood to mean that a local custom, which is admittedly good, nevertheless will not prevail against ordinance, even in that place where it is observed, unless there the conditions described in D. 8 c. 7 are present.

this see is not to be overturned through any contrary customᵃ in order to follow one's own desires, rather it is to be firmly and inviolately obeyed.

Also, Pope Julius to the bishops of the East, in Letter *I:*[141]

C. 3. *Its members may not deviate from the custom of the Roman Church.*

Do not fall into error, my dearest brothers; do not be led astray by diverse and alien teachings. For you have the provisions of the Apostles and other apostolic men, and the canons: depend on these, surround yourself with these, delight in these, arm yourselves with these, that, supported, surrounded, delighted, and armed by these against all enemies, you might withstand any attack.[142] For it is quite unsuitable that any bishop or member of the lower clergy oppose a rule he has seen observed and taughtᵇ by the see of St. Peter. For it is very fitting that the entire body of the Church be at one in drawing authority from where the Lord has placed the primacy of his whole Church.

Also, Emperor Constantine Augustus to Proculus in Cod. 8. 53:[143]

C. 4. *Usage and custom may not prevail over ordinance and reason.*

The authority of longstanding custom and practice is not insignificant; but its power is certainly not of such moment as to prevail overᶜ either reason or ordinance.

Part 2.
*Now,*ᵈ *when custom transgresses neither the sacred canons nor human ordinances,*ᵉ *it is to be preserved undisturbed.*
From the sayings of Basil:[144]

C. 5. *Custom is inviolable when it does not transgress human ordinances or sacred canons.*
§1. We have received certain ecclesiastical institutions from the Scriptures, others from the Apostles, and others from the apostolic

Dicta Gratiani post c. 4. **CASE.** From here to the end he treats good custom.
ᵈ*Now*—This is the second part where it is proven by seven capitula that good custom is to be accepted. Io. de Fan.
ᵉ*ordinances*—C. 25 q. 1 c. 16.[(38)] Arch.

C. 5. CASE. Some did not follow custom unless the fathers had put it in writing. In this capitulum, Augustine [*recte*

Basil] rebukes them, showing that there are three types of institutions in the Church: those in writing, those handed down by the Apostles, and those confirmed only by custom. All these are owed equal observance and respect. Otherwise, if custom were not observed in the Church, the Christian religion would suffer a great loss. That is said in this section. The second section begins, "Where in Scripture. . . ." It shows that what was described earlier is to be

tradition[a] confirmed by their successors in the ministry;[b] practice has approved certain others confirmed by custom,[c] and these are owed equal observance and the same pious respect. Wherefore,[d] may anyone, or[e] may he with even the least knowledge of sacred Scripture, be in doubt?[f] For, if we counted[g] as naught the customs of the Church that are not found in the Scriptures[h] but are handed down from the fathers, it would be obvious to those who examine the matter with careful consideration[i] how great a loss religion would bear.[j]

§2. Where in Scripture[k] (as we commence from there) are the faithful taught to mark themselves with the sign of the life-giving cross? Or what commended either the triple[l] formula of the long prayer over the bread and wine or the words of consecration? For we say in the silent prayers not only what is contained in the Gospels or added by the Apostle, but we make many other[m] commendations in the mysteries, which seem very weighty. What[n] taught us to pray composed prayers facing east? We bless the baptismal font with the oil of anointing. In addition, we anoint three times with oil[o] those being baptized and tell them to renounce verbally Satan and his angels. So, do we not peacefully observe these and many other similar things in the mysteries[145] more because of the unspoken and hidden tradition reverently received from the fathers through ecclesiastical usage than because they were promulgated in writing?

observed in the Church, and this is proved by six examples. The first is the sign of the cross. The second is the words of the triple formula, that is, the one repeated three times over the bread and the chalice. The third is prayer facing east. The fourth is the baptismal blessing with oil. The fifth is the anointing with oil done at baptism. The sixth is the renunciation of Satan and his angels. The case of the next capitulum is clear by itself.

[a]**tradition**—unwritten. Io.

[b]**ministry**—the divine ministry.

[c]**custom**—not from the Apostles, but it is not known from whom.

ADDITION. "observance" means "obedience." Hug.

[d]**Wherefore**—that is, concerning this observance or obedience.

[e]**or**—that is, "indeed."

[f]**in doubt**—that is to say, even the ignorant cannot doubt this.

[g]**counted**—that is, valued.

[h]**in the Scriptures**—but in custom.

[i]**consideration**—that is, thought.

[j]**bear**—that is, suffer.

[k]**Scripture**—the Old or the New Testament. Be it noted that it is not the Scriptures of the Old and the New Testament but rather the canons that teach that the sign of the cross be made on the forehead and the other parts of the body. De cons. D. 4 c. 63; De cons. D. 5 c. 33. Nevertheless, it would seem that the sign of the cross has its origin in the Old Testament, because, when the angel was to kill the first born of Egypt [Exod. 12: 7], the children of Israel were ordered to anoint both doorposts with the blood of the lamb in the shape of the letter tau, which has the shape of a cross. Moreover, it says [Gen. 48: 14] that Jacob blessed the sons of Joseph, that is, Ephraim and Manassas, with his hands crossed. Again, one can read in Ezekiel [9:4–6] that when six men appeared to him with vessels in their hands, a certain man appeared in their midst having an ink well at his waist, and the Lord said to him that he should sign the foreheads of those who sigh and pine with the letter tau. But this was commanded only as a figure. C. 12 q. 2 c. 71.

[l]**triple**—The words are said to be threefold because the same word is repeated three times in the silent prayer, namely, "holy victim, pure victim, spotless victim." This formula is set down neither in the Old Testament nor in the New, but it is handed down through usage from the holy fathers. Or it is said to be threefold on account of the three periods of silence [in the Mass]: the first before the Sanctus, the second before the Lord's Prayer, and the third before the Agnus Dei.

[m]**other**—You find these in X 3. 41. 6.

[n]**what**—namely, in the New and Old Testaments. But nevertheless one reads [Dan. 6:10] that Daniel during the Babylonian Captivity prayed toward the temple, and so did the Jews, and the temple was toward the east. In Solomon [cf. Wisdom 16:28], one reads: "In the morning, pray toward the sun." But you may say that this was done out of respect for the temple.

ADDITION. Nevertheless, according to John of Damascus there are eight reasons that the Church has ordained that the faithful should pray facing the east, which you can find at this point in the work of Archid.[(39)]

[o]**oil**—oil on the shoulders and chest. De cons. D. 4 c. 70. The third anointing is on the top of the head, but this is done with chrism. De cons. D. 4 c. 88. But in a broader sense, as here, oil is called chrism and vice versa. D. 95 c. 3. Ioan.

C. 6. CASE. The case of this capitulum is clear in itself.

ᵃ**custom**—D. 12 c. 8; D. 12 c. 12. There, however, it says that even a custom not opposed to the faith is to be rejected. The solution is that here, one is speaking of tolerable customs, and there, of superstitious and intolerable ones. All authorities which seem to oppose this capitulum should be understood this way.

ᵇ**faith**—that is, against good morals. To show that it is to be expounded in this way, see *De cons.* D. 4 c. 72, where one must give the same exposition.

C. 7. CASE. Casulanus asked Augustine whether customs should be followed where nothing certain was established in divine Scripture. He responded yes, that they are to be observed as ordinance. Just as those who violate ordinances are punished, so those who scorn ecclesiastical customs also ought to be punished.

ᶜ**as ordinance** — Long-standing usage is always to be observed as ordinance. D. 12 c. 6; D. 11 c. 4.

ᵈ**customs** — Note that those who transgress custom are punished in the same way as those who transgress ordinance. C. 1 q. 7 c. 2; D. 11 c. 5. Accordingly, as it is not permitted canonically to disregard ordinance without the pope's permission, neither is it permitted to disregard custom, as it says in the same capitulum. Nevertheless, by common consent, one may go against a custom, even one confirmed by oath, if there is cause. X 3. 11. 1. But the contrary is true in the case of statutes. C. 15 q. 6 c. 2. Ioan.

C. 8. CASE. There are three things by which the Church throughout the world lives and is governed, namely, the Scriptures of the Old and New Testaments, the tradition of the fathers, and universal or local arrangements and customs. The first two govern the entire Church everywhere. Local arrangements or customs rule and govern, not everywhere, but only in various places, as everyone can see.

ᵉ**particular**—To the contrary, see D. 100 c. 8, where it says that local custom does not provide a defense, but only

general custom. But that is true only of those things that may be had as a privilege over which only universal custom prevails.

ᶠ**authority**—namely, Scripture.

ᵍ**the whole**—the Church.

ʰ**ruled**—because each province may follow its own views. D. 76 c. 11; X 3. 28. 9.

Also, among the decretals, Pope Pius I, in Decretal *VII:*[146]

C. 6. *Custom that does not encroach on the faith is laudable.*

We praise customᵃ when, however, it is known not to impinge on the Catholic faith.ᵇ

Also, St. Augustine to Casulanus, in Letter *LXXXVI:*[147]

C. 7. *When an authority is lacking, the usage of the people and the arrangements of previous generations are to be observed as ordinance.*

In matters about which the divine Scriptures determine nothing certain, the usage of God's people and the arrangements of previous generations are to be observed as ordinance.ᶜ And,[148] as violators of the divine ordinances are to be corrected, so too are those who scorn ecclesiastical customs.ᵈ

Also, in a book on the Christian faith:[149]

C. 8. *The Church is ruled by authority and by universal and local traditions.*

The Catholic Church throughout the world lives by three things. For all her observances clearly come either from scriptural authority or universal tradition, unless they are a particularᵉ and local arrangement.[150] Now, by an authorityᶠ the wholeᵍ is bound, and by universal tradition of previous generations, nothing less than the whole; but each, according to the diversity of place, submits to and is ruledʰ by enactments particular to their own establishment, as anyone can see.

Also, in the book against the Manicheans:[151]

C. 9. *The authority of the Catholic Church prevails in matters of faith.*

Itⁱ is clear that what prevails as to the faithʲ in doubtful matters is the authority of the Catholic Church,ᵏ an authority that has held firm from

C. 9. CASE. The Manicheans said that the authority of the Roman Church ought not to be invoked to establish the faith in doubtful matters. Augustine attacked them, saying that the authority of the Roman Church has force in establishing the faith because it has been confirmed by the Apostles and their successors.

ⁱ**It**—These three capitula speak of a general custom of the Roman Church that has been laid down to be observed even in other churches.

ʲ**as to the faith**—that is, in elaborating it.

ᵏ**Catholic Church**—that is, the Roman Church, to which one should refer in cases of doubt. D. 20 c. 1. And so the

ordinances of the Apostles should be observed as the ordinances of Peter. D. 19 c. 2.

ᵃ**so many**—Thus it may be argued that a privilege given
by many bishops prevails over one given by fewer. This
may also be argued from D. 19 c. 6.

C. 10. CASE. Some bishops wanted to abandon the
establishments and customs of the Roman Church. Pope Leo

the very foundation of the Apostles' own sees until the present day,
through the line of bishops succeeding them and by the consensus of so
many ᵃ peoples.

Also, Pope Leo, to the bishops of Sicily, in Letter *IV, 6:*[152]

C. 10. *It is not permitted to depart from apostolic provisions.*

We point out to Your Charity that one may not depart by further diverging from apostolic provisions, so that, after this,ᵇ no one will be
guiltless, if he thinks apostolic norms should be ignored in any way.

*Also, Innocent I to Decentius,*ᶜ *bishop of Gubbio, in* Letter *I:*[153]

C. 11. *What the Roman Church observes ought to be observed by all.*

Who could not know or recognize that something should be observed
by all when it has been handed on to the Roman Church from Peter, the
Prince of the Apostles, and preserved till this day? Or that nothing may
be added or introduced that lacks this authority[154] or follows someone
else's example? For it is manifestly clear that no one established any
church in the whole of Italy, Gaul, Africa, Sicily, and the adjacent isles,
unless the venerable Apostle Peter ᵈ or his successors had made them
priests. Let them check if any other ᵉ Apostle went, or is said to have
taught, in these provinces. If they find this not to be the case—because
it never happened—it is fitting that they follow the Roman Church's
practices, since there is no doubt they have accepted her governance.
Otherwise, while chasing after erring ideas, they will disregard the source
of their orders.

Your Charityᶠ often visited the capital city and joined us in church and
learned what usage is followedᵍ in consecrating the sacraments and
performing other sacred acts.[155] We would have judged this sufficient for
instructing and correcting your church, had your predecessors been doing
anything less or something different. Had heʰ not decided to consult us
on certain matters, we would have thought this had sufficed.ⁱ We are
responding to these questions, not because we believe you to be ignorantʲ
of something, but so that you might instruct your church with greater
authority;ᵏ if anyone has departed from the practices of the Roman

ᶜ**Decentius**—This person had been elected a bishop. Although he knew the customs of the Roman Church, nevertheless he asked the pope to write them down to give them
greater authority. D. 23 c. 6.

C. 11. CASE. Someone to whom the establishments and
customs of the Roman Church were known was elected bishop in a certain city, where men had introduced other
establishments and cus-
toms than those taught by
St. Peter and his suc-
cessors. The bishop dis-
closed this clearly to the
lord pope, asking that he
write him about the establishments of the Roman
Church, concerning which
he wanted to instruct his
people. The pope an-
swered him saying that
you know our customs,
with which you have had
much contact, well e-
nough to inform your
church. Nevertheless, as
you wish to inform your
people about our authori-
ty, we will do as you ask
that your people may be
instructed and the erring
be corrected, or you will
tell us who they are.

ᵈ**Peter**—or by someone
under his command such
as Paul. For Peter gave
Paul license to preach by
the authority of the Lord
when he said [Acts 13:2],
"Set apart for me Paul and
Barnabas." D. 75 c. 5.

ᵉ**other**—that is, con-
trary. And so you should
take C. 11 q. 3 c. 2.

ᶠ**Your Charity**—Con-
strue it this way: "We
thought it sufficed that
Your Charity. . . ."

ᵍ**followed** — that is, by
the Roman Church; or "is
to be followed, that is, by
Your Charity. . . ."

ʰ**he**—Your Charity.

ⁱ**sufficed** — that is, for
Your Charity.

ʲ**ignorant** — This indicates that he both knows
and does not know. But

commands them not to do so, because as to such matters
they would not be held guiltless.

ᵇ**after this**—So it may be argued that a wrong is more
severely punished when it is repeated. C. 15 q. 8 c. 2.

he is speaking colloquially, as if to say, "I would certainly
have believed you knew, if you had not asked me."

ᵏ**greater authority**—But a bishop may do this by his own
authority, and no new right is given by the pope's confirma-

tion, D. 12 c. 2, and he is indeed confirming, not giving, X 2.22.6. From what then arises this greater authority? Some say that people will now show more respect. D. 23 c. 6. I say, the authority of the pope or his confirmation may give more force to what has less force. X 1.36.1. Also, no one now may revoke it without the Roman pontiff's authority. X 20.30.2.

ᵃ**novelties**—D. 30 c. 16[40]; Dig. 1.4.2[41]; D. 4 c. 2.

ᵇ**some church**—that is, if contrary to good morals, and so one may solve the difficulty raised by D. 12 c. 10. Against this is Instit. 4.11.7.[42]

Against this statement of Lau. is D. 56 c. 2 (*in fine*). Hu. holds the contrary.

C. 1. CASE. Some bishops deviated from the rules of the Roman Church. For this reason Pope Calixtus wrote to all the bishops that they, insofar as they are members of the Roman Church, which is their head, ought not dissent without consideration, but should do its will as that of a

Church, you can warn them, and do not fail to report it to us, so that we might learn who has either introduced novelties[a] or thinks that he should follow the custom of some church[b] other than Rome.

DISTINCTION TWELVE

D. 12. This distinction is divided into three parts. In the first he proves that good custom is to be obeyed. The second part begins, "This should be understood. . . ." The third part begins, "Concerning those who. . . ."

Dicta Gratiani ante c. 1. **CASE.** In the previous distinction he showed that the custom of the Roman Church is to be observed. Now he shows that one may not disregard the custom of the Roman Church without consideration. In order to prove this he first presents two capitula in support of the opposite position. Then he adds that good custom is to be obeyed, bad custom rejected. Moreover, the custom of the metropolitan church is to be observed in the whole province except for monasteries.

ᶜ**act**—that is, observe a new custom. In this twelfth distinction the master continues the topic of the preceding distinction, namely, that custom is to be obeyed that is not contrary to natural law or enactment. At the end, he says that every church ought to follow the custom of its metropolitan church, D. 12 c. 13, except for monasteries, as is said there. He begins, however, by presenting two capitula through which he intends to elaborate on the last capitulum of the previous distinction, where it says that we ought not to deviate from the custom of the Roman Church. He understands that to mean that we ought not to deviate without consideration, but one may when one has a reason. This he proves from the two capitula that follow and take the contrary position. Ioan.

ADDITION. And incorrectly, for these texts do not contain an argument to the contrary according to Lau.

Part 1.

No one may act[c] without consideration of justice.

Thus, Pope Calixtus I says to all the bishops in his first letter to Bishop Benedict:[156]

C. 1. *No one may act, without consideration of justice, against the discipline of the Roman Church.*

A member[d] must not dissent from the head; rather, in accord with the testimony of sacred Scripture, let all members obey the head. Now, no one doubts that the Apostolic Church is the mother of all[e] churches and that you may in no way deviate from her norms. As the Son of God came to do the will of his Father, you should also fulfill the will of your mother, that is, the Church, whose head, as was said above, is the Roman Church. Therefore, whatever has been done without consideration[f] for justice, against her discipline, may in no way be considered valid.

Also, Pope Gregory IV:[157]

C. 2. *Let no one oppose apostolic precepts through pride.*

Let obstinate pride not oppose itself to apostolic precepts;[g] rather, in

mother, just as Christ came to do the will of his Father.

ᵈ**member**—*De cons.* D. 3 c. 22; Nov. 131 [Coll. IX. 6] pr. And it may be argued from this that the law is the same for the whole as for the part. C. 1 q. 3 c. 3.

ᵉ**all**—therefore, also of the Greeks. C. 24 q. 1 c. 15.

ᶠ**consideration**—Is it true, therefore, that with consideration it is permitted to act against her? Surely not. *Dicta Gratiani ante* C. 17 q. 4 c. 30. An argument from contraries is not valid here.

C. 2. CASE. Certain patriarchs and archbishops were appointing some bishops and deposing others, against the statutes of the Roman Church and without the permission of [continued on next page]

ᵍ**precepts**—However heavy and intolerable they are, they must be performed, D. 19 c. 3; D. 100 c. 8, or a reason is to be given why performance is impossible. X 1.3.5.

C. 2. CASE. (continued) the Apostolic See. Gregory rebukes them, saying that, like questions of faith, the accusation and deposition of bishops pertains to the Apostolic See, as ancient statutes declare and Gregory confirms in this capitulum, laying down nothing new concerning this matter. Therefore, Gregory commands them not to neglect their head, from which they ought to accept their norms. Whoever acts contrary is to be deposed.

obedience, let what has been commanded by the holy Roman Church and apostolic authority be fulfilled unto salvation, if you want to maintain communion with the same holy Church of God that is your head.

And much further on: We command nothing new[a] in this present order; rather we reassert things that previously appear to have been overlooked, since there is no doubt that, not only a case concerning a bishop,[b] but every matter concerning holy religion,[158] should be referred to the Apostolic See as the head of the churches. Hence, also, a church should take its rule from where it takes its origin, lest it appear to disregard its institutional head. Let all priests, who do not want to abandon the security of that apostolic rock on which Christ founded the universal Church [cf. Matt. 16:18], accept the sway of her authority. If anyone does not observe these precepts of the Apostolic See, let there be no doubt that he is an enemy to the office he has received.

Also, Leo IX to Michael, bishop of Constantinople, Letter *I, 29, and Nicholas I in his second letter to Photius:*[159]

C. 3. *There may be no resistance to customs that canonical authority does not oppose.*

The holy Roman Church knows that customs[c] diverse according to time and place are no obstacle to the salvation of believers if there is no canonical authority standing against them that requires us to abandon them. Thus, we rule that nothing should or may oppose them.

Also, Jerome to Lucinius, Letter *XXVIII:*[160]

C. 4. *Let customs that do not offend the faith be observed because they have been handed on from previous generations.*

I want to remind you briefly that ecclesiastical traditions,[d] in particular[e] those that do not offend the faith, are to be observed because they have been handed down from previous generations and the custom of one group is not overturned by the contrary usage[f] of another.

although he may be absolved by another. C. 3 q. 6 c. 7; C. 3 q. 6 c. 9; C. 5 q. 4 c. 2. Again, only the pope may reinstate him. C. 2 q. 6 c. 10. Again, only the pope may act on his resignation, C. 6 q. 3 c. 3, on his transfer, C. 7 q. 1 c. 34, and on his exemption, C. 16 q. 1 c. 10.

C. 3. CASE. Gratian returns to his topic, showing that custom that is not contrary to natural law or enactment should be followed. It says in this capitulum that different customs may be observed in different places and times, as long as there is no canonical authority against them, and they do not impede the salvation of the faithful.

[c]**customs**—D. 31 c. 14; *De cons.* D. 4 c. 80; *De cons.* D. 2 c. 13.[(43)]

ADDITION. On the same, D. 12 c. 11.

CC. 4–7. CASE. Lucinius found many diverse customs and therefore wondered which should be observed to the prejudice of others. He asked the advice of Jerome on this, who responded that customs handed down from the holy fathers ought to be observed when they are not against the faith. Nor are the customs of one place to overturn those of another. The next three capitula are clear.

[d]**traditions** — that is, customs. D. 8 c. 2.

[e]**in particular**—that is, "but only." In that way you should take C. 11 q. 3 c. 6; C. 16 q. 3 c. 1; C. 7 q. 1 c. 24; C. 27 q. 2 c. 20, and take "they do not offend" to mean "that are not against the faith or good morals." D. 12 c. 12.

[f]**usage**—If bishops argue against any church that it should do this or that because another church does so, an argument in response can be found here. The response to them is that one church's custom is not to be overturned by the contrary customs of others. The opposing argument in their favor is D. 100 c. 8; X 3. 39. 18. To the contrary see X 3. 37. 2 (*circa fine*). Io. The solution is that every church should do what others do according to common law, D. 61 c. 5, unless there is a longstanding custom, X 2. 26. 15, or it has a privilege, C. 16 q. 1

[a]**nothing new**—So it may be argued that something is not new if it has already been established but is renewed in some way. C. 24 q. 1 c. 1; C. 34 q. 1 c. 3. Wherefore if a bishop swore not to alienate a new fief, nevertheless he may lawfully alienate the fief when it becomes vacant again. X 3. 20. 2. Also you find here that the pope's confirmation does not give a new right. X 2. 30. 4. We spoke concerning this right in D. 11 c. 11.

[b]**bishop**—Indeed, only the pope may condemn a bishop,

c. 39. B. It may be seen from these two capitula that the judge-delegate will judge according to the custom of the place. See D. 12 c. 11; D. 8 c. 2 at "No one, whether citizen or foreigner"; X. 1. 4. 6 (*in fine*); X 4. 11. 3, and, most aptly, X 2. 15. 3 and Cod. 8. 10. 3, where it says that the judge will follow what is done more frequently in the city. The legate will observe the custom of the province because people will think highly of one who observes their customs. Dig. 1. 16. 4. Again, ordinance prescribes that the judge follow the custom of the province, Dig. 29. 1. 3 (*in fine*). On the contrary, it may be shown that he should judge according to Roman law. D. 11 c. 11; D. 11 c. 4. And, dealing with security given in litigation, an ordinance says that the custom of the city of Rome is to be observed. Instit. 4. 11. 7; X 2. 27. 19; X 2. 27. 8; C. 25 q. 2 c. 6 (*in fine*). Again, the delegate does not act for himself but for the person delegating. D. 93 c. 26; X 1. 29. 11; Dig. 1. 21. 1; Dig. 1. 21. 3. Again, great disadvantages would ensue if judgment were given according to the custom of the place because, if a place had different customs for giving judgment, it would follow that the same case was to be governed by contrary customs. C. 12 q. 2 c. 18. Again, it would seem that judgment should be given according to the custom of the defendant because the plaintiff must always go to the defendant's forum. C. 11 q. 1 c. 15. And it should favor the defendant over the plaintiff. Dig. 50. 17. 125. As to this, some say that if people voluntarily submit themselves to the judgment of someone, or voluntarily petition the judge-delegate, judgment should always be made according to the custom of the one delegating. If, on the other hand, someone is given a judge against his will, then he should be judged according to the custom of the litigant, and preferably according to the custom of the defendant rather than the plaintiff, as in the law cited, Dig. 50. 17. 125. It would be better, however, to distinguish whether an appeal to the pope has been made or not. If a judge has been granted to hear an appeal, I say this judge-delegate ought to follow the custom of the place from which the appeal came, for a judge on appeal is bound to follow the ordinance applied in the previous decision. Nov. 115 [Coll. VIII. 12] pr. This position may be argued from X 3. 26. 16, where the appellate judge follows the custom of the place from which the appeal was taken. But if they receive a judge other than in the course of an appeal, he

must follow the custom of the person delegating him. Dig. 35. 1. 39 (*in fine*). Io. I believe that the judge should judge according to the custom of the defendant, as the plaintiff must take the defendant's forum, X 2. 2. 8, except in case of a contract made or wrong done in the other's forum, for then one follows the custom of the place where the contract was made or the wrong done. D. 8 c. 2; X 2. 2. 20. Bar.

To the contrary, see Cod. 2. 52. 6 [2. 53. 6], where it calls

Also, Nicholas to Archbishop Hincmar:[161]

C. 5. *Traditions instituted by the fathers are not to be infringed.*

It is a ridiculous[a] and abominable disgrace that in our times we permit the holy Church of God to be slandered and that we suffer the traditions we have received from the fathers of ancient times to be infringed at will by those wandering from the truth.

Also, Justinian in Instit. 1. 2:[162]

C. 6. *Long-standing usages are to be observed like ordinances.*

Long-standing[b] usages[163] approved by the consent of those following them are like ordinances.

Also, in Cod. 8. 52. 1:[164]

C. 7. *Whatever is against long-standing custom ought to be revoked.*

An established custom[c] and the reasons underlying the custom are to be observed. And the provincial governor shall take special care to revoke anything done contrary to long-standing[d] custom.[165]

Also, Gregory to all the bishops of Numidia, in Letters, I, LXXV:[166]

it absurd that diversity arise because of difference of place. The solution is that a difference in law should not arise from difference of place unless there is some other reason underlying it. D. 29 c. 1.

[a]**ridiculous**—Dig. 48. 22. 7. 22.[(44)]

[b]**Long-standing**—This is said in Instit. 1. 2. 9.

[c]**custom**—where it is not contrary to written law.

[d]**long-standing**—"Long" is what has lasted ten or twenty years. Cod. 7. 33. Therefore, it is not required that the custom be immemorial, as some say, or that it be established by prescription. That is so, however, where the custom is not contrary to law. When it is so ancient that it does exceed the memory of man, Dig. 39. 3. 2. 5, it has the status of an enactment, Dig. 43. 20. 3. 4 [43. 19. 3]. Where it is contrary to law, it requires what was noted in D. 8 c. 7.

C. 8. CASE. In Numidia there were many Donatists who, when they had returned to the Church, were promoted to archbishop and primate, according to the custom of the bishops. This custom was contrary to ecclesiastical enactments. Therefore, the pope says that custom is to be followed here only partially. It may not be followed in the promotion of Donatists, although, by dispensation, they might be tolerated in positions of dignity when they already held such positions.

^a**unchanged**—This is contrary to X 1.4.7. But that text

C. 8. *Let custom not impinging on the Catholic faith remain unchanged.*

We allow custom to remain unchanged^a when it does not impinge on the Catholic faith, whether it concerns the creation of primacies^b or other matters. There is an exception for those that entered the episcopacy from among the Donatists. We absolutely prohibit^c them to be raised to the dignity of primate (even when^d clerical order^e places them in that position).[167] It is enough that they take care of the people entrusted to them and not advance themselves for promotion to primacy in preference to those bishops who taught and nourished the Catholic faith within the fold of the Church.

Also, Gregory to Maximus, bishop of Salona, in Letters, *VII, LXXXI:*[168]

C. 9. *Let what is customary not be rejected.*

As we do not allow what is unlawful to be perpetrated in any way, so^f we do not reject what is customary.

Also, to Augustine, bishop of the English (Reply 3):[169]

C. 10. *Place does not approve a custom, custom approves a place.*

Your Fraternity knew the custom of the Roman Church, in which, you remember, you were nurtured. But it pleases me that, when you find something that would be pleasing to almighty God in the Roman Church, in that of the Gauls,^g or in any other church, you should take care to adopt it. Since the church of the English is as yet young in the faith, introduce into it, as its own discipline, whatever you select from any of the other churches. For practices^h are not admirable because they are in a place, but places are admirable because of the practices in them. Therefore, glean from each and every church whatever is pious, religious, and proper, and then instil as custom in the English mind whatever you have gathered, as it were, in your sheaf.

Dig. 48.22.7.22; C. 15 q. 8 c. 1.

^c**prohibit**—C. 23 q. 4 c. 24 § 6. To the contrary, see C. 1 q. 1 c. 42; C. 1 q. 7 c. 1; C. 1 q. 1 c. 4. The solution is that, by the common law, no one returning from heresy may be ordained. C. 1 q. 7 c. 1. But they are given dispensations in many ways. Sometimes they are given a dispensation that is partial, for example, for promotion to minor orders. C. 1 q. 1 c. 42. A full dispensation is given when they may become priests but go no further. C. 1 q. 7 c. 4. A fuller dispensation is when, as in this case, they may become bishops but not primates. It is most full when they may be promoted to all offices and dignities. C. 23 q. 4 c. 24. Io.

^d**even when** — that is, "although."

^e**order**—Although they are in orders such that they could become primates.

C. 9. CASE. This capitulum is clear of itself.

^f**so**—for a similar comparison, see C. 2 q. 1 c. 3. Io.

C. 10. CASE. Gregory sent his monk Augustine to preach to the English. He went, converted them, and became their bishop. Accordingly, he asked Gregory whether he ought to instruct the English in the customs of the Roman Church, with which Augustine was well acquainted. Gregory responded that wherever he found good customs he was to accept them and, gathering them together into unity, to shape the customs of the English. Nor ought he to approve them because of the dignity of the

treats custom involving a canonical statute. C. 22 q. 1 c. 7.

^b**primacies**—So one may argue that custom is to be followed in elections. C. 24 q. 1 c. 33 (*in fine*); X 1.6.18; X 1.6.31. Again, it may be argued that an ineligible person may be eligible because of custom. X 3.3.6; Dig. 50.2.11 (*in fine*). The contrary argument may be made from X 1.4.7. You also find here that one dispensed as to some matter for one office may not be promoted to a superior office. D. 34 c. 18; C. 1 q. 5 c. 1; C. 1 q. 7 c. 21. Indeed, a person who may not receive a greater honor may receive a lesser.

place, for practices are not admirable because they are in a place, but places are admirable because of their practices and customs.

^g**Gauls**—D. 11 c. 11 is to the contrary. But this concerns general custom. Or it concerns matters pertaining to orders. This text and D. 54 c. 9 concern matters belonging to observances.

^h**practices**—that is, customs, for he is saying that bad custom should not be approved because the place is good. D. 40 c. 4.

ADDITION. Nor is a good custom to be rejected because the place is insignificant or ignoble, according to Hugo.

C. 11. CASE. This capitulum is divided into two sections. In the first section Januarius asked Augustine why the Lord's Passion, Resurrection, and Ascension and similar things are observed everywhere throughout the world when there is no authority that prescribes this. Augustine responds that they are to be observed because we understand and believe that their observance has been handed down from the Apostles or prescribed by councils. Therefore, they ought to be observed universally. In the second section, which begins, "There are...," it says that the following of local custom is of free observance and does not apply to those who do not live there: for example, fasting on Saturday, taking the Body of Christ daily, and similar matters. This is proven by the example of Ambrose. For when Augustine's mother went to Milan and doubted whether she ought to fast on Saturday because the church there did not fast, Augustine consulted Ambrose. He responded, "When I am in Rome, I fast on Saturday. When I am in Milan, I do not fast. You, Augustine, ought to observe the custom of whatever church you come to, in order that no scandal be caused to anyone on your account." When Augustine related this advice to his mother, she freely accepted it.

^a**considered**—So it may be argued that a custom is to be presumed just and established for a just reason unless the contrary is proven. The contrary may be argued from D. 12 c. 12; D. 68 c. 5; X 3. 39. 5, where you see that, although the order of chorbishops⁽⁴⁵⁾ was established for a long time among everyone, it was abolished because the cause of its institution was unknown. But this was an evil and onerous custom, and so it was eliminated. Here, however, he is speaking of good custom that is not onerous. Nov. 10 [Coll. II. 5] § 2. Again, from this text you may argue that the passage of time creates a presumption that a debt is owed. C. 18 q. 2 c. 31.

^b**and retained**—that is, "to be retained."

^c**as commended**—as having been commended.

^d**free**—Here Augustine says that the freedom from fasting on Saturday pertains to outsiders, not to those where such a custom is observed. But the contrary is said by Innocent. *De cons.* D. 3 c. 13. But there he is giving a counsel. Or that was specially prescribed for the Romans. D. 76 c. 11.

^e**community**—So it may be argued that everyone is bound

Also, Augustine to Januarius, in Letter *CXVIII, 1–2:*[170]

C. 11. *What is incontestably shown not to be against the faith and good morals, is to be accepted without prejudice.*

§1. Those unwritten but traditional practices that we follow, which are also observed throughout the entire world, should be considered^a and retained^b as commended,^c either by the Apostles themselves, or by the plenary councils (to which belongs salvific authority in the Church). An instance of this are the annual festivities to celebrate the Lord's Passion, Resurrection, and Ascension into heaven and the descent of the Holy Spirit from heaven; similar is whatever else comes to mind that is observed by the universal Church wherever it extends.

§2. There are other things that vary according to the places and regions of the world. For example: some fast on Saturday and others do not; some receive the communion of the Lord's Body and Blood daily, others do so only on certain days; in one place no day passes when the Body and Blood is not offered, elsewhere this happens only on Saturday and Sunday, or only on Sunday. Anything else similar that you discover belongs to the same category of free^d observances. In such matters there is no more weighty, prudent, or Christian habit than to do what one sees to be the practice of the church wherever one is.[171] For anything enjoined that is not against the faith and good morals should be accepted without prejudice and complied with on account of the community^e where one is living.[172] My mother followed me to Milan and found that the church there did not fast on Saturday. She began to vacillate about what to do. I then consulted Ambrose, the man of blessed memory, about this matter. He said, "When I go to Rome, I fast on Saturday; when I am in Milan, I do not fast. So then, observe the usage of the church where you are,^f so that you do not become a scandal to anyone, or they to you." When I related this advice to her, my mother gladly^g accepted it.

to live according to the custom of those among whom he lives, as here and D. 8 c. 2; D. 41 c. 1. B. Hence the verse: "When in Rome, do as the Romans do, and when elsewhere, live as they."

^f**where you are**—So it may be argued that travelers are bound to follow the custom of the place where they are, as here and in D. 8 c. 2. To the contrary, see Dig. 5. 1. 19. The solution is as noted in D. 100 c. 8,⁽⁴⁶⁾ because it depends on whether they will stay or leave quickly, and whether the custom is obvious or not.

^g**gladly**—But perhaps she did not fast gladly.

Part 2. This is the second part, in which it says that, although a custom is not against the faith, nevertheless, if it is blameworthy it should be removed when that can be done without scandal. Ioan. de Fant.

***Dicta Gratiani post c. 11.* CASE.** Here Gratian explains that the previous capitulum spoke of general customs or of local ones that are reasonable and always to be observed. If

Part 2.

This[a] *should be understood of custom that has been confirmed either by the use of the universal Church or by long passage of time. On the other hand, if different customs are introduced according to changing times, opinions, or places,*[173] *it is better to abrogate them than observe them after the circumstances have changed.*

So Augustine wrote in reply to the questions of Januarius, in Letter *CXIX, 19:*[174]

C. 12. *Things that are not sanctioned by authority or universal practice are to be abrogated.*

I think that, when it is suitable,[b] one may abrogate without hesitation those things[c] that are not encompassed by the authority of sacred Scripture, found established in episcopal councils, or confirmed by the custom of the universal Church and that vary so much according to the different habits of various places that the purpose[d] of the men who instituted them can be discovered only with great difficulty or not at all. For, even if they are not contrary to the faith, they oppress the very religion[e] that God's mercy freed from servile burdens[175] so that it could employ brief[f] clear[g] rites of praise. But today even the condition of the Jews is more tolerable since, although they do not acknowledge the age of freedom, they are subject only to the rites of the Law and not to human impositions.

Also, from the Eleventh Council of Toledo, c. 3:[176]

Part 3.

C. 13. *Let each province observe the mode of psalmody used by its metropolitan see.*

§1. Concerning those who, contrary to the Apostle's will,[h] are blown

oppressed by the servile burdens that today oppress the Church to such an extent that the Jews' condition is more tolerable than ours. For, although they reject the law of Christ, their rites are from the Law and not imposed by human presumption.

[b]**suitable**—that is, when it can be done without scandal. D. 50 c. 25.

[c]**those things**—He is speaking of irrational custom. It is not contrary to D. 12 c. 4.

[d]**purpose**—So it may be argued that it does not suffice to say that such a rule has been established unless the reason for its establishment is given. X 3. 39. 5; C. 2 q. 5 c. 20; *De cons.* D. 1 c. 26; D. 68 c. 5. The contrary may be argued from Dig. 1. 3. 20.

[e]**very religion**—Christianity.

[f]**brief**—So one may argue against those who pour out prayers excessively. Dig. 4. 2. 1. And modern writers rejoice in brevity, as is also noted in Dig. 4. 2. 1.

[g]**clear**—D. 4 c. 2.

Part 3. This is the third part, in which it says that the metropolitan church's customs in celebrating the office should be observed in all churches, except for monasteries where office is celebrated according to the rule of St. Benedict. Hug.

C. 13. CASE. There were some bishops who did not follow the order of the divine office followed by the metropolitan church. Therefore, the Council of Toledo ruled that all bishops must observe the way of saying office used in their metropolitan church. Abbots saying the public office, that is, vespers, matins, and Mass, will celebrate them as they are celebrated in the principal church. They may say other offices as their rule prescribes. This is said in the first section. In the second section, which begins, "Any violator . . . ," it says that if anyone acts contrary to this he shall be subject to excommunication for six months. In the third section which begins, "Therefore, not. . . ," it says that metropolitans ought to make the bishops of their province observe the policy just described, and that these bishops should make their rectors observe this rule also.

[h]**Apostle's will**—that is, he does not want one to be led

customs are evil or onerous, they are to be rejected when that can be done. As proof, he presents the following capitulum.

[a]**This**—the preceding concerned the observance of custom.

C. 12. CASE. Some customs were onerous and had not come into force through the authority of the Scriptures, councils of bishops, or universal custom. It was impossible to discover why they had been introduced. Accordingly, Januarius asked Augustine whether they should be tolerated. He responded they should not. They were to be removed when one could do so. For God wanted the Christian religion to be free for brief rites, and he did not want it astray by variety of doctrine. D. 11 c. 3.

^a**citizens**—The citizens therefore chant with the clerics and say amen. D. 38 c. 12.

^b**bishop**—So it may be argued that the governance of all monasteries pertains to the bishop. C. 9 q. 3 c. 2; C. 16 q. 1 c. 12; D. 61 c. 16. But are not the monks of the monastery to be ruled by the abbot, to whom all power over the monastery belongs? C. 18 q. 2 c. 9. But that text concerns rules for living, not for chanting. C. 12. q. 1 c. 11.

^c**public offices**—that is, those of the secular clergy, whose office is public because the people are present, whereas monks do not always have the people present and thus do not have public office. C. 16 q. 1 c. 10.

^d**restrain**—So it may be argued that the metropolitan may suspend and excommunicate his suffragan. D. 18 c. 10.

C. 14. CASE. This chapter is clear because the same material has been discussed earlier.

^e**pleased all**—De cons. D. 5 c. 13.⁽⁴⁷⁾ Nevertheless this capitulum may be set aside by contrary custom.

D. 13. This distinction is divided into two parts. The second part begins, "Nevertheless, there is a subtle way. . . ."

about by every wind of doctrine, it pleased this holy council that, by the authority of their metropolitan see, the citizens^a of the province[177] and the rectors of its churches be compelled to follow the same mode of psalmody instituted in the metropolitan see; and let them not diverge from the metropolitan see through any difference of order or office. Thus it is just that one be guided by rules derived from the place where one was consecrated to one's office, so that the see that is the mother of everyone's sacerdotal dignity according to the decrees of previous generations, also be the mistress of the ecclesiastical order. When abbots have been favored by the will of the bishop^b with offices to conduct regularly, they are certainly not permitted to celebrate the public offices,^c that is vespers, matins, or Mass, differently than they are celebrated in the principal church.

§2. Any violator of these decrees is to remain for correction under penitential censure at the metropolitan's residence deprived of communion for six months. There he is to wash away the guilt of past transgressions by his tears and carefully master the necessary principles of the office.

§3. Therefore, not only should the metropolitan restrain^d the bishops and priests of his whole province under this rule of discipline, but the other bishops should also make the rectors of churches subject to them conform to these arrangements.

Also, from the First Council of Braga, c. 19:[178]

C. 14. *One and the same order is to be observed in the offices of matins and vespers.*

It pleased all,^e by general consent, that one and the same order of psalmody be observed at both matins and vespers, and that alien and private, or monastic,[179] customs not be intermingled with ecclesiastical norms.

DISTINCTION THIRTEEN

Part 1.

No dispensation ^f *is permitted from natural law except perhaps when one is compelled to choose between two evils.*

***Dicta Gratiani ante* c. 1. CASE.** Previously, Gratian showed in D. 5 that natural law ranks above other laws in origin and dignity, and in D. 8 that it ranks above them in scope. In this thirteenth distinction he shows that it also ranks more highly according to the force of its provisions, for there is no dispensation from the precepts or prohibitions of natural law, except, perhaps, when two evils so press on one that he must choose between them. To prove these matters he presents what follows.

^f*No dispensation*—The master identified the difference

between natural laws and other laws in origin, dignity, and scope. Now he identifies a difference between this law and other laws in the force of its provisions, for a dispensation is permitted from the other laws, C. 25 q. 1 c. 25, but it is never permitted from the provisions of the natural law consisting of precepts and prohibitions. Nevertheless, the master makes one exception in the case of doubt, but he does so badly. Let us examine what the law is in this case of doubt. Some say that one can be in doubt when faced with two mortal sins. For example, the Jews who crucified Christ sinned mortally. *De poen.* D. 1 c. 23. If they did not kill him, they would also sin mortally for they would have acted against their conscience which told them the contrary, for it had been said to them that whoever calls himself the son of God must suffer death. And whatever is against conscience leads to Gehenna. *Dicta Gratiani ante* C. 28 q. 1 c. 1 pr. (at *His*); X 2. 26. 20. Furthermore, they say that one can be in doubt between mortal and venial sin. For example, someone is seeking his enemy, and I know where the enemy is. If I reveal where he is, I sin mortally, for I have betrayed him. If I deny that I know, I sin at least venially, or even mortally if I am living in the state of perfection. C. 22 q. 2 c. 14. If I am silent then it will be presumed from my silence that he is in that place. Here is another example. If a wife asks the marriage debt from her husband and he refuses, he sins mortally. If he grants it, he appears to sin venially, because one may not have this physical pleasure without venial sin. C. 33 q. 4 c. 7. So he is in doubt. Similarly it seems that one can be in doubt between two venial sins. For example, one can make a mere promise to drink more than he is able. If he drinks that much, he sins venially. *Dicta Gratiani* § 4 *post* D. 25 c. 3. If, on the contrary, he breaks his word, he sins venially. C. 22 q. 2 c. 8.

But it must be stated that no one can really be in doubt between two evils in this way. For it would then follow that necessity can make one do something evil. But the canons say that God will never punish anyone unless he has done wrong voluntarily. C. 23 q. 4 c. 23. Furthermore, if necessity really requires us to do something evil, then the ordinance that prohibited this would be impossible to obey. But every ordinance must be possible. D. 4 c. 2. Therefore, the person's doubt cannot really arise from the matter itself, but it must arise in the mind and from foolish opinion. Accordingly, the Jews were not in doubt except in their minds, and therefore they should have consulted those who had knowledge such as the Apostles or the sacred Scriptures. In the second example, the one asked ought to be silent, for then it would not be he who injured the other person if a presumption were drawn from his silence. C. 23 q. 5 c. 8 (at *Absit, ut ea*). Moreover, it does not always follow that silence gives consent. D. 86 c. 24. As to what the wife wants, I do not believe that this enjoyment is a sin. C. 32 q. 2 c. 3. Nevertheless, if you still insist on considering it a venial sin, then you should treat it as H. does: If a wife requests the marriage debt, her husband should prudently elude her while she is boiling with passion by promising to grant her request later. Then, if she still does not desist, the man should give her the use of his body in such a way that her desire will be quickly satisfied, so that he can break off immediately and not consummate the act.

C. 1. CASE. It was ruled by the council of Toledo that when two evils press upon one so that one of them must be chosen, the less serious should be chosen and the greater avoided. This is said in the first section. The second section begins, "We should investigate. . . ." There it is shown what is more serious and what is less. For if I swore to kill a man, it is a greater sin to kill him than to desist, for in killing one sins three times but in desisting only twice, and therefore that is to be chosen.

Thus, the Eighth Council of Toledo, c. 2, reads:[180]

C. 1. *The lesser of two evils is to be chosen.*

§1. Although one must carefully guard against being forced to choose between two evils,[a] if an inescapable[b] danger compels one to perpetrate one of two evils, we must choose[c] the one that makes us less[d] guilty.

§2. We should investigate which of the two is less and which is more serious by the acuity of pure reason. For when we have to lie,[e] we offend the Creator, but we stain only ourselves. When we perform a crime because of a promise, we hold God's commands in contempt through pride, harm our neighbors with faithless cruelty, and cut ourselves down with a still crueler sword.[181] In the former case[f] we perish by a twofold[g] lance of guilt, in the latter[h] we are slain three ways.

[a]**evils**—This should be understood as the idea of the one who foolishly believes himself to be in doubt, and you should so understand everything said here. Indeed, it is not really true that both courses of action are evil, even though the interpretation given here is that both are evil.

[b]**inescapable**—This refers to the reasons for acting, or this is a misinterpretation.

[c]**choose**—that is, "do."

[d]**less**—according to the interpretation given here, but he is not obligated to either alternative.

[e]**lie**—according to this interpretation, but it is not really a lie because one is permitted not to fulfill such an oath. C. 22 q. 4 c. 16.

[f]**case**—that is, of the oath.

[g]**two-fold**—Do not understand it to mean that in the murder three sins are committed, and in the lie, two sins. Instead, it says there that in the murder, offense is done in three ways, and in the lie, in two ways. One may argue, therefore, that whoever offends in more ways sins more. D. 94 c. 2; C. 11 q. 3 c. 3. Again, it may be argued from this that one should decide on the course of action for which more reasons can be given. X 2. 19. 9 (*in fine*). Thus he that can show the greater right shall prevail. D. 21 c. 1; Cod. 6. 33. 3. So also the poorer case is the one against which more can be said. D. 28 c. 13. The contrary is indicated by C. 24 q. 5 c. 5, where it says that lying is greater than homicide, but the contradiction is resolved there.

[h]**in the latter**—that is, in the murder.

C. 2. CASE. This capitulum is divided into three sections. In the first section it is shown that this kind of doubt comes from the suggestions of the Devil. The second section begins, "This can be better shown. . . ." It presents three examples of doubt. One is that of a person who has sworn not to reveal any of the secrets of his associate and knows that this person wants to kill the husband of the woman with whom he is committing adultery. The one who swore is afraid to reveal the actions of the other on account of his oath. The second example is a person who promises obedience to an evil prelate and is fearful to disobey him, even in evil, because of the obedience he has promised. The third example is a person who acquired a prelacy through simony and who fears that he will sin if he abandons the care of his flock. In the third section which begins, "Nevertheless, there is. . . ," advice is given as to what one should do when in this kind of doubt. It says that the lesser of the two evils is to be chosen. This is shown by the example of Paul who on account of incontinence permitted the lesser, that is, matrimony and conjugal relations, in order to avoid the greater and more serious, namely fornication [1 Cor. 7:1–2].

ᵃ**sinews** — that is, the suggestions of the Devil, which are sinuous, that is, sly and ensnaring.

ᵇ**Leviathan's** — that is, the Devil's.

ᶜ**loins**—His suggestions are called "loins" because the loins are the ministers and instruments of human generation and contain in themselves the incentive to lust, and so the suggestions of the Devil generate vices in man and lead him to whatever is unlawful. D. 6 c. 2.

ᵈ**are entangled**—that is, "entangling"; and so we are to understand all of the verbs as active in voice.

ADDITION. Entangled is said because they entangle man. In the truth, however, there is no entanglement. Archid.

ᵉ**tangled**—that is, "entangling."

ᶠ**devices**—that is, "devisings."

ᵍ**become an accomplice**—Understand this as according to

the same foolish misinterpretation of some, as above.

ʰ**transgression**—He should admonish him not to do it. C. 2 q. 1 c. 19. If the other does not desist he should do what is explained in C. 22 q. 5 c. 8,⁽⁴⁸⁾ and so free himself, for the oath was not invented to be a chain of iniquity. C. 22 q. 4 c. 22. Accordingly, a person who has sworn not to accuse another may, nevertheless, denounce his crime. X 2. 24. 25. If, however, he is not able to prove it, he ought to remain

Also, Gregory on Job 40 in Moral Reflections, *XXXII, XVIII–XX:*¹⁸²

C. 2. *Concerning the same matter.*

§1. The sinewsᵃ of the Leviathan'sᵇ loinsᶜ are entangledᵈ because the purpose of his suggestions is entangled with tangledᵉ devices.ᶠ Thus, many commit sins when, because they want to avoid one sin, they cannot escape the snare of another, and thus they commit one fault to avoid another. They find no way to escape one sin without consenting to the other.

§2. This can be better shown by giving examples from people's behavior. *And after some intervening texts:* Take a certain man who, while seeking worldly friendships, tells another man leading a similar life that he will keep his confidences a solemn secret and binds himself under oath to do so. He discovers, however, that the one to whom he swore is committing adultery and, what is more, trying to kill the husband of the adulteress. Now, the one who took the oath considers the matter and is beset by differing concerns. He is afraid to keep silent lest by his silence he become an accompliceᵍ to adultery and homicide; and he hesitates to divulge it lest he be guilty of the crime of perjury. Therefore, he is enmeshed in the sinews of the tangled loins because, no matter which way he turns, he fears incurring the stain of transgression.ʰ

Another, abandoning the things of the world and seeking to break his will in everything, wants to place himself under another's direction. But he picks the one who will direct him before God with less than careful inquiry. And, when the one he has injudiciously selected begins to direct him, that man forbids doing the things of God and commands those of the world. So the subordinate, weighing the wrongs of disobedience and of worldliness, hesitates to obey but fearsⁱ not obeying, lest, by obeying, he forsake God's commandments or, conversely, by not obeying, he hold in contempt God who is present in his chosen director.

And further on: Another, not considering the great burdens of ecclesiastical office, rises by bribes to a position of authority. But, inasmuch

silent. C. 2 q. 7 c. 27. If he can prove it, he should do what is explained in C. 2 q. 1 c. 19.⁽⁴⁹⁾ Or he ought to speak to the other person in this way, "Know, brother, that someone wishes to kill you. . . ," but without giving any name. X 1. 31. 2. To the contrary, however, is X 5. 18. 4,⁽⁵⁰⁾ but it is not really contrary, because a thief would not disclose anything to a person who informs on him.

ⁱ**fears**—What if a subject thinks that his prelate's precept is against God? Surely he should not obey for although he swore in general terms to obey him in everything, neverthe-less, that is to be understood only of whatever is lawful and just and honest. C. 11 q. 3 c. 92; C. 11 q. 3 c. 93; C. 11 q. 3 c. 94; X 2. 24. 20; X 2. 24. 19; Dig. 20. 1. 6. But if he is in doubt whether it is against God, he ought to obey. C. 23 q. 1 c. 4 (*in fine*). As to whether one is bound to receive orders from one he knows to be a simoniac, C. 1 q. 1 c. 108.[(51)]

indeed leave without the authority of the pope, because he has something that was stolen and therefore is bound to give it back immediately. Otherwise he could not receive the sacrament of penance. C. 7 q. 1 c. 34; C. 7 q. 1 c. 46. A thief is always in default. Dig. 13. 1. 7. 2.[(52)] A contrary argument may be made from X 1. 9. 10, but that is to be understood of those who do not enter by the door [John 10:1–10]. C. 1 q. 1 c. 113.[(53)]

as every eminent position is more painful on account of its problems than delightful on account of its honors, his heart becomes weighted down by cares, and he recalls his guilt. He grieves that he has attained his position guiltily, recognizes how evil it was to do so, and is broken by the strain. Knowing himself guilty of bribery, he wants to abandon the high position he has gained, but he fears causing even greater harm by abandoning the flock entrusted to him. He wants to care for the flock entrusted[a] to him, but he fears it would be a greater crime to keep a purchased office of pastoral care. He sees that he has become bound by guilt on all sides through his ambition for office. Neither alternative seems without fault: either he abandons his flock or he retains a sacred duty purchased in a worldly manner. Thus, he is horrified, frightened by both dubious al-ternatives, lest, staying unworthily in the purchased office, he feel sorry for not making amends by abandoning it; or, abandoning his authority, he make up for the one fault by committing the other of abandoning his flock.

Part 2.

§3. *Further on:* Nevertheless, there is a subtle way to destroy the Behemoth's craftiness: when the mind is torn between greater and lesser sins, if absolutely no path of escape lies open without sin, lesser evils are always to be chosen. For, when there are walls on all sides and the way of escape is closed to prevent flight, the one fleeing throws[b] himself off where the wall is lowest. Hence, Paul, when he saw there were in-continent people in the Church, conceded[c] a lesser[d] evil so they could avoid a greater,[e] saying [1 Cor. 7:2], "On account of fornication then, let every man have his own wife." Then,[f] because having relations with one's spouse is sinless only when done for the procreation[g] of children and not for the satisfying of desire, and so what he conceded might not appear devoid of guilt (however small), he added [1 Cor. 7:6], "This I say by way of indulgence, not as a commandment." For something should be only indulged, not commanded, if it is not without vice. Surely, he considers what he declares susceptible of indulgence to be a sin. So, when we are torn between dubious choices, we expediently submit to the

Part 2. This is the sec-ond part of the distinction, in which advice is given as to what one in the doubt just described should do. Arch.

[b]**throws** — What if one in flight throws himself off a wall and dies? Has he sinned mortally? A distinction should be drawn, for if the wall was not high and he could justifiably presume that he would escape, then he does not sin mortally, but otherwise he does. Argu-ment for the first proposi-tion from C. 23 q. 5 c. 8; for the second from C. 23 q. 5 c. 9; C. 23 q. 5 c. 11. That is especially so if he threw himself off for a good reason, as in X 3. 28. 11.

[c]**conceded** — that is, "shown to be conceded"; as elsewhere "give" has been explained to mean "to be given by pro-nouncement." *Dicta Gra-tiani* pr. *post* C. 23 q. 5 c. 49.

[d]**a lesser**—that is, mat-rimony.

[e]**a greater** — that is, fornication. Or, the lesser evil is the immoderate ex-action of the conjugal debt, which the Apostle permits rather than forni-cation. C. 32 q. 2 c. 3. According to this interpre-tation, "conceded" should properly be understood as explained earlier where "conceded" meant "shown to be conceded."

[f]**then**—One may argue from this text against H., who says that a man may never know his wife without sin. C. 33 q. 4 c. 7.

[g]**procreation**—and to render the debt. C. 32 q. 2 c. 3.

[a]**entrusted**—If this person wishes to save himself, he will leave that place and enter perpetual penance. C. 1 q. 1 c. 115; C. 1 q. 7 c. 5; X 5. 3. 23. Nevertheless he is not to leave without the authority of the pope. C. 7 q. 1 c. 34; C. 7 q. 1 c. 46. But I believe, as Ion. de Fan. says, that he may

^a**the lesser**—Insofar as neither can be done without some impropriety, what involves less should be done. Dig. 50. 17. 200; Dig. 50. 17. 9.

^b**indulgence**—as was said elsewhere. What we permit, we allow against our will. C. 31 q. 1 c. 9.

D. 14. This distinction is divided into two parts, of which the first shows that no one may commit a lesser sin to avoid a graver or more serious one. The second part begins, "The rigor of custom. . . ."

Dicta Gratiani ante **c. 1.**
CASE. Here Gratian says that the previous distinction about choosing a lesser sin must be understood to apply to two evils by a single person. In this distinction it is asked whether a lesser evil may be chosen and done by one person to avoid a greater one by another. In the following capitulum it is shown that this may not be done. It also says that customary or enacted law may sometimes be relaxed.

^c*The preceding*—In this fourteenth distinction it is asked whether one may commit a lesser evil in order to prevent another's greater evil. It says that one may not, as below in the following capitulum. This section continues what was said in the previous distinction—namely, that when two evils press upon us, the lesser of them is to be chosen—by showing that this is not true when two different persons are involved.

C. 1. CASE. It is written in Genesis [19:1–11] that God sent two angels in the form of young men to destroy Sodom. When they were guests in the house of Lot, the men of Sodom came to his house wishing to abuse them. So that they would not be violated, Lot brought out his two daughters for the men of Sodom to fornicate with, rather than allow his guests to suffer anything, in this case, sodomy. Augustine asks whether such a substitution could be permitted, that is, whether Lot could consent to his daughters' fornication to prevent the sodomizing of his guests. He responds that this substitution would be perilous and that what happened should be attributed to Lot's distress.

^d**said**—The first words are Augustine's, and he picks up again at, "Since, in this substitution. . . ."

^e**substitution**—So it may be argued that the substitution of evil for evil is not to be permitted. C. 14 q. 5 c. 3; C. 23 q. 5 c. 1; C. 32 q. 8 c. 1; C. 1 q. 1 c. 27. Nevertheless, such substitution occurs in criminal trials when a defense is raised. C. 32 q. 6 c. 1; Dig. 24. 3. 39.⁽⁵⁴⁾ The truth is that such a substitution is allowed before a court but not in the

lesser^a evil, lest we sin without indulgence^b by committing the greater.

And so, the tangle of that Behemoth's sinews is frequently unraveled as one passes to greater virtues through the commission of lesser faults.

DISTINCTION FOURTEEN

Part 1.

The preceding,^c however, concerns one and the same person. In addition, we must ask whether there is the same dispensation when more than one person is involved, that is to say, whether we may commit a lesser sin so that another will not fall into a greater one.

Concerning these things, Augustine writes in Questions on Genesis, *LI, XLII:*¹⁸³

C. 1. *We should not commit crimes so that others not commit greater ones.*

Lot said^d to the men of Sodom [Gen. 19:7], "I have two daughters who have never known man; I will bring them out to you; use them as you will, but do no evil to these men." Since, in this substitution, he was willing to prostitute his daughters so that his guests not suffer evil from the men of Sodom, it may rightly be asked if the substitution of one evil or sin for another may be allowed, so that we may do something evil in order that another not do something worse. Or we can say that what Lot said was more to be attributed to his emotions than to his judgment. To allow this kind of substitution^e would be perilous^f indeed. He should in no way be imitated since his actions are to be ascribed to his human emotions and the unbalancing of his mind in the face of so great an evil.

penitential forum. C. 34 q. 5 c. 4.

^f**perilous**—Here Augustine says that no one may commit a lesser evil so that another will avoid a greater evil. Some people understand this to mean that no one may commit a lesser mortal sin so that another may avoid a greater mortal sin, but that one may commit a venial sin so that another may avoid one that is mortal. One ought to lay down one's life for one's neighbor. Consequently, one may suffer temporal death to prevent another from incurring an eternal penalty. De poen. D. 2 c. 5 § 4. But for venial sin, one is liable only for a temporal punishment; for a mortal sin, eternal punishment. C. 11 q. 3 c. 41. Therefore, one may sin venially to prevent another from sinning mortally. Furthermore, the Apostle says, "I have prayed to be anathema for my brothers." But no one is anathematized except for a

mortal sin. C. 11 q. 3 c. 41. Furthermore, as virtue and vice are opposites they cannot exist together. C. 32 q. 1 c. 9. But venial sins exist in man along with virtues; so, they are not properly to be called vices. *De poen.* D. 3 c. 23. Others say that one should commit no sin for his own good or for another's. C. 23 q. 5 c. 19. Indeed God does not want such a loss to be set against such a gain. C. 33 q. 5 c. 1. No one should perpetrate a crime for another's benefit. D. 46 c. 10.

Part 2.

The rigor of custom or enactment should sometimes be relaxed.
Wherefore Pope Leo said to Rusticus, bishop of Narbonne, in the preface of Letter *XC:*[184]

C. 2. *Which enactments may be tempered and which may not.*

As there are certain things[a] that may not be modified for any reason, so there are many that should be tempered, either for the necessity of the times,[b] or in consideration[c] [185] of age.[d] But, although this logic still holds, we have decided that, in those things doubtful[e] or unclear, one should act in a way neither contrary to the precepts of the Gospel nor in conflict with the decrees of the holy fathers.

DISTINCTION FIFTEEN

Part 1.

Since,[f] *to this point, we have been discussing natural law, enactment, and custom, and we have identified the differences that distinguish one from another, let us now turn our pen to ecclesiastical enactments, briefly identifying where possible their origins and authority from the writings of the holy fathers:*[186]

C. 1. *When the canons of the general councils begin.*

§1. Canons of the general councils (*as Isidore says in* Etymologies, *VI, XVII*) commence at the time of Constantine.[g] For in earlier years, since persecution was raging, there was hardly any way to instruct the people.

Furthermore, no one should sin venially for another's temporal or eternal salvation, for no one should be saved with the help of lies. C. 22 q. 2 c. 15; C. 22 q. 2 c. 8. Io. But why isn't Lot commended by Augustine when elsewhere he is commended by Ambrose? C. 32 q. 7 c. 12. Ambrose was considering the respect he had for his guests, and Augustine, the wrong to his daughters. D. 26 c. 1; D. 26 c. 2.

Part 2. This is the second part of this distinction, in which it says when rigor may be relaxed and when not. Io. de Fan.

***Dicta Gratiani ante* c. 2. CASE.** This section continues to treat the matter discussed earlier at the beginning of D. 13, where it said that no dispensation is permitted from natural law. Here, in contrast, it says that the rigor of custom or enactment may sometimes be relaxed, as is shown in the following capitulum.

C. 2. CASE. Pope Leo was asked whether a dispensation could be given from custom or enactment. He responded that, as there are certain things from which no dispensation may be given, such as the natural law, so there are certain things, such as custom and enactment, from which one may dispense on account of the times or age. But one must use discretion so that in doubtful matters nothing be done against the Gospel or the decrees of the fathers.

[a]**certain things**—such as precepts of the Decalogue, the form of baptism, and the form of confecting the Body of Christ. *De cons.* D. 4 c. 13; *De cons.* D. 2 c. 88.

[b]**times**—C. 1 q. 7 c. 7; D. 81 c. 12; D. 34 c. 7.[(55)]

[c]**consideration**—D. 29 c. 1.[(56)]

[d]**age**—C. 33 q. 2 c. 14; D. 86 c. 24.[(57)]

[e]**doubtful**—X 4.1.3.[(58)]

D. 15. This distinction is divided into two parts. In the first, the question of when the councils took place is asked and answered. The second part begins, "I also. . . ."

***Dicta Gratiani ante* c. 1. CASE.** Gratian spoke above about natural law, custom, and enactment and identified the differences among them. In this distinction he turns to ecclesiastical enactments and shows briefly their origin and authority.

[f]**Since** — Up to this point, the master has treated natural law. Here he begins to treat canon law. He identifies its basis and origin, and he shows which writings are received by the Church and which are not received.

C. 1. CASE. This capitulum is divided into three sections. In the first section, it is shown that the canons of general councils began in the time of Constantine. He, be it noted, first gave Christians the authority to meet together, as previously the Church had suffered persecution. In the second section, which begins, "Among. . . ," it says that four universal councils were held under four emperors, namely, under Constantine, Theodosius I, Theodosius II, and Marcian. He shows what was condemned by these councils and that these four councils and others like them must be followed inviolately. In the third section which begins " 'Synod.' . . ," he gives the etymology of names such as synod, council, and caucus.

[g]**Constantine**—On the contrary, in D. 16 c. 4 (in Isidore's

Letter), it says that councils were held from the time of Clement. I answer that earlier they were not generally held, and the word "generally" resolves the contradiction.

^a**Apostles**—The Apostles made the first symbol (that is, creed) that begins "I believe in God the Father. . .," but the Synod of Nicaea produced the one that begins "I believe in One God. . . ." Symbol is so-called from *syn*, which means "with," and *bolus*, which means "piece," because each Apostle contributed his piece.[(59)]

^b**318**—300 bishops are mentioned elsewhere. C. 10 q. 1 c. 15. But you may say that the lesser number does not exclude the greater. Dig. 12. 3. 9.

^c**inequality** — He said that the Father is greater than the Son and that the Son is greater than the Holy Spirit. C. 24 q. 3 c. 39 § 42. Hug.

^d**Constantinople**—D. 15 c. 2.

^e**Macedonius**—He said that the Holy Spirit is subservient to the Father and the Son. C. 1 q. 1 c. 21; C. 24 q. 3 c. 39 § 43.

^f**that**—We do not have this one, for we possess only the creed of the Apostles, that of Nicaea, and that of Athanasius, which begins "Whosoever. . . ." [(60)]

^g**the first at Ephesus**—This distinguishes it from the second, which is rejected. D. 16 c. 7.

^h**persons** — the Word and the man.

ⁱ**one**—He is one person, but he has two natures, namely, divine and human. D. 15 c. 3 § 1.

^j**Eutyches** — who said that Christ had one nature after the Resurrection, namely, a divine one. D. 16 c. 9 § 4 [§ 5].

ADDITION. He has both. X 5. 7. 7. Alanus notes there that, before the definition included in the decree itself, it was permitted to say the opposite because it was not yet prohibited, but that afterwards it was not. Therefore, what previously was not an article of the faith became an article of the faith when it had been defined as one. Archid.

^k**defender**—Therefore, he sinned against the faith inasmuch as he was a defender of heretics, C. 24 q. 1 c. 1; C. 24 q. 3 c. 32; X 5. 7. 10, as the law says concerning a thief. Cod. 39. 9. 1. Against this see D. 21 c. 9; C. 24 q. 2 c. 6, especially § 7. There, be it noted, it says that Dioscorus did not sin against the faith, but you should understand the words "he did not sin against the faith" to mean that he did not sin only against the faith, for he also sinned in daring to excommunicate Pope Leo. D. 21 c. 9.

^l**of the faith**—of its articles.

^m**this work**—that of Isidore. Nor is it contrary to D. 19 c. 1 (at "This is above all evident [*Presertim*]").

Hence Christianity was sundered into various heresies because before the time of the aforesaid emperor the bishops had no freedom to meet as a body. He granted Christians permission to gather freely. Under him, holy fathers from all over the world gathered at the Council of Nicaea and established, in accord with the evangelical and apostolic faith, that creed which is second after that of the Apostles.^a

§2. Among other councils, we recognize four venerable synods that, before all others, shelter the whole of the faith, like the four Gospels or the like-numbered rivers of Paradise.

Of these, the first is the synod at Nicaea of 318^b bishops conducted under the emperor Constantine Augustus. There the blasphemous Arian perfidy, in which Arius asserted the inequality^c of the Holy Trinity, was condemned, and the holy synod defined in a creed that the Son was God, consubstantial with God the Father.

The second is the synod of 150 fathers at Constantinople^d convoked under Theodosius I. Condemning Macedonius,^e who had denied that the Holy Spirit was God, it resolved that the Holy Spirit is consubstantial with the Father and the Son, producing the form of the creed that^f proclaims the full profession of belief in the Latin and Greek churches.

The third is the synod of two hundred bishops, the first at Ephesus,^g proclaimed under Theodosius II Augustus. It condemned with just anathema Nestorius, who was asserting that there were two persons^h in Christ, and made plain that the person of Our Lord Jesus Christ remains[187] oneⁱ in two natures.

The fourth is the synod of 630 clergy at Chalcedon held under the emperor Marcian. There, a single decree of the fathers condemned the abbot Eutyches^j of Constantinople, who was saying that the Word of God and the flesh were of one nature; his defender^k Dioscorus, once bishop of Alexandria; and, for a second time, Nestorius and the other heretics. The same synod proclaimed that Christ the Lord was so born of the Virgin that in him we confess one substance of divine and human natures.

These four chief synods proclaim most fully the doctrine of the faith.^l But, if there are any other synods that the holy fathers, filled with the Spirit of God, have decreed, let those whose acts are contained in this work^m preserve their full force subject to the authority of these four.

§3. "Synod," from the Greek, means "company" or "caucus." But the word "council" was taken from Roman practice. Then, when matters were being decided, all gathered as one and worked for a common purpose. "Council" is so called from "counsel" on account of the common purpose; "counsel" being like "consult," changing the letter "e" to "u." Or it is called "council" from the common purpose because they direct the entire gaze of their minds to one thing, for they are the eye's "cilia." Hence those who differ among themselves cannot form a "council" since they cannot reach agreement on one thing. Now a "caucus" is a "convention" or "congregation," being taken from "to caucus," that is, "to convene" as one. Because of this, indeed, something is called a "convention" because there men convene as one. As "convention" denominates a "caucus," so also "council" denominates the association of many as one.[188]

Concerning the four councils, St. Gregory writes thus in Register, *I, XXIV:*[189]

C. 2. *Concerning the authority of the four councils.*

§1. Like the four books of the Holy Gospel, so, too, I confess that I accept and venerate the four councils. They are: Nicaea, where the perverse teaching of Arius was destroyed; Constantinople, where the error of Eunomius and Macedonius was defeated; the first at Ephesus, where the impiety of Nestorius was condemned; and Chalcedon, where the depravity of Eutyches and Dioscorus was rejected. I embrace them with full devotion and I adhere to them with undivided approval since on them, as on a four-square foundation, the edifice of the holy faith rises and the norm of every life and activity stands.[190]

Part 2.

§2. I also venerate equally the Fifth Council, where the error-filled letter ascribed to Ibas[a] was rejected; Theodore was convicted of having fallen into the impious perfidy of separating the person of the Mediator[b] between God and man into two substances;[c] and in which were refuted the writings of Theodoret,[191] produced in rash insanity, through which the faith of St. Cyril was rejected. Moreover, all those whom the aforesaid councils spurn, I spurn; whom they venerate, I embrace. Because they have been established by universal consent, anyone who presumes[d] either to loose what they bind, or to bind what they have loosed, destroys, not them, but himself.

Concerning the same things Pope Gelasius writes in a council held at Rome with seventy bishops:[192]

C. 3. *Which councils the holy Roman Church receives.*

§1. The holy Roman Church does not forbid the following to be received after the Scriptures of the Old and New Testaments that we

C. 2. CASE. In the first section of this capitulum Gregory says that he wishes to follow the four councils like the four books of the Gospels. He shows what was condemned in each. In the second section, which begins, "I also. . . ," Gregory says that he also wishes to venerate the Fifth Council, in which three matters were condemned, namely, the error-filled letter ascribed to Ibas, the opinion of Theodore that separated the person of Christ the Mediator between God and man into two substances, that is, persons, saying that Christ had two persons, and the writings of Theodoret, which condemned the life and faith of St. Cyril. Whoever does not accept these councils destroys himself.

[a]**ascribed to Ibas** — as its originator.

[b]**the Mediator**—that is, Christ. Ioan.

[c]**two substances** — that is, persons.

[d]**presumes**—It appears, therefore, that the pope may not annul the statutes of councils since the world is greater than the capital city. D. 93 c. 24 (*circa medium*). Therefore, the pope requires the consent of a council. D. 19 c. 9. An argument to the contrary may be made from *dicta Gratiani* pr. [§ 1] *post* D. 17 c. 6; X 1. 6. 4, where it says that the council may not impose an ordinance on the pope. C. 35 q. 9 c. 5. But you should understand what is said here as pertaining to articles of the faith. C. 25 q. 1 c. 6.

C. 3. CASE. In this capitulum the same matters are treated as in D. 15

cc. 1 and 2. Gelasius, be it noted, says he wishes to venerate the four councils mentioned above and whatever else is ordained by the holy fathers. He shows which writings of the holy fathers the Church receives.

accept as normative: the holy synod of the 318 fathers at Nicaea, under the moderation of the Augustus Constantine the Great, where the heretic Arius was condemned; the holy synod at Constantinople, under the moderation of the Augustus Theodosius I, where the heretic Macedonius received due condemnation; the holy synod at Ephesus, where Nestorius was condemned with the consent of the most blessed Pope Celestine, under the moderation of Bishop Cyril of the See of Alexandria and Bishop Arcadius dispatched from Italy; the holy synod at Chalcedon, under the moderation of the Augustus Marcian and Bishop Anatolius of Constantinople, where the Nestorian and Eutychian heresies were condemned, along with Dioscorus and his accomplices. And then, if any other councils have since been instituted by the holy fathers, we declare and command that they should be both obeyed and received, but after these four in authority.[193]

§ 2. And now, indication must be made of the works of the holy fathers that are received in the Catholic Church:

§ 3. The works of St. Cyprian, martyr and bishop of Carthage.

§ 4. Also, the works of St. Athanasius, bishop of Alexandria.

§ 5. Also, the works of St. Gregory, bishop of Nazianzus.

§ 6. Also, the works of St. Basil, bishop of Cappadocia.

§ 7. Also, the works of St. John, bishop of Constantinople.

§ 8. Also, the works of St. Theophilus, bishop of Alexandria.

§ 9. Also, the works of St. Cyril, bishop of Alexandria.

§ 10. Also, the works of St. Hilary, bishop of Poitiers.

§ 11. Also, the works of St. Ambrose, bishop of Milan.

§ 12. Also, the works of St. Augustine, bishop of Hippo.

§ 13. Also, the works of St. Jerome, priest.

§ 14. Also, the works of St. Prosper, a most devout man.

§ 15. Also, the letter of Pope St. Leo, sent to Bishop Flavian of Constantinople. Should anyone question one iota of it or not reverently receive this text in its entirety, let him be anathema.

§ 16. Also, we prescribe for reading the works and treatises of all orthodox fathers who have in no way departed from the holy Roman Church and have not separated themselves from its preaching of the faith, but have remained, by God's grace, partakers of its communion until the last day of their lives.

§ 17. Also, the decretal letters, that the most blessed popes have issued at various times from the city of Rome for consultation by various fathers, are to be received reverently.[194]

Also, the acts of the holy martyrs, who endured the sufferings of numerous torments and shine with the marvelous triumph of their confession.

§ 18. What Catholic could doubt that the martyrs endured such great things in their sufferings, not by their own strength, but by the grace and help of God alone? But, because the names of those who compiled these acts have been completely forgotten, and they are thought to contain extraneous matter written by unbelievers and fools, or incidents that are less fitting than the true course of events, from ancient custom and singular caution these are not read in the Roman Church. Of this kind are passions like that of a certain Quiricus and Julitta, or like that of Gregory and certain others, which are thought to have been compiled by heretics. For this reason, as was explained above, these are not read in the Roman Church lest they give occasion to scoffing. Nevertheless, we, with the entire aforesaid Church, venerate with full reverence all the martyrs and their glorious struggles, which are known better to God than to men.

§ 19. Also, the lives of the fathers Paul, Anthony, Hilarion, and all the hermits, which St. Jerome composed, we receive with honor.

§ 20. Also, the acts of St. Silvester, bishop of the Apostolic See, which, although we do not know the name of its compiler, we know to be read by many Catholics in the city of Rome, a practice many other churches also imitate on account of ancient usage.

§ 21. Also, the description of the finding of the Lord's holy cross, other writings about the finding of the head of John the Baptist; there are also other new revelations that some Catholics read, but when they come into the hands of Catholics, let the saying of St. Paul be the guide [1 Thess. 5:21], "Test all things and retain what is good."

§ 22. Also, the pious Rufinus composed many books on ecclesiastical matters and interpreted some of the Scriptures; but, since St. Jerome criticized his treatment of free will in some of these, we believe what St. Jerome maintained. This is the case, not only with Rufinus, but also with any others whom that oft-remembered man censured out of zeal for God and devotion to the faith.

§ 23. Also, certain works of Origen that St. Jerome did not repudiate, we accept for reading. The remainder, however, we declare to be spurned along with their author.

§ 24. Also, the chronicle of Eusebius of Caesarea and his books of ecclesiastical history. Although in the first book of this history he was favorable to, and later compiled a book in praise and defense of, the schismatic Origen, we still say that he is not to be completely spurned, on account of his singular knowledge of matters that are useful for instruction.

§ 25. Also, we praise the learned Orosius, because he composed a history very necessary for combatting the calumnies of the pagans and edited it with marvelous succinctness.

§ 26. Also, we suggest with high praise the *Opus Paschale* of the venerable Sedulius, which he also rendered into epic verse.

§ 27. Also, we do not spurn the truly difficult work of Juvencus,[195] but rather admire it.

On the other hand, the Catholic and Apostolic Roman Church in no way receives what has been written or proclaimed by heretics or schismatics.

§ 28. Of these, we believe we should add a list of a few that come to mind that Catholics should avoid:

First of all, the Synod of Rimini, convened by the Caesar Constantine,[196] the son of Constantine, under the moderation of Prefect Taurus, we confess to be condemned now, then, and unto eternity.

Also, the travels under the name of the Apostle Peter that is called the eighth[197] book of St. Clement, is apocryphal;

the acts under the name of the Apostle Andrew, apocryphal;

the acts under the name of the Apostle Philip, apocryphal;

the acts under the name of the Apostle Peter, apocryphal;

the acts under the name of the Apostle Thomas, apocryphal;

the gospel under the name of Thaddaeus, apocryphal;

the gospel under the name of the Apostle Thomas, which is used by the Manicheans, apocryphal;

the gospel under the name of Barnabas, apocryphal;

the gospel under the name of the Apostle Bartholomew, apocryphal;

the gospel under the name of the Apostle Andrew, apocryphal;

the gospel that Lucian forged, apocryphal;

the gospel that Hyrcius forged, apocryphal;

ADDITION. Apocryphal means hidden and secret, as the word comes from *apo* meaning "of" and *crysis* meaning "concealed." Therefore, a book is called apocryphal, that is, concealed and secret, when its author is unknown. It is not received by the Church but, one might say, rejected, in that it may be read, not in church, but elsewhere privately. This follows Hug. So it is called apocryphal in Greek and *secreta*, that is "concealed places" in Latin. And, according to Io. de Fan., because virgins are accustomed to hide in their rooms and remain there concealed, a virgin is called *alma* in Hebrew, *apocrypha* in Greek, and *secreta*, that is, hidden, in Latin.

ᵃCyricus—Elsewhere, Quiricus.

the book concerning the infancy of the Savior, apocryphal;

the book concerning the birth of the Savior, St. Mary, and the midwife of the Savior,[198] apocryphal;

the book called *The Shepherd*, apocryphal;

all the books composed by Lenticius,[199] the disciple of the Devil, apocryphal;

the book called *The Foundation*, apocryphal;

the book called *The Treasure*, apocryphal;

the book called *Concerning the Daughters of Adam* or *Of Genesis*, apocryphal;

the hundred stanzas on Christ written in Virgilian verse, apocryphal;

the book called the *Acts of Thecla and Paul the Apostle*, apocryphal;

the book called of Nepos, apocryphal;

the book of proverbs that was compiled by heretics and passed off under the name of St. Sixtus, apocryphal;

the revelation called of Paul the Apostle, apocryphal;

the revelation called of Thomas the Apostle, apocryphal;

the revelation called of Stephen, apocryphal;

the book called the *Passing*[200] *of St. Mary*, apocryphal;

the book called the *Penitence of Adam*, apocryphal;

the book called by the name of the giant Ogyges, who is considered by the heretics to have fought with the dragon after the flood, apocryphal;

the book called the *Testament of Jacob*,[201] apocryphal;

the book called the *Penitence of Origen*, apocryphal;

the book called the *Penitence of St. Cyprian*, apocryphal;

the book called the *Penitence of Jannes and Jambres*, apocryphal;

the book called the *Lots of the Apostles*, apocryphal;

the book of Lusana,[202] apocryphal;

the book of *Canons of the Apostles*, apocryphal;

the book *Physiologus*, which was compiled by heretics and transmitted under the name of St. Ambrose, apocryphal;

the history of Eusebius Pamphilus, apocryphal;

the works of Tertullian or Africanus, apocryphal;[203]

the works of Postumianus and Gallus, apocryphal;

the works of Montanus, Priscilla, and Maximilla, apocryphal;

all the works of Faustus the Manichean, apocryphal;[204]

the works of the other Clement of Alexandria, apocryphal;[205]

the works of Cassian, the priest of Gaul, apocryphal;

the works of Victorinus of Poitiers, apocryphal;

the works of Faustus of Riez in Gaul, apocryphal;

the works of Frumentius,[206] apocryphal;

the letter of Jesus to King Abgar, apocryphal;

the passion of George, apocryphal;

the passion of Cyricusᵃ and Julitta, apocryphal;

the text called the *Contradiction of Solomon*, apocryphal;

all phylacteries, since they are not of the angels, as some pretend, but were compiled by the magical arts of demons, apocryphal.

§ 29. These writings and everything similar to them that were taught or written by Simon Magus, Nicholas, Cerinthus, Marcion, Basilides, Ebion, Paul of Samosata, Photinus (with Bonosus and those who spewed out similar errors), Montanus and his obscene followers, Apollinaris, Valentinus or the Manichean Faustus,[207] Sabellius, Arius, Macedonius, Eunomius, Novatus, Sabbatius, Celestius,[208] Donatus, Eustathius, Jovinian, Pelagius, Julian and Latiensis,[209] Celestine, Maximinus, Priscan of Spain,[210] Lampedius, Dioscorus, Eutyches, the two Peters (one of whom defiled Alexandria and the other Antioch), Acacius of Constantinople with his associates; as well as all the heresies that they, their disciples, or the schismatics (whose names can hardly all be remembered) taught or wrote, ought to be not only repudiated but also eliminated from the entire Roman and Apostolic Church. Along with their authors and the followers of their authors, we confess them to be condemned under the bond of indissoluble anathema.[211]

§ 30. In addition, we have decided to list the books read in ecclesiastical offices throughout the year for the instruction of the faithful (since the Apostolic See does not reject that practice but follows it).

Some appoint the Pentateuch[212] from Septuagesima up to the fifteenth day before Easter, and from the fifteenth day until Holy Thursday, Jeremiah.

On Holy Thursday they read three lessons from Lamentations 1:1 and following,[213] three from St. Augustine's Tract on Psalm 54,[214] and three from the Apostle at 1 Corinthians 11:20 and following. The second lesson begins at 1 Corinthians 11:25; the third at 1 Corinthians 12:1.

On Good Friday: three readings from the Lamentations of Jeremiah, three from Augustine's Tract on Psalm 63, and three from the Apostle, beginning at Hebrews 4:11. The second reading begins at Hebrews 5:1; the third at Hebrews 5:11. On Holy Saturday: three readings from the Lamentations of the Prophet Jeremiah, and three from St. Augustine's same Tract on Psalm 63, and three from the Apostle, starting at Hebrews 9:11. The second reading begins at Hebrews 9:16; the third at Hebrews 10:1.

Easter: the homily pertaining to that day, and the homilies for the days of that week. From the Octave of Easter until the Octave of Pentecost, they appoint the Acts of the Apostles, the Catholic Epistles, and the Apocalypse.

From the Octave of Pentecost until the first of August, they appoint the books of Kings and Chronicles. From the first Sunday of August until the first of September, they appoint Solomon. From the first Sunday of September until the first of October, they appoint Job, Tobit, Esther,[215] and Ezra. From the first Sunday of October until the first of November, they appoint the books of Maccabees. From the first Sunday of November until the first of December, they appoint Ezekiel, Daniel, and the Minor Prophets.

From the first Sunday of December until the Nativity of the Lord, they appoint the Prophet Isaiah. On Christmas they first read three lessons from Isaiah. The first begins at Isaiah 9:1, the second at Isaiah 40:1, and the third at Isaiah 52:1. Then, they read the sermons or homilies pertaining to that day. On the feast of St. Stephen: the homily pertaining to that day. And likewise on the feast of St. John. Likewise, on the feast of the Holy Innocents. On the Octave of Christmas: the homily of the day. From the first Sunday after Christmas until Septuagesima, they appoint the letters of Paul. On Epiphany: three readings from Isaiah. The first begins at Isaiah 55:1, the second at Isaiah 60:1, the third at Isaiah 61:10. Then, they read the sermons or homilies pertaining to that day.

DISTINCTION SIXTEEN

Part 1.

There are fifty[a] Canons of the Apostles *that some assert to have been passed down through*[216] Pope Clement of Rome.

Isidore writes that these should not be received but counted as apocrypha:[217]

D. 16. This distinction is divided into two parts. The second begins, "This synod. . . ."

***Dicta Gratiani ante* c. 1. CASE.** In this sixteenth distinction, Gratian shows that the *Canons of the Apostles* are to be received. First, however, he presents a difference of opinion as to the *Canons of the Apostles*. First, he presents the view that they are not to be received, then the view that they are to be received, and then his solution.

[a]***There are fifty***—Here begins the sixteenth dis-

tinction in which it is proven that the canons of the Apostles are to be received; then it is shown at what time and in the incumbency of which pope or emperor each council was held. Note also that Gratian presents a difference of opinion concerning the *Canons of the Apostles* but does not resolve it. He proves by the authority of Isidore that the *Canons of the Apostles* are not received because they are apocryphal. Then he proves by the authority of Zephyrinus and Leo that they are received and are not apocryphal. The solution is simple: those canons should be received that were imposed by true Apostles, but those composed by pseudo-apostles should not. D. 15 c. 3 § 17 [§ 18].

C. 1. CASE. Isidore asks whether the canons which are called "apostolic" are to be approved. He answers that, since they were composed by heretics under the name of the Apostles and were not approved by the Roman Church or the holy fathers, they are taken to be apocrypha, although many useful things are to be found in them.

[a]**canons**—Construe the passage this way: "Although those canons are said to be canons of the Apostles and. . . ."

[b]**useful**—So it may be argued that the useful is vitiated by the not useful. D. 9 c. 7.

[c]**apocrypha**—that is, having no definite author, such as the Wisdom of Solomon, the book of Jesus ben Sirach that is called Ecclesiasticus, the book of Judith, the book of Tobit, and the books of Maccabees are called apocrypha. Nevertheless they are read but not, perhaps, generally.[(61)]

CC. 2–4. CASE. The following capitula are clear.

[d]**Clement**—that is, which was composed by heretics under the name of Clement.

[e]**travels**—which are contained in the acts of Peter who went traveling throughout the world.

[f]**exception**—This exception seems improper because the exception is either for true canons or for false ones. But it cannot be for false ones for nothing in these should be observed. Nor can it be for true ones for none of these are apocryphal. You may say that the term "canons" is taken in a broad sense for both true and false ones together. *Dicta*

Gratiani pr. *post* D. 32 c. 6.

[g]**orthodox**—that is, "right"; "orthos" meaning "right" and "doxa" meaning "glory." On this account the faith is said to be orthodox, that is, Catholic and right, because in it we rightly glory. Ioan. de Fan.

[h]**It pleased**—Conflicting views, which Gratian neither discusses nor resolves, are found in these three capitula. The Sixth Synod says that eighty-five capitula of the *Canons of*

C. 1. *The canons called "apostolic" are rejected by apostolic authority.*

The canons[a] that are said to be of the Apostles, although useful[b] things are found in them, are to be discarded and relegated to the apocrypha[c] along with their version of apostolic affairs. This is either because the Apostolic See has not received them and the holy fathers have withheld assent from them or because they were compiled by heretics under the name of the Apostles.

But Zephyrinus writes the opposite to the bishops in Sicily, in Letter 1:[218]

C. 2. *The* Canons of the Apostles *are to be received.*

The Apostles, along with many other bishops, rendered sixty [219] decisions and ordered that they be observed.

Also, Pope Leo IX against the letter of the Abbot Nicetas: [220]

C. 3. *Except for fifty capitula, the* Canons of the Apostles *are counted among the apocrypha.*

The fathers count among the apocrypha the book of Clement,[d] that is the travels[e] of the Apostle Peter, and the *Canons of the Apostles*, with the exception[f] of fifty capitula that they decided were to be added to the orthodox[g] faith.

The Sixth Synod, c. 2:[221]

[C. 4.]

It pleased[h] this holy synod that the eighty-five capitula of the *Canons of the Apostles* be henceforth confirmed and ratified.

the Apostles are to be followed, but Zephyrinus speaks of sixty and Leo of fifty. Some resolve the difficulty by saying that the Sixth Synod was before Zephyrinus, and Zephyrinus before Leo, and that eighty-five canons were followed as the Sixth Synod says, but afterward twenty-five fell into desuetude, thus sixty remained as Zephyrinus says; in the period afterward ten more were eliminated, and so there remained only those fifty as Leo says. But this solution does not stand up. Zephyrinus came before the Sixth Synod, for the Sixth Synod was held at the time of Agatho, D. 16 c. 9, which was a long time after Zephyrinus, as appears from the chronicles. Leaving aside other solutions, you may say that there is no contradiction, for the synod said there were eighty-five capitula, Leo said there were fifty capitula, Zephyrinus did not speak of capitula but of decisions, and it could be that in one capitulum there were many decisions.

Isidore's letter. **CASE.** In this capitulum Isidore shows that the canons of the Apostles are to be received for three reasons. First, because many have received them. Second, because the holy fathers have confirmed their decisions and placed them among the canonical enactments. Third, because they have been inserted and placed in the digest with the decrees of the various councils from Clement to Silvester. The rest is clear.

D. 19 c. 6. Accordingly, although the Synod of Ancyra was prior to Nicaea, nevertheless Nicaea is placed first on account of its greater authority. D. 16 c. 9; D. 16 c. 11; argument from X 1. 3. 41.

C. 5 is dubious. **CASE.** Gratian shows that the Sixth Synod formulated canons and proves this by the next capitulum.

bSixth Synod—The text is wrong. It must have been the Seventh Synod. For how could there be a doubt about what the Sixth Synod did? [(62)]

C. 6. CASE. It says in this capitulum that the Sixth Synod made canons and was held under the emperor Constantine, rebuking the perfidy of the heretics who were saying that Christ acted only in the works of his humanity, such as eating and walking. His other works and powers, such as to raise the dead and to walk on water, were delusions and not the truth. This is said in the first section. The second section begins "This synod was dissolved . . . ." It says that this Sixth Synod was later held under Justinian, the son of Constantine, and that it adopted many canons that had been formulated at this same Sixth Synod. In the third section, which begins, "The same. . .," what was said in the second section is repeated.

Isidore's letter before the canons.

Isidore, a servant of Christ, to his fellow servant, the reader.[222]

On account of their authority, we have placed ahead^a of the other councils the canons that are said to be of the Apostles, although they are called apocryphal by some, because a greater number receive them and the holy fathers have confirmed their decisions by synodal authority and placed them among the canonical enactments. *Also below*: There is included, as was said above, first the order for celebrating a council, then the *Canons of the Apostles* and the earliest apostolic decretals (that is, those from St. Clement to St. Silvester), and then we have inserted a digest of the various councils, following their order.

Also, because Pope Adrian receives the Sixth Synod with all its canons, the eight holy and universal councils have been confirmed by the profession of the Roman pontiffs, and the Sixth Synod or Seventh Council[223] has received and approved the Canons of the Apostles, *it is evident that they are not to be relegated to the apocrypha.*

Thus, Pope Adrian writes to Patriarch Tarasius:[224]

C. 5. *The Sixth Synod is confirmed by the authority of Adrian.*
I receive the holy Sixth Synod^b with all its canons.

Although there is a doubt whether it composed any canons, this doubt is easily removed by the fourth session of the Sixth[225] *Synod.*
There Peter, bishop of Nicomedia, says:[226]

C. 6. *The Sixth Synod composed canons.*
§1. I have a book containing the canons of the holy Sixth Synod. The patriarch said, "Are some scandalized through ignorance of these canons, saying that the Sixth Synod never made any canons? Let them know then that the holy Sixth Synod was convoked under Constantine [IV] against those who said that there is one operation and one will^c in Christ, and that the holy fathers there anathematized these as heretics and explained the orthodox faith."

Part 2.
§2. This synod was dissolved in year fourteen of the reign of Constantine^d [IV]. Then, after four or five years, the same holy fathers were

C. 6 § 1. CASE. The case of this section is clear.
cwill—Some were saying that there was only one will in Christ. But it should be said that insofar as he was man he had two wills, one sensual, according to which he said [cf. Matt. 26: 39], "Father, if it may be done, let it pass from me. . .," and the other rational, according to which he said [Matt. 26: 39], "Not as I will, but as you will." [(63)]

^a**placed ahead**—So it may be argued that those who are of greater authority ought to have the first voice in elections.

^d**Constantine**—The contrary appears from Instit. 2. 7. 3, and from Instit. 2.12.4,[(64)] where Justinian calls his father Justin. But this text speaks of another Justinian [II], under whom the Sixth Synod was held in the time of Pope Agatho. D. 16 c. 9. The Fifth Synod was held under Justinian [I], whose laws we read. D. 16 c. 9.

[a]**Justinian**—But certainly one cannot resolve the contradiction in this way, because both Leo and the synod speak of capitula. You may make a distinction concerning the times to reconcile the texts. C. 2 q. 1 c. 18.

[b]**same**—Note that the synod is said to be the same because the same fathers convened. This is as in C. 7 q. 1 c. 9; Dig. 5.1.76. Thus it may be argued that something takes its name from that which brings it into existence. *Dicta Gratiani* § 1. *post* C. 2 q. 6 c. 39.

CC. 7–13. CASE. In the next capitulum it says that the Fifth and Sixth Synods did not issue canons like the other synods. This is because the holy fathers of this Sixth Synod met at Constantinople under Justinian, as the Sixth Synod, to formulate canons, although they had already assembled earlier. It is said that the Fifth Synod was reconvened under Justinian for the sake of giving greater authority, because in it, as the Sixth Synod, the canons issued under Constantine were confirmed. The remaining capitula are clear until c. 14.

[c]**eight holy** — These councils are called eight, because eight of them were held, and here it says they were held in four places. D. 15 c. 2.

convoked under Justinian,[a] the son of Constantine, and promulgated the aforesaid canons. Concerning this, there is no doubt. The very same bishops, who were at the synod under Constantine, subscribed to the same canons under Justinian. For it is fitting that a universal synod also promulgate ecclesiastical canons.

Also: The holy Sixth Synod reconvened—after the definition promulgated by it against the Monothelites under the emperor Constantine, who convoked it—not long after his death and when his son Justinian was ruling in his place.

§3. The same[b] divinely inspired holy synod was convoked again at Constantinople four or five years later and promulgated 102 canons for correction of the Church.

Therefore, it can be inferred from this that the Sixth Synod was convoked twice, first under Constantine, when it issued no canons, and again under his son Justinian, when it promulgated the aforesaid canons. So the holy fathers, gathered a second time at the synod, decreed:[227]

C. 7. *The enactments of the Sixth Synod.*

Since the holy and universal synods—the fifth under Justinian [I] Augustus, the sixth under your father Constantine [IV] Augustus—while discussing very amply the mystery of the faith,[228] have not issued any canons as did the other four universal synods. We, coming together in this imperial city, have drawn up sacred canons. *Also:* It pleased this holy synod that the 85 capitula of the *Canons of the Apostles* be henceforth confirmed and ratified.

Also:[229] We also confirm[230] the other canons and synods of the saints, that is, Nicaea, Ancyra, Neocaesarea, Gangra, Antioch, Laodicea, Constantinople, First Ephesus, Chalcedon, Sardica, Carthage,[231] along with the works of Theophilus, bishop of Alexandria; of Dionysius,[232] bishop of Alexandria; of Peter, bishop and martyr of Alexandria; of Gregory the Thaumaturge, bishop of Neocaesarea; of Athanasius, bishop of Alexandria; of Basil, bishop of Caesarea in Cappadocia, of Gregory, bishop of Nyssa; of Gregory the Theologian; of Amphilochius, bishop of Iconium; of Timothy, bishop of Alexandria; of Gennadius,[233] bishop of Constantinople; of Cyril, bishop of Alexandria; and of Cyprian, bishop of Carthage and his synod.[234]

Also, the Roman pontiff's profession from the Liber Diurnus:[235]

C. 8. *Eight holy councils are confirmed by the authority of the Roman pontiff.*

I profess that eight holy[c] universal councils, that is, first, Nicaea; second, Constantinople; third, Ephesus; fourth, Chalcedon; fifth and sixth, Constantinople; seventh, Nicaea; and eighth, Constantinople, are to be preserved complete to the last letter and held worthy of equal honor and veneration; and all they proclaim and establish, I completely accept and proclaim, and whatever things they condemn, I also confess as to be condemned with mouth and heart.

Now, as to when the Sixth, First, Second, Third, Fourth, and Fifth Synods, were convened, Bede wrote in the Book on the Times, *LXV:*[236]

C. 9. *Concerning the dates of the councils.*

§ 1. The Sixth[a] Universal Synod was celebrated at Constantinople, and drawn up in the Greek language at the time of Pope Agatho, with the attendance and presence within his palace of the most pious emperor Constantine [IV], and with the legates of the Apostolic See and 150 bishops.

§ 2. The First Universal Synod, of 318 fathers, was convoked at Nicaea against Arius in the time of Pope Julius,[237] under the emperor Constantine.

§ 3. The Second, of 150 fathers at Constantinople, against Macedonius and Eudoxius, in the time of Pope Damasus and Emperor Gratian, when Nectarius was ordained bishop of the same city.

§ 4. The Third, of 200 fathers at Ephesus, against Nestorius, bishop of the imperial city, under Emperor Theodosius the Great and Pope Celestine.[238]

§ 5. The Fourth, of 630 fathers at Chalcedon, under Pope Leo, in the time of the emperor Marcian, against Eutyches, leader of the evil monks.

The Fifth, also at Constantinople in the time of Pope Virgilius,[239] under the emperor Justinian [II], against Theodore and all the heretics.

[C. 10.][240]

Now, the First Synod was that of the 318 fathers at Nicaea, against the priest Arius of Alexandria, who had asserted three grades in the Trinity, the Father being greatest, the Son less, and the Holy Spirit a creature: in the time of the emperor Constantine, Pope Silvester of Rome, Macarius of Jerusalem and Alexander [241] of Alexandria. Having condemned that same heresy, they promulgated twenty canons, of which the principal author was the

aforesaid Bishop Alexander.

The Second was[242] at Constantinople, against Bishop Macedonius of Constantinople, who denied that the Holy Spirit was God: in the time of the emperors Gratian and Theodosius, Pope Damasus of Rome, Cyril of Jerusalem, and Nectarius of Constantinople.[243] Having condemned the aforesaid heresy, it promulgated three canons, of which the principal author was Nectarius of Constantinople.

The Third was at Ephesus, of 200 [244] fathers, against Bishop Nestorius of Constantinople, who said that the Blessed Virgin Mary was not the Mother of God, but of a man only, thus making one person of the flesh and another of the Deity: in the time of Emperor Theodosius II,[245] Pope Celestine of Rome, Bishop Juvenal of Constantinople, and Bishop Cyril of Alexandria. They compiled twelve[246] capitula against the like numbered capitula of the blasphemies of Nestorius, the same author who had been anathematized by St. Cyril.

The Fourth was at Chalcedon, of 630 fathers, against Abbot Eutyches of Constantinople, who said that Christ, after the assumption of the flesh, did not exist in two natures, but that the divine nature alone remained in him: in the time of Emperor Marcian, Pope Leo of Rome, Juvenal of Jerusalem, and Anatolius of Constantinople. Having condemned the above heresy, they promulgated twenty-seven canons, of which the principal author was St. Anatolius, bishop of Constantinople.

The Fifth was at Constantinople against Theodore of Mopsuestia and all the heretics, Theodore having said that the Word of God was one thing and Christ another [247] and having denied that the holy Virgin Mary was the Mother of God: in the time of Emperor Justinian [II], Pope Virgilius of Rome, Domninus of Antioch, and Eutyches of Constantinople. They wrote fourteen capitula of anathemas against the blasphemies of Theodore and his followers.

The Sixth was at Constantinople, of 150 fathers, against Bishop Macarius of Antioch

^a**greater**—So it may be argued that the one first in time is not first in right. Preference should be given to the better person, for one should approve not noble rank but the deeds of a better life. C. 23 q. 4 c. 48; D. 40 c. 4; D. 40 c. 12 (*in fine*); Nov. 5. 9 [Coll. I. 5]. Note that honors ought to go to the honorable. Argument from D. 25 c. 1 (*in fine*); Dig. 50. 4. 10. The contrary may be argued from Cod. 1. 31. 2; D. 61 c. 5.⁽⁶⁵⁾ Argument to the contrary from D. 65 c. 8; D. 65 c. 9 (*in fine*), and from the note concerning this matter in D. 67 c. 2. Archid.

and his associates, who asserted the false proposition that there was only one will and operation in Christ: in the time of Emperor Constantine [IV], Pope Agatho of Rome, and George[248] of Constantinople. Having condemned the aforesaid heresy, they wrote nine[249] capitula anathematizing it, which are appended below.

[C. 11.][250]

First, note is made of the Synod of Ancyra, which is held to have occurred before that of Nicaea, but which is placed after it, because of its greater[a] authority, where twenty-eight fathers promulgated twenty-four[251] canons, whose principal author was Bishop Vitalis of Antioch.

Second, Neocaesarea, which is read to have been after Ancyra but before Nicaea,[252] where sixteen[253] fathers promulgated fourteen canons, whose principal author was Bishop Vitalis of Salamis.

Third, Gangra, which is read to have been after Nicaea, where sixteen[254] fathers promulgated twenty canons on account of ecclesiastical necessities, in particular, against Eustathius,[255] who asserted that no one in the married order and none of the faithful had any hope before the Lord unless he renounced all his possessions, and many other harmful things that are too long to enumerate here.

Fourth, Sardica, where sixty[256] fathers promulgated twenty-one canons, whose principal authors were Bishop Hosius of Cordova, Bishop Vincent of Capua, Bishop Januarius[257] of Benevento, and Calepodius of Naples, legates of the holy Roman Church.

Fifth, Antioch, where twenty-nine[258] fathers promulgated twenty-five canons, whose principal author was Bishop Eusebius of Palestine.

Sixth, Laodicea, where thirty-two[259] fathers promulgated fifty-nine[260] canons, whose principal author was Bishop Theodosius.

Seventh,[261] Carthage in the time of Emperor Honorius, where three-hundred-twelve[262] fathers promulgated thirty-three canons, whose principal author was Bishop Aurelius of Carthage. It is read that St. Augustine, bishop of Hippo, also attended this synod.

Eighth, that of Africa under Emperor Theodosius II, where one-hundred-seventeen[263] fathers reviewed and confirmed one-hundred-five canons that, it is read, were drafted by various synods of the African province during the time of Bishop Aurelius of Carthage.

Ninth, Arles in the time of Emperor Constantine, as some say, where two hundred[264] fathers promulgated four[265] canons, whose principal authors were Silvester, bishop of the city of Rome, and St. Marinus, bishop of Arles.

Tenth, also at Arles, where nineteen fathers promulgated canons, whose principal author was St. Caesarius, bishop of Arles.

Eleventh, also at Arles, where sixteen[266] fathers promulgated the canons.

Twelfth, also at Arles, in the Garden Quarter, where eleven fathers promulgated canons, whose principal author was St. Caesarius, bishop of Arles.

Thirteenth, also at Arles, where nineteen fathers promulgated canons, whose principal author was Bishop Sarpaudus of Arles.

Fourteenth, Orange, where sixteen fathers promulgated canons, whose principal author was Bishop Hilary.

Fifteenth, Albon,[267] where twenty-six fathers promulgated thirty-nine[268] canons, whose principal author was Bishop Caesarius.

Sixteenth, Agde, where twenty-nine[269] fathers promulgated canons, whose principal author was Bishop Caesarius.

Seventeenth,[270] Orleans, where seventy-two fathers promulgated canons, whose principal author was Bishop Aurelius[271] of Arles in the time of King Clovis.[272]

Eighteenth, also at Orleans, where thirty-one fathers promulgated canons, whose principal author was Bishop Melanius of Rennes.

Nineteenth, also at Orleans, where thirty [273] fathers promulgated canons, whose principal author was St. Aubin, bishop of Angers.

Twentieth, Auvergne, where fifteen fathers promulgated canons, whose principal author was Bishop Honoratus of Bourges.

Twenty-first, Mâcon, where twenty-one fathers promulgated canons, whose principal author was Bishop Priscus of Lyons.

Twenty-second, also at Mâcon, where eighty-six [274] fathers promulgated canons, whose principal author was the same Bishop Priscus of Lyons.

Twenty-third, Lyons, where eighteen [275] fathers promulgated canons, whose principal author was Bishop Philip of Vienne.

Twenty-fourth, also at Lyons, where twenty fathers established canons, the principal author of which was the same Bishop Priscus of Lyons.

But, what is said above, that the Synod of Nicaea promulgated twenty canons, seems to contradict what is found in a letter of Athanasius. For Athanasius, bishop of Alexandria, wrote to Pope Mark:[276]

C. 12. *Athanasius' letter requesting approval for the capitula of the Council of Nicaea.*

We hope that we will be found worthy to receive, by the authority of your Holy See through the present legates, the seventy [a] capitula of the Council of Nicaea, which were burned by fire, that I offered at the command of my lord Alexander and by the decree of all the bishops.[277]

Also: While we were present eighty [278] capitula were treated at the aforementioned synod: forty [279] from the Greeks, prepared in the Greek language, forty [280] from the Latins, similarly prepared in the Latin language. But it seemed to the 318 bishops, filled with the Holy Spirit, and to the said Alexander, secretary of the Apostolic See, that ten capitula should be combined with others and inserted in suitable places, so that the capitula of such a great and excellent council, which instructs the entire Christian world, would be seventy, after the number of the seventy disciples or the languages of the whole world.

So how is it said that twenty capitula were promulgated at the Synod of Nicaea, when it can be shown (as Athanasius writes) that seventy capitula were there promulgated? The response to this is: Certain capitula of the Synod of Nicaea have fallen into disuse, while twenty are followed in the Roman church.

So Pope Stephen wrote to Bishop Luitbert of Mayence:[281]

C. 13. *Only twenty capitula of the Council of Nicaea have been received.*

Only twenty capitula[b] of the Council of Nicaea have been received by the Roman Church. It is uncertain through what neglect the others have lapsed; many declare that they have been mixed in with those of the Council of Antioch.

The Council of Sardica is received by the authority of Pope Nicholas.

So he writes to the clergy of Constantinople:[282]

C. 14. *The Council of Sardica is received by apostolic authority.*

What you say, that you do not observe or receive the Council of Sardica and other decrees of the holy pontiffs, is difficult for us to believe. Since the Council of Sardica was held

[a]**seventy**—D. 21 c. 2; D. 68 c. 5, where it says that there were seventy-two disciples. According to Hugo. you may say that the lesser number does not exclude the greater. Argument from C. 10 q. 1 c. 15; D. 15 c. 1 § 2 [§ 2].

[b]**twenty capitula**—from Sardica.

C. 14. CASE. Clerics of Constantinople were saying that they neither possessed nor received the statutes of the Council of Sardica or the holy fathers. The pope argues against them, saying that it is hard to believe that they do not have these statutes, as they were promulgated in their area. As the entire Church has received them, Constantinople ought to receive them.

^a**area**—Here the argument is twofold. First it is argued that, because everyone else does something, you should do it, too. D. 12 c. 4; D. 12 c. 9. Again, it is argued that no one should be ignorant of what is done publicly. C. 12 q. 2 c. 24; C. 8 q. 1 c. 15; C. 11 q. 3 c. 20; D. 20 c. 2; D. 87 c. 9; C. 33 q. 1 c. 2; Dig. 14. 3. 11. 3; Cod. 7. 16. 37; X 5. 1. 1. The contrary may be argued from D. 82 c. 2; C. 1 q. 1 c. 108; C. 24 q. 1 c. 41. The former is normally done, and the latter is occasionally done in the case of one who was ignorant. X 4. 18. 6.

D. 17. This distinction is divided into three parts. In the first of these, the master wishes to prove that a general council is of no force if it is held without the permission of the pope. The second part begins "Therefore. . . ." The third part begins, "Hence, by. . . ."

***Dicta Gratiani ante* c. 1.** **CASE.** Above, in D. 15 c. 1 and D. 16 c. 6, it was shown when the general councils were held and how their authority exceeds that of other councils. In this seventeenth distinction, it is shown that they may be held only by authority of the Apostolic See. This is proven in the following capitula.

^b*It*—In this seventeenth distinction it is shown who may call councils. Some councils are universal, some local or provincial, and some episcopal. Universal ones are ordained by the pope or his legate with all the bishops. A local or provincial council is held by the metropolitan or primate with his suffragans. D. 19 c. 1; D. 92 c. 8. A universal council may not be held without the authority of the pope, as is shown here; a particular one without the authority of the metropolitan or primate; or an episcopal council without the authority of the bishop. Nevertheless, a metropolitan may hold a council without the authority of the primate. D. 92 c. 8. Similarly, the bishop may do so without the authority of the metropolitan. D. 38 c. 2; C. 12 q. 2 c. 51. That is so, notwithstanding what it says in D. 18 c. 4 (*in fine*); D. 18 c. 15, because that is to be understood of provincial councils, or you may understand it to refer to the promulgation of canons. Ioan.

C. 1. CASE. The Bishop Maxentius wished to hold a general synod to formulate canons, and Marcellus says that, although he might hold a local synod, he could not do this.

^c**synod**—that is, a general one.

ADDITION. or, indeed, a provincial synod that is to establish something general. Archid.

^d**assemble**—when the bishops convene to consider the case of a cleric's crime in sacred matters. Accordingly, one may

under you in your area^a and the whole Church receives it, how does it accord with reason that the holy church of Constantinople rejects it and does not fittingly observe it?

DISTINCTION SEVENTEEN

Part 1.

It^b *has been shown above from the writings of the saints when the general councils were celebrated and that their authority is greater than that of other councils. Authority for convoking councils, however, belongs to the Apostolic See.*

So Pope Marcellus wrote to Maxentius:[283]

C. 1. *A synod of bishops may not be lawfully conducted without the authority of the Holy See.*

A synod^c of bishops may not be lawfully conducted without the authority of this Holy See (although you may assemble^d the bishops).[284] Nor may any bishop who has appealed to this Apostolic See be condemned until its definitive sentence has been delivered. For, if secular people lodge appeals during criminal trials, how much more is it permitted to priests to do the same? About them, after all, it says [Ps. 81:6], "I have said you are gods."

Also, Pope Julius I in his rescript favoring Athanasius against the bishops of the East, 29: [285]

C. 2. *A council that has not been confirmed by the authority of the Roman Church is not valid.*

Your rule has no force, nor could it have any, because this council was not conducted by orthodox bishops, nor was the legate^e of the Roman

argue that such a meeting of bishops may not be called a general synod.

CC. 2–3. CASE. Heretical oriental bishops held a council that enacted many things. Neither the pope nor his legate went to this council. Therefore, Pope Julius says that it has no force, nor does anything it established. He proves this from the authority of the canons, which say that a council may not be held without the authority of the Apostolic See. The case of the next capitulum is clear.

^e**legate**—one specially assigned this task. Otherwise, a legate may not hold a council. *Dicta Gratiani* pr. [§ 1] *post*

D. 3. 2; X 1. 30. 4.

^a**valid**—So it may be argued what is void may not be made valid, as noted in C. 9 q. 2 c. 1; X 1. 6. 29.

^b**without**—Here one can find expressly that what belongs to the pope alone may not be committed to another by a general mandate but only by a special mandate. X 1. 30. 4.

Church present. For the canons order that no council occur without its authority. And no council has been valid,^a nor will one be valid, that has not been confirmed by its authority.

Also, Pope Damasus I to Stephen, in Letter *III:* ²⁸⁶

C. 3. *Let none treat matters reserved to the Roman Church.*

Let no one who does not want to be declared unworthy of ecclesiastical honors as insubordinate presume, without^b its permission, to treat matters reserved to this see alone.

*Also, Gregory:*²⁸⁷

C. 4. *Without the authority of the Apostolic See, a local synod may not be convoked against a general one.*

To convoke a local synod^c was not allowed to anyone at any time nor will it be allowed.²⁸⁸ But occasionally some hesitate out of ignorance whether the teachings of a general synod should be received.^d Others, out of concern for the salvation of their souls, spontaneously have recourse to the Apostolic See to receive²⁸⁹ its teaching. Still others (of whom it has been written [Prov. 18:3], "The sinner, when he has reached the depths of sin, is contemptuous") are so stubborn and contemptuous that they refuse to be instructed. In that case, it is necessary that the Apostolic See draw them to their salvation, or, in accord with the canons, that they be restrained²⁹⁰ through the secular^e powers (lest they became the ruin of others).

Also, Pope Pelagius II to the bishops who had convened at the illicit call of John of Constantinople, Letter *I, 1:* ²⁹¹

C. 5. *An assembly without the authority of the Apostolic See is not a council but a conventicle.*

§1. We have again established from many apostolic, canonical, and ecclesiastical norms that councils are not to be celebrated without the decision of the Roman pontiff.

These matters are explained in D. 12 c. 2. You may also consult X 1. 30. 4.

C. 4. CASE. When the Fifth Council had been held at Constantinople, the bishops of Venetia, Istria, and Liguria, wishing to adopt the statutes of this council, convened to examine whether the statutes were good or bad. Gregory attacked them, saying that if any doubt had emerged as to the statutes of this council, it ought to have been submitted

to the Apostolic See. For if any are contumacious, they ought to be constrained by the Church. If the Church cannot do so, then they ought to be restrained by the secular power.

^c**local synod**—to decree something generally or to revoke something decreed by a universal council, as in the case of those bishops who wanted to retract the statutes of the Synod of Constantinople. It appears here that it belongs to the pope alone to interpret the statutes of a universal council. X 3. 8. 12. For the contrary argument, that an interpretation may be made by all the bishops or by the most senior of those present, because those who laid down a law ought to be judges of its interpretation, see X 5. 39. 31; X 2. 1. 12.

^d**received**—One is not said to be a heretic simply because he errs if he is willing to be corrected. C. 24 q. 1 c. 14. But if he doubts the faith he is said to be a heretic. X 5. 7. 1.

^e**secular**—Therefore, there are cases in which laymen may constrain clerics, even when they have not been deposed. C. 23 q. 5 c. 20. Otherwise, a layman may not punish even a deposed cleric unless that cleric is incorrigible. X 2. 1. 10. Be it noted, that a cleric, even when he is a criminal, is never to be delivered to a secular court, as long as he may be corrected by the ecclesiastical power. D. 81 c. 8; X 2. 1. 4. An exception is the crime of falsifying apostolic letters. X 5. 20. 7. It is also shown by this text that, whenever the ecclesiastical power fails, one may always have recourse to the secular arm. C. 11 q. 1 c. 19; C. 23 q. 5 c. 43. ADDITION. On the same, see C. 23 q. 5 c. 26.⁽⁶⁶⁾

C. 5. CASE. This capitulum is divided into two sections. In the first section, it says that the bishops of Constantinople held a council, called by John, who was then patriarch. This was done without the permission of the Apostolic See. Consequently, the pope voided and quashed this council and whatever was enacted by it, and forbade others of this sort to be held. In the second section, which begins, "If disputes. . . ," it says that if the bishops disagree on any matter, the question should be referred to the see of the archbishop or patriarch. If it cannot be resolved there, it is to be referred to a synod of bishops. More difficult questions are to be referred to the Apostolic See.

^a**exhortation**—So it may be argued that a superior's authority is no excuse. C. 12 q. 2 c. 4. The contrary may be argued from C. 12 q. 2 c. 22; D. 63 c. 24. You may say that in small matters it is an excuse but not otherwise.

^b**to a greater**—that is, to the metropolitan. Accordingly, since matters are appealed from all the bishops of a province to the metropolitan, it appears that the metropolitan alone is greater than all the bishops of the province, since an appeal is not taken from equals to equals. C. 2 q. 6 c. 28. Moreover, it seems there is an appeal from a metropolitan to the metropolitan's council. C. 2 q. 6 c. 3. And so the council is greater than the metropolitan himself. Moreover, there may be an appeal from someone to that person himself together with others, and so it is similar to Dig. 49. 4. 1. 3. But how should we understand what is said here, that if the bishops disagree one should have recourse to a superior? Why is a ruling not made according to the judgment of the greater number? D. 65 c. 1. Some think that this is said of the criminal cases of bishops where it is necessary for all the bishops to consent. C. 6 q. 4 c. 1; C. 6 q. 4 c. 2. But it may be understood to concern a case where there is doubt among the bishops over some matter in the province. Then one is to have recourse to the see of the superior. Or this case may be one where the bishops disagree as to a decision, with some on one side and some on the other, not a case where they make a decision.

^c**greater**—concerning the faith, C. 24 q. 1 c. 12.

C. 6. CASE. Each year certain bishops held councils without the Apostolic See. Consequently Pope Symmachus quashed them, as nothing may be enacted without the

authority of the Apostolic See. Indeed, great matters are always to be referred to it.

^d**priests**—that is, bishops.

^e**have lost**—Note that one may lose what he never had. C. 5 q. 6 c. 3; C. 23 q. 4 c. 30; D. 23 c. 14; C. 32 q. 2 c. 8;[67] C. 32 q. 2 c. 9.

Part 3. This is the second part [*sic*] of the distinction,

Part 2.

Therefore, as has already been said, let that conventicle or assemblage—for it cannot rightly be called a council—of yours be quashed and anything enacted there held null and void. Also, see that you do not heed anyone's exhortation^a to do such things unless you would fall from communion with the Apostolic See.

§2. *And below:* If disputes have arisen in any province and this has become such a cause of discord among the bishops of that province that they cannot agree among themselves, let the affair then be referred to a greater ^b see. And if it cannot be easily and justly decided there, let it be judged canonically and justly at a properly convoked synod. But let greater ^c and more difficult questions always be referred to the Apostolic See (as a holy synod has established and blessed custom demands).

Also, Pope Symmachus:[292]

C. 6. *Provincial synods lack force without the concurrence of the Roman pontiff.*

The councils of priests,^d which are required by ecclesiastical ordinances to be held each year in the provinces, have lost^e their force when they lack the concurrence of the pope.[293] Have you, in mad delusion, ever read that anything has ever been promulgated in them contrary to the sanction of the Apostolic Crown, or that, in major matters, whatever had been done was not subject to inquiry according to the judgment of the aforesaid see?

Part 3.

§1. *"Hence, by King Theodoric's authority it was ordered^f that priests from various provinces gather in the city of Rome for a holy council to*

where the law concerning synods is set forth.

***Dicta Gratiani post* c. 6. CASE.** This passage is divided into two sections. In the first section, it says that Pope Symmachus was accused of crimes. Therefore, King Theodoric, having come to Rome, held a council to examine the accusations against the pope. There the bishops of Liguria, Emilia, and Venetia rose and said to the emperor that it belonged to the pope to convene a council. To this, the emperor benignly responded that everything is within the power of the synod. He committed [continued on next page]

^f**ordered**—These bishops came at the summons of the king, not because they were bound to come, but in order to call him back from his error. Similar is X 2. 25. 7.

Dicta Gratiani post **c. 6. CASE.** (continued) the matter to the authority of the pope, so that peace in the city of Rome could be preserved. In the second section, which begins "The bishops. . .," it says that the bishops brought together there by the authority of this same Symmachus absolved him from human judgment, leaving him to be judged by God alone, and decreed that the clerics who had withdrawn from Pope Symmachus were to have their offices restored, after

pass judgment on the accusations concerning the conduct of the venerable Pope Symmachus, bishop of the Apostolic See. The bishops of Liguria, Emilia, and Venetia replied that the accused himself had to convoke the synod. They knew this, first, because of the merit of the Apostle Peter and, second, because in accord with the Lord's command,ᵃ venerable councils had decided to give his see such unique power among the churches that the bishop of the aforesaid see was not subject to the judgment of inferiors." And further on: "In reply to this, the most serene king, inspired by God, responded that it was up to the judgment of the synod to decide what should be done in such matters, and that he wanted to show nothing but respectᵇ in ecclesiastical affairs. He left it to the pontiffs' discretion whether to consider the proposed business or not, and to determine what they thought most useful, so long as they gave peace to the city of Rome through their venerable council's decisions.

§2. "The bishops, when they had assembled in a synod convoked by Symmachus' own authority, said: 'Let Pope Symmachus, bishop of the Apostolic See, whose case we hand over to God's judgment, be clearedᶜ and free of these accusations insofar as they concern human affairs.' " And further on: "But in the case of the aforementioned pope's clerics who, contrary to the norms, prematurelyᵈ abandoned their bishop and created a schism, we rule that those who have made satisfaction to their bishop shall receive mercy and enjoy restoration to ecclesiastical office."

And further on: " 'I, Lawrence, bishop of the church of Milan, subscribed to this decision of ours, by which we handed the whole case over to God's judgment.' Peter, bishop of the church of Ravenna, subscribed in the same words, and, after him, seventy-five bishops. It is evident that the clerics were treated mercifully and indulgently to restore peace to the city.

"This is also to be noted: it is read that in this council and in Pope Symmachus' other synod ᵉ the bishop of Milan subscribed and spoke before the bishop of Ravenna. From this it is gathered that the former's see also takes precedence over the latter's."

But Gregory I says to Syagrius, bishop of Autun, in Register, VII, CXII:²⁹⁴

C. 7.

We determine that bishops order themselves according to the dateᶠ of their consecration when they sit in council, subscribe to documents, or attend to any other matter. And it is up to them to establish this prerogative of their orders.

they had made satisfaction to Symmachus. Lawrence, the bishop of Milan, subscribed to this decree first, followed by the bishop of Ravenna, and then by seventy-five bishops. All that follows is clear until D. 18.

ᵃ*command*—The Roman Church, therefore, has authority from councils and the emperor from the people. D. 93 c. 24 (*in fine*). The opposite appears from D. 21 c. 3; D. 22 c. 1, where it says that the Roman Church has primacy from God, not from councils. But you may say that it has primacy principally from God and secondarily from councils.

ᵇ*respect*—The emperor must respect the Church. He has no power to distribute the things of the Church. D. 96 c. 1. Therefore, he may not grant dignities or prebends. C. 16 q. 7 c. 12. An argument to the contrary may be made from X 1. 4. 5 (*in parte decisa*), where it says that the king confers deanships. But this is perhaps by custom and privilege. C. 16 q. 1 c. 39.

ᶜ*cleared*—To the contrary is *dicta Gratiani* pr. *ante* C. 2 q. 7 c. 42 (*in fine*), where it says that a simoniac, after making restitution, is obligated to respond to his accusers. But you may say that first he was accused of heresy, but when the calumny of his accusers was later discovered, he was absolved, as it says here.

ᵈ*prematurely* — which should not to be done. C. 8 q. 4 c. 1 § 1.

ᵉ*synod*—D. 96 c. 1.⁽⁶⁸⁾

ᶠ*date*—It is generally the case that whoever first receives a dignity has precedence over the others. D. 74 c. 5; D. 75 c. 7; X 1. 33. 1; for his rank precedes the others like one whose labor was longer and therefore has earned a greater reward. Cod. 1. 31. 2. Except for someone who receives a dignity from the prince, for then he may be placed above others. X 1. 33. 7; Dig. 50. 3. 2; and except for the rank of metropolitan or other greater dignity that preceeds another although his ordination was later. D. 18 c. 1.

D. 18. This distinction is divided into three parts. In the first he shows that episcopal councils ought to be held twice a year. The second part begins, "Because a rule. . . ." The third part begins, "Let each bishop. . . ."

Dicta Gratiani ante **c. 1.**
CASE. It was stated and shown above that without the approval of the Roman see, bishops may not hold councils where anything is to be generally determined or decreed. Nevertheless, councils may be held for correction and to declare what has already been enacted generally or particularly.
ᵃ*Episcopal*—This is the beginning of the eighteenth distinction, in which the master shows that provincial councils may not make general enactments. Accordingly, he shows what purpose they do serve. He then explains how many times a year, at what times of the year, and under whose authority they are held. Then he shows that the metropolitan may not exact anything from the bishops convened in council. He then treats the punishment of bishops who do not come to a synod when called. Finally he says that the bishop must inform his subjects within six months of the matters decided in the council.
ᵇ*enact*—This is not true, because the bishop may certainly issue episcopal canons, and the archbishop, provincial canons, because any people and any church may make law for itself, D. 1 c. 8; D. 8 c. 2; D. 11 c. 8; D. 12 c. 11; *De cons.* D. 3 c. 1; X 2. 9. 5, but they may not make rulings as to greater matters, as is seen here and in D. 12 c. 2, where this is treated.

C. 2. CASE. In this capitulum, Leo ruled that episcopal councils be held twice a year, and that the problems of the clergy be settled there. If these cannot be settled there, they

are to be referred to the primate, and if they cannot be solved there either, then they are to be referred to the Apostolic See.
ᶜ**twice**—This has been amended. D. 18 c. 7; X 5. 1. 25.
ᵈ**all the complaints**—that concerned them.
ᵉ**orders**—that is, the laity or the clergy. He is speaking to a primate or patriarch.
ᶠ**metropolitan**—Note that in important matters the arch-

The time of consecration, then, refers not to that of churches but to that of persons, as appears clearly both from the custom of the cardinals of the holy Roman Church and from that of the bishops in every province.

DISTINCTION EIGHTEEN

Part 1.
*Episcopal*ᵃ *councils, therefore, as appears from the preceding, may not validly define or enact,*ᵇ *but they may correct. Episcopal councils are needed for exhortation and correction, because, although they do not have the power to enact, they do have the authority to impose and declare what has been otherwise decreed and commanded to be generally or particularly observed.*
[*From the Council of Châlons, c. 6:*[295]

[**PALEA. C. 1.**
[It was agreed that, saving the primacy of the metropolitan, other bishops give place to one another according to the time of their consecration.]

So Leo I to Anastasius, bishop of Thessalonica, in Letter *LXXXII, 7:*[296]

C. 2. *Assemblies are to be celebrated by the bishop twice each year.*
Concerning episcopal councils, then, we enjoin nothing other than what the holy fathers have salutarily ordained, that is, there are to be assemblies twiceᶜ each year, where all the complaintsᵈ that are wont to arise among the various ordersᵉ of the church can be adjudicated. But, if perchance among those who preside some case concerning (God forbid) graver sins arises that cannot be resolved through provincial inquiry, your metropolitanᶠ will take care to explainᵍ the character of the entire matter

bishop always consults his primate, as here and in D. 65 c. 5; C. 6 q. 4 c. 3. Furthermore, it may be seen here that the primate ought not to take part in the council of the metropolitan. D. 92 c. 8; C. 11 q. 1 c. 46.
ᵍ**explain**—Therefore, a judge from whom an appeal is taken may explain the case, and why he did not accept the appeal himself, to the judge to whom it is taken. He ought to place the court record before that judge, Dig. 49. 5. 6, but not, however, act as a witness. C. 2 q. 6 c. 38.

CC. 3–5. CASE. In the next three capitula, the case is plain.

ᵃLent—In the following capitulum it says that this should be done after the third week of Eastertide, but this canon does not derogate from the other. This is either because it is from the Council of Nicaea, or because what this text says comes from a different custom. D. 16 c. 9 § 1 [§ 2].

to Your Fraternity; and let whatever it concerns be transferred for our examination if the matter cannot be settled by your decision in the presence of the assembled parties.

Also, from the Council of Nicaea, c. 5:[297]

C. 3. *When episcopal councils are to be celebrated.*

Let there be one council before Lent,ᵃ so that, when all dissensionsᵇ have been put to rest, a pure and solemn fast might be offered to God. Let the second be conducted during the autumn.ᶜ

Also, from the Council of Antioch, c. 20:[298]

C. 4. *Let an episcopal council be held twice yearly for the correction of morals and settling of controversies.*

For settling the ecclesiastical cases and controversies that arise, it seems sufficient for a council of bishops to be held twice yearly in every province, the first being after the third week of the feast of Easter so that it conclude[299] during the fourth week that follows, that is in the middle[300] of Pentecost. Let those who dwell in larger, metropolitan cities admonishᵈ the other bishops of the province.

Let the second council be held on the Idesᵉ of October, that is, on the tenth[301] of the month called Hyperberetaeus ᶠ by the Greeks. Let priests and deacons and allᵍ who consider themselves wronged attend these councils to await synodal judgment. None are to hold a councilʰ by themselves without consent of the metropolitan bishop, to whom judgment has been granted in all cases.ⁱ

Io. But that is not true. X 1. 10. 3. There it seems to say that delay may not be made up for. But certainly a new decretal says that in the payment of a sum of money, a delay may be made up for within a brief period of time. X 3. 18. 4. But this text is speaking of a different case than the decretal, or you may say that it corrects the decretal. B.

ᵉIdes—This appears to be false because the Ides always falls on the 13th or the 15th of the month depending on the number of days that precede the Nones. If, then, the Nones are preceded by four days, then the Ides fall on the 13th day of the month. If the Nones are preceded by six days, then the Ides fall on the 15th day. Consequently the Ides never fall on the tenth day. That is true among us, but among the Greeks it might well be that Ides is on the tenth day. Some say that the term "Ides" may sometimes be used, as here, in an extended sense, to mean the entire time that we begin to count after the Nones, as when we call the day after Nones the "eighth before the Ides," the next as the "seventh before the Ides," and so forth, until the Ides arrives. This is just as the first day of the month is called the Kalends and the day after is counted as the fourth before the Nones, or the sixth before the Nones, and so forth, until the Nones is over. So we say the "eighth before the Ides," "the seventh before the Ides," and so forth. Why then does this text refer to the tenth? You may say that here the day that is called by the name "Ides" is any day among those days that are said to be "before the Ides" and not that last day which is properly and strictly called the Ides. The other explanation presented here is wrong.

ᶠ**Hyperberetaeus**—that is, October.

ᵍ**and all**—that is, "on behalf of all." Otherwise, if everyone from the province had to meet, why would the bishop inform them of everything done in the synod, as below in c. 17?

ʰ**council**—a provincial council, for any bishop may hold a council of bishops without permission from his metropolitan. D. 38 c. 2.

ADDITION. See also D. 18 c. 16 (*in fine*). Arch.

ⁱ**all cases**—that concern the condition of the province.

ADDITION. This may be argued from D. 76 c. 11. Archidiaconus.

ᵇ**dissensions**—If there was much personal ill feeling. D. 65 c. 3.

ᶜ**autumn**—The Ides of October, as in the following capitulum.

ᵈ**admonish**—that is, convoke on his own. So it may be argued that the delay may be made up for, even though a certain day is provided, for otherwise why is he to admonish them? D. 18 c. 7; X 3. 8. 5; Dig. 18. 6. 1. 3. To the contrary, X 1. 6. 7. To the contrary, C. 7 q. 1 c. 3; C. 20 q. 2, c. 2; Cod. 8. 37. 12 [8. 38. 12]; X 2.14.6. The solution is that when the day has been set by the canon, the delay may be made up for. But it is otherwise when the day is set by a person. Dig. 4. 8. 21. 12 [4. 8. 26. 4]; Dig. 4. 8. 23 [4. 8. 28].

ᵃ**taught**—Although they may not formulate doctrine, C. 1 q. 7 c. 4, nevertheless they ought to learn it. C. 24 q. 3 c. 1. Laur.

ᵇ**condemn**—that is, they ought to be excommunicated. C. 2 q. 6 c. 19.

C. 6. CASE. There were some bishops who were not holding councils which was shown by the fact that many affairs in need of correction in the Church had been neglected. For this reason the synod ruled that episcopal councils were to be held twice a year to correct things needing reform. It ruled that all bishops of the province are to come unless they are excused by some necessity. Otherwise they are to be corrected.

ᶜ**many**—So it may be argued that, from what follows, one can know and make presumptions about what precedes. If a person were taken by violence among heretics but stayed with them for a month, it can be presumed that he was not forced there. C. 1 q. 1 c. 111. So too, the vices of subjects argue against their prelates, and those of students against their teachers. D. 28 c. 4; C. 22 q. 2 c. 18; D. 53 c. 1; C. 12 q. 2 c. 27; D. 44 c. 5; C. 34 q. 1 c. 1; Cod. 9. 9. 33 [9. 9. 34].

ᵈ**need** — That necessity excuses may be seen from *De cons.* D. 4 c. 16. Similarly, a person is excused if he is absent because of storm or flood, or because he has been called as a witness or to some office, or if he is on business with the state, or if he is prevented by a funeral in his family, or if more important business draws him away. Dig. 2. 11. 2. 1; Dig. 2. 11. 2; Dig. 2. 11. 4; Dig. 4. 6. 4. The same is true if he is summoned by a higher tribunal, Dig. 42. 1. 54. 1, or kept away by fear of enemies. X 2. 28. 47.

Part 2. This is the second part of this distinction, in which it is shown that it is enough to hold a provincial council once a year. Ioan de Fan. Also, the holding of provincial councils each year is imposed as a precept. Archidiaconus.

C. 7. CASE. This capitulum is divided into two sections.

In the first section it says that the ancient rule prescribed that a synod be held twice a year. But because this was difficult, the Sixth Synod accordingly ruled that it be done once a year. A prince who prohibits this is to be excommunicated. A metropolitan who neglects to hold a council is to be punished canonically. In the second section, which begins, "Then, while. . . ," it says that while the synod is meeting, the bishops ought to devote themselves to the divine com-

Also, from the Council of Laodicea, c. 40:[302]

C. 5. *When those summoned to a synod disdain to attend, they condemn themselves.*

Bishops summoned to a synod may not disdain to come but must be present either to teach or be taughtᵃ what is useful for correction of their church and others. And, if they should disdain to come, they condemnᵇ themselves unless perhaps they were unable to come because of illness.

Also, from the Council of Chalcedon, c. 19:[303]

C. 6. *Let the bishops summoned to a council who refuse to come be corrected.*

It has come to our ears that the episcopal councils appointed in the provinces are hardly held at all. This[304] proves that manyᶜ responsible for correction are neglecting ecclesiastical affairs. Therefore, this holy synod decrees, according to the norms of the fathers, that the bishops of each province shall assemble twice a year so that everything[305] that deserves it be corrected. Furthermore, those bishops who refuse to attend and stay home are to be corrected by loving and brotherly admonition, especially if they enjoy bodily health and are free from any other pressing needᵈ or unavoidable business.

Also, from the Seventh Synod, c. 6:[306]

Part 2.

C. 7. *The metropolitan shall inflict canonical punishments on those who neglect to celebrate a council at least once a year.*

§1. A ruleᵉ exists that requires that regular inquests be made in each province twice a year by an assembly of bishops. But, on account of the inconvenience of this and so that those who must assemble have suitable mandments. The metropolitan is not allowed to exact anything from the bishops coming to the synod. If he is convicted of having exacted something, he must restore fourfold.

ᵉ**rule**—Note that as this synod wishes to correct an ancient enactment, it makes mention of it, and so it may be argued that one enactment may not revoke another unless mention is made of it. It is so in rescripts, because otherwise the pope is not deemed to have revoked the contrary provisions with full knowledge. Nevertheless, I do not believe this to be correct. Although in rescripts and in privileges, mention must be made of prior ones if the prior ones are to be revoked, nevertheless, it is not so with enactments. That is because an enactment proceeds from the free act of the lord pope, and he has the entire law encased in his heart. Cod. 6. 23. 19; argument from X 4. 11. 1. Similarly, in a testament, mention of what was done previously is not required, because a testament takes the place of an ordinance, C. 13 q. 2 c. 32. There are two exceptions: when a testament is made by children, Cod. 6. 23. 21. 3; Auth. *Hoc inter* post Cod. 6. 23. 21. 3, and when the testator binds himself while making

time to travel,[307] the holy fathers of this Sixth Synod have determined that a council must be held at least once a year to correct abuses. This must occur without fail and irrespective of any excuse.[a] So, we now renew this canon, and, if any prince hinders this, let him be deprived of communion.[b] If any metropolitan fails to do this, except on account of need, compulsion,[c] or some reasonable cause, let him undergo canonical punishment.

§2. Then, while the synod is treating matters of the canons or the Gospel, the assembled bishops shall give consideration and care to guarding the Lord's divine and life-giving commandments. *And a little further on:* Moreover, the metropolitan has no right to demand a horse or anything else that a bishop brings with him. If he has been convicted of having done this, let him restore fourfold.[d]

Also, Leo IV to the bishops of Britain, c. 3:[308]

C. 8. *Priests are not to be compelled to bring honoraria to sacred councils.*

Concerning the bringing of honoraria[e] to sacred councils, we find nothing established by earlier generations, but each priest did as he pleased. For, if it were required that gifts be offered on these occasions,

[a]**excuse**—If it is frivolous, for a reasonable exception may always be made. X 1. 29. 13.

[b]**communion**—Note that princes may be excommunicated and, indeed, by priests. D. 96 c. 10; C. 11 q. 3 c. 11; Auth. *Qua in provincia* post Cod. 3. 15. 2.

[c]**compulsion**—It appears, therefore, when a person is detained by another using force and action is taken against him during that time, it may be revoked. It is the same if he does not come because of another person's fraud. X 1. 41. 4. But one can read the contrary in Dig. 2. 11. 2. 9 and Dig. 2. 10. 3, where it says that if, through someone else's force or fraud, a person does not appear in court, what was done is not revoked; rather, the person has an action against the one who impeded him. But you may say that it is not revoked as a matter of law, but through the action to restore the prior state of things, or else that it is revoked in cases where the person detaining him cannot pay. X 2. 13. 12.

[d]**fourfold**—So it may be argued that the clergy may be punished financially and may so punish others. D. 23 c. 6 (*in fine*); C. 17 q. 4 c. 35; C. 17 q. 4 c. 22; C. 23 q. 5 c. 43. The contrary may be argued from X 5. 37. 3. But you might say that where a spiritual penalty is provided by law, one may not inflict a financial one, but one may otherwise. X 2. 6. 5 (*in fine*). He is punished fourfold because he has committed the crime of extorting money which is punished by a fourfold penalty. *Dicta Gratiani ante* C. 1 q. 1 c. 1; C. 1 q. 7 c. 26 (*in fine*). Both laity and clergy are punished by this penalty for extortion. C. 23 q. 1 c. 5. It says that the Church ought not receive back its own property with increase. You may say, however, that here something is not received as payment to the Church but in one's own name. C. 16 q. 6 c. 2.

a testament, by saying, for example, "If I make another testament, it shall not be valid," for then, if he does make a second, it is necessary that he mention the previous one. Dig. 32. 1. 22 pr. In councils, the most ancient is followed if it has greater authority. D. 50 c. 28 (*in fine*). Ioan. What is done with rescripts is correct. To remember everything that has been done belongs more to God than to man. Cod. 1. 17. 2. 13 [1. 20. 2].[(69)] Nor should the pope be presumed to have issued a second rescript after an earlier one on the same subject with full knowledge. Rather it should be presumed that he did this without remembering the first one. X 1. 29. 13. It has been forgotten, as in D. 23 c. 12. But as the gloss of Ioan. mentioned, he has or is presumed to have the entire law encased in his heart. The law consists of ordinances and enactments, and later ones abrogate earlier, even when no mention is made of them. Dig. 1. 3. 26. In testaments, however, the reason is different. It is not to infringe, as one should not, upon the liberty of a last will. Dig. 17. 2. 52. 9–10 [17. 2. 53]. For nothing is owed more to someone than that the written expression of his last will be free and that an unchanged will be left free. Cod. 1. 2. 1 (*in fine*). In the two cases mentioned, however, what is noted in the gloss of Ioan. applies by way of exception. Bar.

ADDITION. C. 33 q. 2 c. 11 (*in fine*).[(70)] Archidiaconus.

C. 8. CASE. Some bishops asked the pope whether at the time of a synod the priests ought to offer honoraria, that is, small gifts, to the bishop. The pope answered that nothing was to be found from earlier generations that settled the matter, and he left it up to each priest's judgment what he would give. For if it had been determined that a priest must make a gift at the time of the synod, they would come to the synod less willingly. Therefore, honoraria ought not to be asked from anyone, but need not be refused when offered.

[e]**honoraria**—Honoraria are gifts given by a subject to his prelate.

^a**less**—Thus it may be argued that teachers should not ask a fee from their students, so that they come more willingly to school. C. 1 q. 1 c. 99; C. 1 q. 1 c. 103; C. 1 q. 3 c. 10.

^b**reject**—Thus it may be argued that we may lawfully receive things that we are prohibited from asking for. C. 1 q. 2 c. 1; C. 1 q. 2 c. 2; C. 13 q. 2 c. 12.

ADDITION. See Dig. 1. 2. 2. 49 (at *Divus*), where this matter is treated. Archidiaconus.

C. 9. CASE. It says here that a bishop must go to a synod when summoned, unless he is impeded by grave necessity, and then he should send a legate, so that he can receive what the synod has ruled.

^c**legate**—So it may be argued that one who is cited before a court and is not able to come is nevertheless bound to send a representative. C. 5 q. 3 c. 1; X 2. 28. 45. The contrary may be argued from X 1. 38. 2. On this question consult C. 5 q. 3 c. 1. But X 1. 38. 2 is speaking of a serious case.⁽⁷¹⁾

CC. 10–13. CASE. It says in this capitulum that, unless there is an impediment, bishops must always go to the synod. If they cannot go, they ought to send letters of explanation. If they neglect to send these to their primate, they should be deprived of communion with their brothers and be limited to the communion of their own church. The same is to be done in the three cases described in the following capitula, as you can see for yourself. Nevertheless, it should be added that they are deprived of communion with their brothers until the following synod.

^d**illness**—serious, as in D. 18 c. 14. Indeed, he is not excused by a light fever or a passing cold. Dig. 21. 1. 1. 7.

ADDITION. For the contrary argument, see C. 7 q. 1 c. 3; X 1. 38. 2,⁽⁷²⁾ where this matter is treated. Archidiaconus.

^e**writing**—or, indeed, send some messenger whom one would believe. D. 97 C. 3; X 1. 29. 21; X 1. 3. 2; X 1. 3. 13.

^f**explanation**—Note that it does not suffice to say that one cannot come unless the reason for the impediment is given.

X 1. 29. 21; X 1. 3. 13. This reason must be demonstrated. C. 4 q. 5 c. 1. It may be demonstrated by one witness. X 1. 38. 3. Granted, an argument to the contrary may be made from X 1. 41. 4. Ioan. But I believe this to be a special case, as one witness along with his oath was believed.

^g**communion**—It would seem that a person may be excommunicated in one church and not in another, as here and in D. 58 c. 2. That is contrary to C. 4 q. 5 c. 1. But you

priests would probably come less ^a willingly to synods and might even resist coming. In my opinion, it is unreasonable to request them, as well as to reject^b them when they are offered spontaneously.

*Also, from the Fourth Council of Carthage, c. 21:*³⁰⁹

C. 9. *Bishops should not delay in coming to a synod without grave necessity.*

Let a bishop not delay in coming to a synod unless he is impeded by grave necessity. If it so happens that he sends a legate^c to take his place, he is to accept whatever the synod determines, always saving the truth of the faith.

*Also, from the Fifth Council of Carthage, c. 10:*³¹⁰

C. 10. *Let those who are impeded from going to a synod send letters of explanation.*

It was approved that bishops who are not impeded by age, illness,^d or other grave necessity duly attend whenever a council is convoked. *And below:* If they cannot attend, let them put down their excuses in writing.^{e 311} And, unless³¹² they have given an explanation^f of their impediment to their primate, they ought to be limited to the communion^g of their own church.

*[Also, from the Council of Tours, c. 2:*³¹³

[PALEA. C. 11.

[A bishop may not compel an abbot^h to come to a synod unless some reasonable cause exists.]

*Also, from the Second Council of Arles, c. 19:*³¹⁴

C. 12. *He is deprived of communion who has disdained to attend a synod.*

If anyone has neglected to attend a synod, or has chosen to abandon the

may say that in this case the person is not excommunicated, but may not take communion with the other bishops since he cannot come to take part in their affairs or to consecrate a bishop along with the others.

^h**abbot**—This may be understood of the abbots of the Cistercian Order, X 3. 35. 1, except in cases of serious crime, C. 11 q. 3 c. 63; argument from X 5. 33. 11. But other abbots must come to the council, C. 18 q. 2 c. 16; D. 18 c.

17. You can find that clearly in *dicta Gratiani post* C. 18 q. 2 c. 31.[(73)]

^a**before**—So *De cons.* D. 1 c. 62; C. 11 q. 3 c. 43.[(74)]

^b**synod**—So, therefore, sometimes a distinction is made in giving absolution so that greater force will belong to absolutions given in the presence of many. Similarly, the absolution of a sacrilegious person is deferred so that he may be

normally to be deferred. X 2. 28. 25.

^c**of a supreme pontiff**—that is, of a bishop, C. 2 q. 7 c. 15, or else to hear what the supreme pontiff has ordained.

^d**king's**—to the contrary, see C. 23 q. 8 c. 28; C. 23 q. 8 c. 27. But this text, unlike that one, speaks of those who have fiefs. But whoever is summoned while on the king's business ought to come. Or that text is to be understood of a bishop who abandons the judgment of the Church and comes to the emperor to request justice, which no cleric ought to do. C. 11 q. 1 c. 11.

assembly of his brethren before^a the council has dissolved, let him know that he is excluded from the communion of the brethren and that he will not be readmitted, unless he is absolved at the following synod.^b

Also, from the Council of Agde, c. 35:[315]

C. 13. *Let him abstain from communion until the next synod who, summoned by his metropolitan, neglected to come without grave necessity.*

If the metropolitan bishop has sent letters to the bishops of his province, inviting them either for the ordination of a supreme pontiff^c or a synod, let all, after putting everything else aside, not fail to present themselves on the appointed day (except in cases of grave bodily infirmity or the king's^d command^e). If any have been absent, let them (as ancient canonical authority has required) be deprived of the love of fraternal charity and ecclesiastical communion until the next synod.

^e**command**—although a bishop is held to obey his metropolitan as he would a superior. D. 8 c. 2. Here, however, deference is given to the dignity of a king. C. 12 q. 2 c. 22; D. 63 c. 24. Again, in summoning to a synod, a single summons is sufficient as here and similarly in C. 4. q. 5 c. 1. In judicial matters, however, three are required. C. 24 q. 3 c. 6.

Also, from the Council of Tarragona, c. 6:[316]

C. 14. *If a bishop summoned to a synod by his metropolitan disdains to come, let him be deprived of communion.*

If any of the bishops, summoned to a synod by the metropolitan, disdains to come, without the intervention of grave bodily necessity, let him be deprived of the communion of charity until the next council of all the bishops, as the statutes of the fathers have decreed.

C. 14. CASE. Nothing is noted.

C. 15. CASE. It says in this capitulum that the metropolitan ought to hold a council twice a year, summoning all of the bishops of the province. Priests, deacons, and all who deem themselves to be injured should come. Those who are found to have done wrong will be excommunicated as is fitting. At the end of the capitulum it says that no bishop may hold a council unless he is a metropolitan.

Also, from a council of Pope Martin:[317]

C. 15. *Let priests, deacons, and any who consider themselves wronged attend the metropolitan synod.*

For the sake of ecclesiastical concerns^f and the settlement of disputes, it was heartily agreed that a council be held twice a year in each province by the metropolitan bishop's summons to the bishops of the province. Then all priests, deacons, and those^g who consider themselves wronged may come,[318] and the cases examined at the council may be brought to just judgment. And, if any bishops, priests, or deacons have been found in offense, let them be fittingly excommunicated until judgment^h has been passed on them by common consent.ⁱ No bishop, except those to whom

^f**ecclesiastical concerns**—Martin, out of public concern, reformed the canons and therefore is called the Reformer of the Canons.

^g**those** — As though to say that all should come, or at least all those who have been injured, not that all must come. D. 18 c. 16.

^h**judgment**—absolution.

ⁱ**consent**—of the bishops. Ioan.

confounded even more. C. 17 q. 4 c. 29. Similarly, the absolution of one who is greatly delinquent is deferred. C. 11 q. 3 c. 39. Wherefore, although he wanted to be absolved beforehand, he is not heard. Otherwise, absolution ought not

^a**councils**—that is, provincial councils, namely, with other bishops. He may hold episcopal councils. D. 38 c. 2; D. 12 q. 2 c. 51.

Part 3. This is the third part of the distinction, in which it says that each bishop ought to inform his churches of what has been decreed at councils.

C. 17. CASE. In this capitulum it says that when the bishop returns from the council of the archbishop, he ought to assemble all his subjects within six months and to inform them of what was done at the synod. If he does not do so, he shall be excommunicated for two months.
^b**while**—that is, "after."
^c**abbots**—Abbots, however, are not summoned to the synod. D. 18 c. 11.
^d**excommunication**—that is, suspension from office for two months. D. 86 c. 24; C. 10 q. 3 c. 3 (*in fine*).

D. 19. This distinction is divided into two parts. In the first it says, as noted, that decretals have the force of canons. The second part begins "Therefore, let anyone. . . ."

Dicta Gratiani ante **c. 1. CASE.** Above in D. 18 Gratian treated the authority of canons and sacred enactments. In this nineteenth distinction he treats letters that come from the pope. He shows that decretal letters have the same force and authority as canons. This appears in the following capitula.
^e***There is a question***—

The master dealt with the authority of canons above in a previous distinction. Here he treats the authority of decretals. He shows here that decretals and canons have the same authority. Accordingly, one must know that some decretal letters are general, some particular. The general letters are those directed to everyone. C. 2 q. 5 c. 19. Particular letters are those sent to someone in particular. C. 35 q. 3 c. 20;⁽⁷⁵⁾ C. 7 q. 1 c. 17. Whether they are general or particular, however, when something is decided by them,

the decision is received as general law, C. 16 q. 3 c. 5; X 2. 27. 19, unless the decision is made on account of time, place, or particular reason. D. 29 c. 1. If, however, there is doubt as to whether a letter is a decretal, one must have recourse to the [papal] register. D. 9 c. 6. Nevertheless, it is presumed that a letter is a decretal if it is found among other decretals, in the same way that one who is found among nuns is presumed on that ground to be a nun.

metropolitan sees have been entrusted, is permitted of himself to hold particular councils.^a

[*Also, from the Council of Bylon:*³¹⁹

[**PALEA. C. 16.**

[Let the bishop hold each year in his diocese a synod of his clerics and abbots, and let it examine the other clerics and monks.]

Part 3.
Let each bishop take care to inform his churches about what has been decreed at councils.
*So in the Sixteenth Council of Toledo, c. 6:*³²⁰

C. 17. *Let each bishop inform his churches of what has been established in councils.*
We determine that, while^b councils are held in each province, every bishop, within a space of six months and without delay, is to assemble before him by his summons all the abbots,^c priests, deacons, clerics, and even the whole population of the city where he presides, as well as the whole people of his diocese. Then,³²¹ let him explain everything completely in their presence so that they know what was done or determined in the council that year. *And below:* If anyone thinks these matters unimportant, let him be punished with a sentence of excommunication^d for a period of two months.

DISTINCTION NINETEEN

Part 1.
There is a question^e *whether decretal letters have authoritative force, because they do not appear in the corpus of canons.*
*Concerning these, Pope Nicholas writes to the archbishops and bishops of Gaul:*³²²

Argument from C. 20 q. 1 c. 6. Or if many people accept the letter, then it is to be accepted. D. 16 c. 4 is to be distinguished as is indicated in X 2. 22. 8.⁽⁷⁶⁾

C. 1. CASE. This capitulum is divided into three sections. In the first, Nicholas rebukes those who will not accept decretal letters because they are not found in the corpus of canons made by Isidore. Nicholas gives three reasons. The first is that, as the pope has authority as to the writings of others, still more must he have authority as to his own. The second reason is that as they accept his letters when favorable to themselves, therefore, they must accept them when they are contrary. The third reason is that, if they refuse to accept them because they are not in the corpus of canons, then on the same ground they must reject the writings of St. Gregory and many others who lived both before and after him, as well as the New and Old Testaments, because these

C. 1. *Decretal letters have authoritative force.*

§1. Works of other writers were approved or rejected[a] by decree of the Roman pontiffs, and so today what the Apostolic See approved is taken as received and what it rejected is now considered of no force. So how much[b] more, then, should what it has written at various times on the Catholic faith, sound doctrine, the diverse and various needs of the Church, and the usages of the faithful be held in all honor and reverently accepted by everyone in its entirety under every circumstance, on account of its magisterial discernment and stewardship? Some of you, however, have written that the decretals of the ancient pontiffs are not transcribed anywhere in the entire corpus of the collection of canons.[323] And, although these used the same letters without hesitation when they found them to support[c] their own ends, they now accept them only if they diminish the power of the Apostolic See and increase their own privileges.[324] *And below:* So if they say that the decretal letters of the ancient Roman pontiffs should not be received because they are not found transcribed in the collection of canons, then nothing promulgated or written by St. Gregory, or by anyone before or after him, should be received when it is not found transcribed in the collections of canons. So, let the teachings and sanctions of those who are venerated by every tongue be erased from their books since they are not found transcribed in the collections of canons. To what end are they occupying parchment[d] when they have not been received? Why should we stop there, since, if we adopted such a course, would we even receive the divine Scriptures of the New and Old Testaments? Neither is included in the collection of ecclesiastical canons.

§2. But those more defiant than obedient will reply that among the canons there is a capitulum of Pope St. Innocent,[325] by authority of which it seems[e] that we should receive both Testaments, even though the text of neither is included among the same canons of the fathers. One can suitably reply to them that if the Old and New Testaments are to be received, not because they are found annexed as a whole to the collection of canons, but because of Pope St. Innocent's decision cited on receiving them, it follows that the decretal letters of the Roman pontiffs are even

nevertheless they have been received because there is a capitulum of Innocent that approves both Testaments and says that they are to be received even if they are not found in the corpus of canons. Nicholas answers these people, saying that on the same grounds decretal letters ought to be received because a capitulum of Pope Leo commands that all decretal letters are to be observed and that if anyone has violated them, he is to be punished. On this matter, he cites a capitulum of Pope Gelasius. The third section begins with the words, "From the preceding. . . ." In this section, he concludes from the decretal just mentioned that letters are to be received like canons, briefly recapitulating what has already been said.

[a]**rejected**—So it may be argued that, what the pope approves or rejects, we also must approve or reject. C. 24 q. 1 c. 14; C. 35 q. 9 c. 5.

[b]**how much** — For it is patently absurd that one who may assist others cannot assist himself. Cod. 5. 27. 11 (*in fine*).

[c]**support**—So it may be argued that one who introduces something in his own favor may not reject it when it is introduced against him, be it a document or anything similar. Argument from D. 9 c. 10; *dicta Gratiani* § 42 *post* C. 4 q. 3 c. 2; C. 3 q. 8 c. 1 § 2; X 3. 39. 19. The contrary may be argued from C. 2 q. 7 c. 26. To the contrary: D. 37 c. 13; D. 10 c. 1. The first normally applies; the second is a special case and is applied because of aversion to heretics and to favor the faith and piety.

[d]**parchment**—Although abrogated ordinances do not bind us, nevertheless acquaintance with them is

are not found in the corpus of canons. The first of these reasons is at the beginning of the capitulum. The second of them begins with the words, "And although these. . . ." The third begins with the words, "So if they say. . . ." The second section begins, "But those more defiant. . . ." It contains an answer to those who reply that, even if the New and Old Testaments are not found in the corpus of canons,

necessary. D. 7 c. 2. It may also be argued that no word put in a writing should be vacuous or superfluous. C. 28 q. 1 c. 9; X 1. 33. 6; Dig. 22. 1. 4. The contrary may be argued from Cod. 8. 40. 3 [8. 41. 3].

[e]**it seems**—as though it were said that what obtains in one case should obtain in similar cases. D. 4 c. 6 (*in fine*); D. 26 c. 3.

^a**capitulum**—This capitulum is C. 25 q. 1 c. 12.⁽⁷⁷⁾ Nevertheless, all of it is attributed to Pope Damasus. It may be that it was issued by both, and so it is like C. 1 q. 1 c. 109; *De cons.* D. 1 c. 46.

^b**By saying**—So it may be argued that a general proposition applies to all cases. C. 1 q. 1 c. 114; C. 14 q. 3 c. 2; C. 12 q. 1 c. 2; C. 13 q. 2 c. 19. To the contrary, *De cons.* D. 2 c. 69; D. 75 c. 5.

^c**absent**—So it may be argued that if the pope in some privilege or rescript confirms for some church a privilege of exemption or something else belonging to its privileges, the privilege will then have force by this act alone, even though it cannot be proved otherwise. Note that it says here that decretals are received, although they themselves are not in the corpus of canons, because the capitulum of Leo, which is in the corpus of canons, says this. I discussed this above at D. 9.

^d**various**—Note that a word used indefinitely is to be understood generally. C. 1 q. 3 c. 8; C. 15 q. 1 c. 11; C. 28 q. 1 c. 5; C. 31 q. 1 c. 13. The contrary may be argued from C. 1 q. 1 c. 114.

ADDITION. On the first section, see X 5. 33. 22; X 3. 26. 12 pr. Archidiaconus.

C. 2. CASE. The case put in this capitulum is clear.

more to be received. Although they are not inserted in the collection of canons, a capitulum^a of St. Leo is incorporated among those same canons, and by this it is commanded that all decretals promulgated by the Apostolic See are to be observed and that, if anyone has violated them, he should know that he will receive no pardon.

For he says in c. 10 of his decretals: "Lest we be thought perchance to have omitted anything, we command that Your Charity observe all decretals promulgated by Innocent of blessed memory and all our predecessors, which were issued concerning the ecclesiastical order and canonical discipline, so that all who have infringed them can know that they will receive no pardon."³²⁶

By saying,^b "all decretals promulgated," he excluded no decretal promulgated from his command that they all be kept. And again, by saying, "of all our predecessors," he did not exclude any Roman pontiff before him when he commanded that the decretals promulgated by all of them must be observed, so that all who have infringed them know that they will receive no pardon. Thus, it does not matter whether or not all decretals promulgated by the Apostolic See have been incorporated among the canons of the councils, because they could never all be compiled into one corpus, and those incorporated lend strength and vigor to those absent.^c This is above all evident because the synodal acts that promulgated the canons themselves are not found in the collections of canons, yet we revere them with all due respect.

Moreover, Pope St. Gelasius,³²⁷ who was most prolific in his decrees, agrees with the most blessed Pope Leo when he speaks thus: "The decretal letters that the most blessed popes have issued at various times from the city of Rome for the consultation of various fathers, are to be received with veneration." Here it should be noted that he did not say, "the decretal letters that are found among the canons," nor even, "that the recent popes have issued," but rather those "that the most blessed popes have issued at various times from the city of Rome." By saying, then, "at various^d times," the holy man included even those times when the raging pagan persecutions prevented most episcopal cases from being referred to the Apostolic See.

§3. From the preceding, with the help of divine grace, we have shown that there is no difference between those decrees of the bishops of the Apostolic See found in the collection of canons and those that can hardly be retrieved from all the volumes of compilations on account of their great number. For we have shown that those excellent bishops, Leo and Gelasius, have commanded that all the decretals promulgated by all their predecessors and the decretal letters issued by the most blessed popes at various times from the city of Rome are to be accepted and observed with veneration.

*Also, Pope Agatho to all the bishops:*³²⁸

C. 2. *All sanctions of the Apostolic See are to be observed inviolably.*

All of the sanctions of the Apostolic See are to be received as confirmed by the voice of St.

^a**Peter**—For the pope receives sanctity from his office. D. 40 c. 1. Io.

C. 3. CASE. This capitulum is divided into two sections. In the first section, it says that, out of reverence for St. Peter, the Roman Church must be so honored that what it commands must be endured even if it is hard to bear. In the second section which begins "Now, if someone. . . ," it says

Peter^a himself.

Also, from the capitula of the emperor Charles:[329]

C. 3. *A yoke that has been imposed by the Holy See is to be endured even if it seems insupportable.*

§1. In memory of the blessed Apostle Peter, let us honor the holy Roman and Apostolic See so that she who is our mother in the priestly dignity might also be our mistress in the ecclesiastical order. Therefore, let humility be observed in meekness so that we bear and endure with pious devotion any yoke,^b however weighty, that the Holy See imposes.

§2. Now, if someone, whether priest or deacon, in order to stir up any unseemly disturbance or to undermine our ministry, is convicted of having presented a false^c letter from the Apostolic See or anything else that did not come from there, saving the faith and our complete humility before the apostolic head, the bishop shall have power to thrust him into prison^d or other confinement until he can consult the apostolic highness either by letter or through the office of suitable delegates. Let him, above all, discover by sending an ecclesiastical messenger whatever Roman law requires in such cases in accord with just order,[330] and then impose it so that the falsifier be corrected and restraint be imposed on others.

Also, Pope Stephen V:[331]

C. 4. *Whatever the Roman Church decrees or ordains is to be observed by all.*

To be sure, because the holy Roman Church, which Christ appointed to rule over us, is set up as a mirror^e and example, whatever she decrees and ordains is to be perpetually and inviolately observed by all.

2. 20. 33 (*in fine*). Again, a document may be said to be false ipso facto, as when it appears erased or altered. In such a case the falsifier is to be deposed. X 5. 20. 3. He, however, who fabricates a new false document is not only deposed but also turned over to the court. X 5. 20. 7. According to ordinance the penalty for falsification by a free man is deposition and the confiscation of all his goods; by a slave, death. Dig. 48. 10. 1. A document is called false when it does not have the names of witnesses. X 1. 38. 1. Again, it is called false when it is subscribed to in a number of hands or when it is not completed in the same hand, X 5. 33. 12 (*in fine*), unless the diversity arises from change in pen or ink. Nov. 73 [Coll. VI. 3] pr. Again, it is called false when it is sealed with another's seal, at least when the person has his own seal, unless he indicated at that time he did not have his own. X 2. 28. 48. Again, an instrument is called false if it contradicts another put forward by the same party. X 2. 22. 13; Cod. 4. 21. 14. Again, letters of the pope are said to be false because of incorrect grammar. X 1. 3. 13. Again they are said to be false if they are suspect and faith in them is not required. Cod. 4. 19. 24. Again, a document will be called false if its seal is broken, or if no indication of the year of the indiction has been placed on it. X 2. 22. 6. Again, if the cord is broken. X 5. 20. 5. Again, when documents have been obtained pending appeal. X 2. 20. 19. Again, if they have been obtained without authorization of the owner. X 1. 3. 28.

^d**prison**—If it is certain that he is a falsifier. D. 50 c. 7; X 5. 20. 7. But, where there is doubt, one should do what this text says.

that if a priest or deacon is shown to have presented false letters from the Apostolic See, it is permitted for the bishop to hold him in prison or other confinement until he consults the pope by letter or delegate as to his decision on correcting him and checking others.

^b**yoke**—D. 100 c. 8; C. 11 q. 3 c. 99,⁽⁷⁸⁾ and also that imposed by other prelates. C. 2 q. 7 c. 8.

^c**false**—A document may be called false on account of what is said or not said. As to such falsehoods, one must distinguish as in X 1. 3. 20.⁽⁷⁹⁾ In such a case, a person is correctly called a forger. Dig. 48. 10. 29. Again it may be called false as to its contents, as when it is written that all or the greater part of the brothers were present although they were not really present. X 3. 10. 5. In such a case the falsifier is to be suspended from his office and benefice. X

C. 4. CASE. The case in this capitulum is clear.

^e**mirror**—"Mirror" refers to teaching, "example" to good conduct. C. 16 q. 1 c. 64; C. 16 q. 1 c. 62; C. 7 q. 1 c. 46; C. 8 q. 1 c. 16; C. 25 q. 2 c. 7; C. 1 q. 1 c. 124;⁽⁸⁰⁾ C. 1 q. 1 c. 78. Lau. D. 12 c. 3. Archid.

C. 5. CASE. There were certain bishops who spurned the

Roman Church and refused to observe the precepts of the Apostolic See. This capitulum rebukes those Greeks and exhorts them not to fall away from the Roman Church. Otherwise they will be deposed. Their judgments are of no account because the more that has been entrusted to them, the more they ought to be punished.

ᵃ**cast down**—Here it appears that all those who do not obey the decrees of the Roman See are heretical. The various types of heresy are noted in *Dicta Gratiani ante* C. 24 q. 3 c. 26; C. 24 q. 3 c. 39. You should, however, understand what it says here to mean that one is a heretic who says that the Roman Church is not the head and may not make canons. D. 22 c. 1; C. 25 q. 1 c. 5; C. 25 q. 2 c. 18. But if one violates the Church's commands in some other way, he is not on that account a heretic, although he sins. X 1. 3. 5. Io.

ᵇ**authority**—to the contrary, see C. 24 q. 1 c. 39. There, however, a person condemned by heretics is not admitted to the Church, but he may be admitted if he repents. This is not because a heretic condemned him, but because he is evil in some other way.

ᶜ**major**—So it may be argued that as a person's offense is greater, so much greater should be the punishment. D. 40 c. 5; C. 11 q. 3 c. 3; C. 25 q. 1 c. 4.

ᵈ**others**—So it may be argued that one who is bound to defend someone against others is even more strictly bound to defend that person against himself. C. 16 q. 1 c. 57; Dig. 8. 5. 15.

C. 6. CASE. This capitulum is divided into two sections. In the first it says that the careful student of divine Scripture ought to follow the authority of the Catholic churches concerning which writings are received and adopted. Among these writings, the first place belongs to those of the Apostolic See. The second section begins, "Accordingly. . . ." It says that writings that have been received by all the churches are to be preferred to those which some have not received. Among those which have not been received by all the

churches, those writings that have been received by the larger number of churches with greater authority are to be preferred to those that have been received by fewer with lesser authority. If, however, some writings have been received by the churches of greater authority and others by the greater number of churches, then their authority is equal, although one will not be able to find such a case easily.

ᵉ**writings**—"canonical writings" means letters.

Also, Gregory IV:[332]

C. 5. *He who refuses to obey apostolic precepts is unsuitable for pontifical office.*

It is wrong that anyone try to transgress or be able to transgress the precepts of the Apostolic See or the ministry that we have arranged for Your Charity to perform.

Part 2.

Therefore, let anyone who would contradict apostolic decrees be cast downᵃ to his sorrow and ruin, and let him no longer have a place among the priests. Rather, let him be banished from the holy ministry. And let him henceforth have no pastoral care under his authority,ᵇ since no one can doubt that he has already been condemned by the authority of the holy and apostolic Church for his disobedience and presumption. He is to be cast out through the imposition of major ᶜ excommunication because the one entrusted with the discipline of the holy Church is not only to appear obedient to the holy Church's commands but also to inculcate them in othersᵈ lest they perish. Let him who refuses to submit to apostolic precepts also be cut off from every divine and pontifical office.

Also, Augustine in On Christian Doctrine, *II, VIII:*[333]

C. 6. *Decretal letters are to be reckoned among the canonical writings.*

§1. In regard to canonical writings, let the careful student of the divine Scriptures follow the authority of the greater number of Catholic churches. Among the canonical writingsᵉ are certainly those that the Apostolic See receivesᶠ and those that others have merited to receive from it.

§2. Accordingly, he will observe this rule concerning the canonical writings: he will prefer ᵍ those that are received by all the churches to those that some do not receive. Among those that are not received by all,

ᶠ**receives**—merited to receive from the Church.

ᵍ**prefer**—So it may be argued that a large number always establishes a presumption. D. 61 c. 13. Again, it may be argued that what is received by many has greater authority than what is received by few. D. 16 c. 4; C. 2 q. 7 c. 35; D. 63 c. 36. But how can what is said here be right? Are not all canonical writings to be received equally, as may be argued from D. 15 c. 3? How then can one be preferred to another? I answer that it may be that all of them are received but nevertheless not all are held in the same veneration. Or you may understand this text to apply to local canons, so that the one received by a greater number is to be preferred to others. You may also understand in this way D. 50 c. 28 (*in fine*), where this matter is treated in the gloss beginning *Nonne* [on the word *discors*].

a**greater number**—Note that here the dignity of people compensates for their number. It is the same with witnesses, X 2. 20. 32, and also with creditors, Dig. 2. 14. 8. In elections, however, the majority always decides, even though the

ADDITION. See Nov. 105 [Coll. IV. 3]; Nov. 95 [Coll. VII. 4]. Archidiaconus.

C. 7. CASE. Some bishops spurned the Roman Church, refusing to obey it and to follow the doctrine it had anciently received. Leo attacked them, showing that one may not fall away from the Roman Church, since it has been confirmed by the Lord and been corroborated by the solidity of Peter so that neither temerity nor the gates of hell can prevail against it. He shows that from the beginning the Lord wanted the preaching of the Gospels to be diffused throughout the entire earth by the Apostles and other preachers in such a way that Peter, whose office is executed by the pope, would be, as it were, the head of this preaching. He wishes to depose whoever falls away from the solidity of Peter.

he should prefer those that have the approval of the greater number a of churches of weightier authority to those adopted by the smaller number of lesser authority.

If, however, one should find that some books are received by the greater number of churches, and others by the churches with greater authority (although this could hardly occur b), I think that they then should be held as having equal authority.

Also, Pope Leo I to the bishops of Vienne, in Letter *LXXXVII*:[334]

C. 7. *Let one who abandons solidarity with Peter know himself to be deprived of the divine ministry.*

Our Lord Jesus Christ, the savior of the human race, determined that the truth contained earlier in the proclamation of the Law and the Prophets should be sounded for the salvation of all through the apostolic trumpet. So it was written [Ps. 18:5]: "Their voice sounds to all the world, and their words to the ends of the earth." The Lord wanted this sacramental burden c to belong to the office of all the Apostles and also that it vest principally in the most blessed Peter, the head of all the Apostles. Thus, since gifts flowed from him as head to the entire body, everyone knew that he would be deprived of the divine mystery[335] if he had dared to withdraw from solidarity with Peter. For he wished that he,d in that chosen companionship of undivided unity,e be named for what he himself was,f when he said [Matt. 16:18], "You are Peter and upon this rockg I shall build my Church," so that the structure of the eternal temple, through a marvelous gift of God's grace, might stand firm in solidarity with Peter. This strengthened his Church by that one's stability, so that no human temerity might oppose it,h and the gatesi of hell might not prevail against it. Indeed, no impious presumption dares violate the sacred stability of this same rock, since its builder, as we have said, is the Lord, no matter who, giving in to his own desires j and not following what he received from his elders,k might try to infringe on his power.

c**this sacramental burden**—that is, "this holy office."

d**he**—that is, Peter.

e**of undivided unity**—that is, of the Church.

f**was**—that is, the Lord wanted Peter to be named after what the Lord himself was, namely, the Rock. *De cons.* D. 2 c. 69.

g**this rock**—I do not believe that by these words the Lord refers to anything other than the words with which Peter answered the Lord [Matt. 16:15]: "You are Christ, the Son of the Living God." For the Church is founded upon this article of the faith. Therefore, God founded the Church upon himself.

other side may be greater in dignity and personal merit. X. 1. 6. 22. Although the opposite may be argued from D. 63 c. 36; *dicta Gratiani post* D. 76 c. 7.

ADDITION. But that authority is not opposed, for there they were equal in number, not in merits. Cy.

b**occur**—So it may be argued that laws are accommodated to what rarely occurs. *De cons.* D. 4 c. 36; Dig. 5. 4. 3. The contrary may be argued from: D. 28 c. 13; C. 14 q. 5 c. 10; Dig. 1. 3. 5.

h**oppose it**—that is, challenge and deprecate it.

i**gates**—that is, neither vices nor heresies, for the Church cannot err. C. 24 q. 1 c. 9. Nor can the Church be brought to nothing. C. 24 q. 1 c. 33. For the Lord himself has asked on its behalf that it not fail. D. 21 c. 1 (*in fine*).

j**his own desires**—that is, "his own will."

k**elders**—So it may be argued that what is said by the elders should be followed. D. 37 c. 14; C. 24 q. 3 c. 33; D. 20 c. 3.

Dicta Gratiani post c. 7. **CASE.** It was stated and proven above that decretal letters have authoritative force. This is true, as Gratian says, of decretals that do not contradict the decrees of the fathers and evangelical Scripture. Thus, the Roman Church repudiated the decree of Pope Anastasius, given as a favor to the emperor Anastasius, because it decreed that persons ordained by the heretic Acacius could rightly exercise their offices according to the common law. Therefore, the Roman Church repudiated his decree.

[a]***This***—namely, that decretal letters have the same authority as canons.

[b]***Acacius***—a heretic and excommunicate, C. 24 q. 1 c. 1. He was excommunicated for heresy by Gelasius and Felix, as is said there.

C. 8. CASE. The heretic Acacius baptized and ordained many people at the time of his heresy. Some said that according to the common law these people could not execute their offices. Consequently the emperor Anastasius, doubting that this was so, asked the pope. He answered that by the common law they could perform their offices and would not be injured because of Acacius's crime, for baptism and orders may be conferred by an evil person, and that his being evil does not of itself prevent this. And this is proved by six reasons. The first reason is that the power of Christ is operative in the sacrament and repels any stain. The second is that, just as the rays of the sun are not tainted when they pass through foul places, so it is with the sacraments administered by evil persons. The third is that Judas, although he was evil, did much that was valid. The fourth is the authority of the Lord who commanded that the words of the Scribes and Pharisees were to be obeyed and put into practice. The fifth reason is that every good thing, whoever may do it, comes from God. The sixth reason is that in a sacrament one does not pay attention to who confers it or how but rather to what is conferred, for the increase is given only by God: that is, not by he who plants or he who waters, but by he who gives the increase [1 Cor. 3:6]. Then he concludes from what he has said that sacraments performed by such a person should be recognized.

[c]**Your Serenity's**—There are various ways of putting the case of this capitulum, which Gratian presents as something that has been abrogated. Melendus agrees with him and with all those who say that the reality of the sacraments does not exist among heretics. C. 24 q. 1 c. 34; C. 1 q. 1 c. 71. H. says that this capitulum should not be rejected and that its author was not condemned because of what it contains. For nothing is contained here that is not said canonically. The author was condemned because he was in communion with the heretic Photinus and because he wanted to rehabilitate the heretic Acacius after his death. For this Anastasius was condemned. D. 19 c. 9. Other people say, however, that this capitulum has been rejected along with its author because he said that those ordained by heretics may exercise their offices without dispensation as a matter of law. Indeed, H. says that heretics have the reality of the sacraments but they do not have the right to exercise them. *De cons.* D. 4 c. 151; *De cons* D. 4 c. 43; as noted C. 1 q. 1 c. 17; C. 1 q. 1 c. 87.

[d]**baptized**—in the Church's form.

[e]**office**—that is, baptism.

[f]**voice**—saying, "This is he who baptizes. . . ." *De cons.* D. 4 c. 26 (*in fine*).

[g]**dove**—that is, the Holy Spirit in the form of a dove. Hu.

[h]**in fire**—that is, with love.

[i]**visible**—C. 1 q. 1 c. 30.[(81)]

This,[a] *however, is to be understood only of those sanctions or decretal letters in which nothing is found contrary to the decrees of earlier fathers or evangelical precepts. For Anastasius II, as a favor to the emperor Anastasius, decreed that those priests or deacons whom Acacius*[b] *had ordained after sentence had been pronounced on him were rightly to exercise the offices they had received.*
Anastasius II to Anastasius Augustus, Letter 1, 7-8:[336]

C. 8. *No share in the offense is attached to one who has been ordained by previously condemned heretics.*

Your Serenity's[c] heart knows that according to the most sacred custom of the Catholic Church none of those whom Acacius baptized[d] or ordained as priests and deacons share, according to the canons, in the offense attached to Acacius's name, lest the grace of a sacrament imparted wrongly seem unreliable.

Were baptism to be administered by an adulterer or a thief (and may the Church be spared this), the office[e] would come unharmed to the recipient, for the voice[f] that the dove[g] caused to sound excluded every stain of human pollution, when it declared [Jn. 1:33]: "This is he who baptizes in the Holy Spirit and in fire."[h] For, if the rays of the visible[i] sun itself are not stained by contact with corruption when they pass through the foulest places, how much less is the power of him who made all visible things limited through a failing of his minister? Also, when Judas acted in virtue of the dignity given him among the Apostles, although he was both sacrilegious and a thief, the graces he unworthily bestowed were not harmed by that since the manifest words of the Lord himself declare [Matt. 23:2–3]: "The Scribes and Pharisees sit in Moses'

^a**whole**—that is, "perfect."

^b**force**—that is, with God's cooperation.

^c**planted**—by preaching.

^d**Apollo**—the disciple of Paul.

^e**watered**—by baptizing.

^f**the increase**—grace and the remission of sins.

^g**how well**—This is to be understood of what is tolerated. Otherwise one should ask as described in D. 42 c. 2.⁽⁸²⁾

^j**the envious**—that is, false apostles.

^k**this**—namely, about envy.

^l**one**—namely, Acacius.

^m**others**—namely, to those ignorant.

ⁿ**power**—as to the reality of the sacrament.

^o**generally**—that is, in every sacrament.

^p**he**—namely, Acacius.

^q**be afraid**—that is, according to their own false opinion. In reality they had received orders, although not the right to exercise them. C. 1 q. 1 c. 113; C. 1 q. 7 c. 24.

seat, so practice what they say, but do not practice what they do, for what they preach, they do not practice."

Therefore, whatever a minister in the Church does in virtue of his office for the perfection of his people is rendered whole^a through the Divinity's fulfilling force.^b Thus the one through whom Christ speaks, Paul that is, affirms [1 Cor. 3:6–7]: "I planted,^c Apollo^d watered,^e but God gave the increase.^f So neither the one who planted nor the one who watered is anything, for God gave the increase." Nor should one ask who the preacher is or how well^g he preaches,^h but rather whom he preaches [cf. Phil. 1:15]. He attestedⁱ that even the envious^j can preach Christ and that through envy the Devil has been thrown down [cf. Matt. 23:2–4]. He himself never stopped preaching this.^k

So therefore, that one^l whose name we forbear to speak harmed himself alone by ministering good things unworthily. For the inviolate sacrament given through him to others^m maintained the fullness of its power.ⁿ

This then is true generally,^o lest anyone be so anxious and insecure that he imagine, because of the judgment passed by Pope Felix, that he^p afterwards acted without efficacy in the sacraments that Acacius had usurped and that those who received the mysteries imparted in consecration or baptism be afraid^q that these divine gifts are void.

Because he gave this rescript illicitly, uncanonically, and contrary to the decrees of ³³⁷ *his predecessors and successors (as, before Anastasius, Felix and Gelasius had excommunicated Acacius, and later the third pope after Anastasius, Hormisdas, condemned the same Acacius), he has been repudiated by the Roman Church and it is read that he was also smitten by God.*³³⁸

C. 9. *Anastasius, reproved by God, was smitten by divine command.*

Anastasius II, a Roman by birth, lived in the time of King Theodoric. At that time, many clerics and priests began to withdraw^r from communion with him, because, apart from the council^s of the bishops, priests, and clergy of the whole Catholic Church, he was in communion with a

Dicta Gratiani post C. 10. CASE. Gratian draws a conclusion from what he has said, saying that because Anastasius decreed this, he incurred the excommunication laid down by Felix, Gelasius, and Hormisdas, as Acacius had earlier.

CC. 9–10. CASE. Photinus, a deacon of Thessalonica, was in communion with the heretic Acacius. After the death of Acacius, Pope Anastasius was in communion with Photinus, apart from the council of his clergy. He secretly wanted to rehabilitate Acacius, who had died in heresy, so that prayers could be said for him in church. So many of the clergy fell away from obedience to him, and he was struck with leprosy. The case of the next capitulum is clear.

^r**withdraw**—that is, they absented themselves. *Dicta Gratiani intra* D. 32 c. 6. To the contrary, C. 8 q. 4 c. 1, where it says that before sentence is passed the clergy may not withdraw from their bishop. But here they did not withdraw before sentence

For no one may preach unless he is sent. C. 16 q. 1 c. 19; X 5. 7. 12. Or else the text is speaking of ancient times when everyone could preach.

^h**how well he preaches**—but what he preaches.

ⁱ**attested**—In the Epistle to the Philippians [1:15] when he says, "Whether Christ is preached in integrity or in some other way, I rejoice and will rejoice."

was passed, for they broke off over a heretic who had already been condemned. C. 24 q. 1 c. 1; C. 24 q. 1 c. 2; C. 24 q. 1 c. 3.

^s**council**—Therefore, it would seem that the pope must hold a council of the bishops. This is true where it is a question of the faith, in which case a synod is greater than the pope. D. 15 c. 2 (*in fine*); argument from D. 93 c. 24.

ᵃ**communion**—To the contrary, C. 11 q. 3 c. 103, where it says that excommunication does not transfer to a third person. Nevertheless, he also participated with him in evil, and therefore it may transfer to a third person. X 5. 39. 29.

ᵇ**secretly**—Therefore, there is a presumption against him. X 3. 12. 1; X 1. 29. 24; Dig. 23. 2. 43; Dig. 26. 7. 54. Lau.

ᶜ**by the divine command**—While he was defecating his intestines fell out, and he died ignominiously.

ᵈ**ordained**—because it was conferred contrary to the Church's form. C. 1 q. 1 c. 71.

ᵉ**with him**—So it may be argued that everything done by those who have forced their way in or who have been defectively elected is invalid. C. 12 q. 2 c. 37; C. 25 q. 1 c. 8. The contrary may be argued from *dicta Gratiani post* C. 3 q. 7 c. 1 (at *Verum*); Cod. 1. 2. 16. This provision, however, is in favor of the guardians of the Church, and, therefore, acts are valid when this is to the advantage of the Church, but not otherwise. C. 16 q. 6 c. 2.

D. 20. Gratian showed above that decretal letters have the same force as the canons of councils. In this twentieth distinction it is asked whether the expositions of the holy fathers are equal to canons and decretals or to be preferred to them. It seems that they should be preferred because of their greater authority, for their authors excel others by being more filled with the grace of the Holy Spirit. Therefore, it would seem

proven in what follows.

ᶠ***Decretal letters***—In this twentieth distinction the master asks whether expositions of sacred Scripture have the same authority as canons and decretals. He solves this problem as follows. The authority of saints prevails in exposition of sacred Scripture, that of the Roman pontiffs in the determination of questions.

ᵍ***knowledge***—So it may be argued that no one may be a

deacon of Thessalonica by the name of Photinus, who was in communionᵃ with Acacius. And because he secretlyᵇ wanted to rehabilitate Acacius but could not, he was smitten by the divine command.ᶜ

Thereupon, it was decreed concerning Bishop Maximus, at the Synod of Constantinople under Pope Damasus, c. 6:[339]

C. 10. *Let everything done by or in conjunction with undisciplined prelates be revoked as void.*

Because of the report of his complete lack of discipline, which was revealed at Constantinople, it is decreed that Maximus is not to be considered to have been a bishop at any time, nor are those ordainedᵈ by him to be so considered, whatever their clerical rank, because all acts done by or in conjunction with himᵉ have been revoked as invalid.

DISTINCTION TWENTY

Part 1.

Decretal letters ᶠ *are thus legally equivalent to the canons of councils. There remains the question of whether expositions of sacred Scripture are equal or subordinate to these. For, when someone draws on greater knowledge, it seems that his words are of greater authority. Furthermore, many writers seem to be more secure because, being more filled with the Holy Spirit, they excel others in knowledge. Whence, it would seem that the opinions of Augustine, Jerome, and other writers are to be preferred to the enactments of some pontiffs.*

Part 2.

But it is one thing to decide an issue, and another to expound the sacred Scriptures accurately. For in determining a matter, not only knowledge ᵍ *is necessary, but power as well. Thus Christ said to Peter* [Matt. 16:19]*: "Whatever you bind on earth is bound in heaven. . . ,"*

that the expositions of Augustine, Jerome, and others are to be placed ahead of the statutes of pontiffs. This is discussed in the first section. In the second section, which begins "But it is one thing. . . ," Gratian solves the difficulty and says that to determine a matter requires not only knowledge but also the power that is signified in the keys that Christ gave to Peter. One key signified knowledge to discern between leper and leper; the other the power to bind and loose. Therefore, since power is necessary to decide an issue, it seems that pontiffs are to be preferred to expositors. This is

judge, especially in the Church, unless he is an expert. X. 4. 14. 1 (*in fine*); C. 1 q. 1 c. 82; C. 11 q. 3 c. 53; C. 24 q. 3 c. 4; *De poen.* D. 5 c. 1; *De poen.* D. 6 c. 1. This is because he must know the ordinances, Nov. 82. 1. 1 [Coll. VI. 10. 1. 1]; because his decision must be made in writing, C. 2 q. 1 c. 7 (*in fine*); and because judges should write their decisions themselves and read them aloud, Cod. 1. 51. 2 [1. 52. 2]. To the contrary is Cod. 3. 1. 17, where it says that knights may be judges, because, from daily practice, they have the skill requisite for judging. A mediocre knowledge is sufficient in a judge, as in a prelate. X 1. 6. 19.

[a]*before*—So it may be argued that a presumption may arise from the order in which deeds are done. C. 23 q. 4 c. 38; C. 1 q. 1 c. 82. So also from the order of words. D. 43 c. 1; X 1. 3. 22. To the contrary, Dig. 46. 3. 6.

[b]*gave*—Gratian here seems to hold that the key of binding and loosing is one key and that of knowledge another, so

14:2-4]. When there was a doubt whether someone was infected with leprosy, he was led before the priests to be received or cast out according to their judgment. C. 11 q. 3 c. 44; *dicta Gratiani* § 1 (at *Moysi*) *post De poen.* D. 1 c. 60.

ADDITION. See Hug. and *dicta Gratiani* § 1 (at *Moysi*) *post De poen.* D. 1 c. 60; X 4. 17. 13 (at *rationibus*). Archid.

before[a] *he gave*[b] *him the keys of the kingdom of heaven, by the one key giving him the knowledge to discern between leper and leper,*[c] *and by the other giving him the power to cast people from the Church or receive them in. Therefore, when any matter is settled, whether by acquittal of the innocent or condemnation of the guilty, the acquittal or condemnation requires not only knowledge but also the power of presiding. It is evident that writers on the sacred Scriptures, although they surpass pontiffs in knowledge and so are to be preferred to them in questions of scriptural interpretation, take second place to them in deciding cases since they have not been elevated to the same high dignity.*

So, Pope Leo IV writes to the bishops of Britain:[340]

C. 1. *The writings of others are not to be preferred to the decrees of the Roman pontiffs.*

It is not suitable that anyone pass judgment using the books or commentaries[d] of others[e] while ignoring the canons of the holy councils and the norms of the decretals, which have been received among us along with the canons. Now, in all ecclesiastical judgments we employ the canons[341] of the Apostles, Nicaea, Ancyra, Neocaesarea, Gangra, Antioch, Laodicea, Constantinople, Ephesus, Chalcedon,[342] Sardica, Africa, and Carthage;[343] and, along with these, the norms of the Roman bishops, Silvester, Siricius, Innocent, Zosimus, Celestine, Leo, Gelasius, Hilary, Symmachus, Hormisdas, Simplicius and Gregory III.[f][344] Using these generally, bishops pass judgment, and both bishops and clerics are judged. If such a problem should arise, or a matter so unusual happen, that it cannot be settled using these, then, when they can be had, the opinions of the writers whom[g] you mentioned, Jerome, Augustine, Isidore, and other similar holy teachers, are to be open-mindedly adopted and promulgated, or recourse is to be made to the Apostolic See about such matters.

For this reason, I am not afraid to declare clearly and with a loud voice

C. 1. CASE. The bishops of Britain were judging cases using only the expositions of Augustine, Jerome, and others, preferring them to the canons of councils and the decretals of pontiffs. Leo refuted them, showing them that in questions to be determined, one must first turn to the canons of councils and the decrees or decretals of pontiffs, and then, only secondly, to the expositions of holy men, such as Jerome, Augustine, and other saints. If the truth cannot be found there, then one must turn to the Apostolic See. One who does not accept these statutes is guilty of heresy.

[d]*books or commentaries*—that is, according to books or commentaries.

[e]*others* — that is, of Jerome and Augustine by whose works one may not judge without using the canons. D. 50 c. 58.

[f]*Gregory III* — Here what was said by Gregory III seems to be approved whereas elsewhere it seems to be rejected, C. 32 q. 7 c. 18, as also in the sections following where Gratian says that it is contrary to the Gospel. But the other capitulum should be understood to concern stricture, and so

that there are two keys. Nevertheless, I say that they are one, although they are called two because of the two effects. But how may knowledge be called a key since a person can have knowledge who does not have the key and vice versa? You may say that, granted that knowledge was not a key before one was ordained, it becomes a key after ordination. If you ask what, properly speaking, the key of a priest is, I say it is the sacerdotal power by which he binds and looses.

[c]*between leper and leper*—that is, between one matter and another. This alludes to what was done in the Law [Lev.

may be accepted. Ioan.

[g]*whom*—Here it appears that one is to judge following the authority of the canons rather than the authority of Jerome or Augustine. That is true unless Augustine has the support of an authority from the New or Old Testament or of some canon. For, although the Council of Aachen established that an abductor may not marry the person he abducted, C. 36 q. 2 c. 11, Jerome favored the opposite position, as in C. 36 q. 2 c. 8. But the former is supported by the authority of the Council of Metz, C. 36 q. 2 c. 10.

ᵃ**convicted**—But has not the Eastern Church received the canons? It appears not. D. 31 c. 14. Is it therefore heretical? You may say that, although it has not received these canons, nevertheless it has not rejected them. Or you may say that the pope has approved its customs. D. 19 c. 1.

C. 2. CASE. The case in this capitulum is clear.
ᵇ**have**—knowledge of.
ᶜ**neglect**—Ignorance of the canons is in no way permitted. D. 38 c. 4; D. 38 c. 6; D. 19 c. 1.
ᵈ**corrected**—The argument is as in D. 16 c. 14.

C. 3. CASE. Someone asked to which writings one should turn if doubt arises in solving some question, and it says in this capitulum that the following order is to be followed. First, one is to turn to the Old and New Testaments and the writings of the Apostles. If it does not appear from these what one is to do, one must turn then to the Greek Scriptures, then to the acts of councils and pontiffs, then to the expositions of the saints, and finally to the elders. This is how Beneventa. puts the case; Hugo. puts it this way: first, one should obtain the Old and New Testaments; second, the canons of the Apostles and the councils; third, the decrees and decretal letters of the Roman pontiffs; fourth, the Greek Scriptures; fifth, the sayings of the holy Latin fathers; last, examples of-

that anyone (be he bishop, cleric, or lay)³⁴⁵ convicted³ of not accepting in their entirety what we have called the statutes of the holy fathers, which among us are entitled the canons, has shown that he does not keep and believe profitably and effectively to their purpose the Catholic and apostolic faith and the four holy Gospels.

*Nicholas I to Photius, in the letter that begins "Afterwards, to St. Peter. . . :"*³⁴⁶

C. 2. *Those who do not have and obey the decrees of the Roman pontiffs are to be corrected.*

If you do not haveᵇ the decrees of the Roman pontiffs, you are to be accused of neglectᶜ and carelessness. If indeed you have them but do not observe them, you are to be correctedᵈ and rebuked for temerity.

*Also, Pope Innocent:*³⁴⁷

C. 3. *Where recourse is to be made when no authority appears in sacred Scripture.*

In those cases where no authority for binding or loosing appears in the four Gospels and all the other writings of the Apostles,ᵉ turn to the Greek sacred Scriptures. If there is nothing there, then consult the canons of the Apostolic See.³⁴⁸ If there is nothing there, then turn your hand to Catholic histories of the Catholic Church written by Catholic authors. If there is nothing there, carefully examine the examplesᶠ of the saints. And if, having checked all these, the state of the question has not been illuminated, gather the eldersᵍ of the province and ask them. For something is more easily discovered by asking many ʰ elders. For the Lord, the true guarantor, said [Matt. 18:20]: "If two or three of you gather in my name on earth, whatever they ask in any matter will be done for them by my Father."

the holy fathers; and finally one must turn to the elders. You, however, should turn to where text indicates second.
ᵉ**the Apostles**—that is, apostolic men.
ᶠ**examples**—So it may be argued that one may judge according to example. D. 37 c. 11; C. 24 q. 3 c. 1. The contrary may be argued from Cod. 7. 45. 13. But that text may be understood to apply when one has a law. Then judgment should not be according to example. Or you may say that the examples of private persons are not followed, but that those of public persons or someone with authority, such as the chief of state or apostolic men, are valid. C. 16 q. 3 c. 5; X 2. 27. 19. Or you may say that the examples of a few people are not to be used, but those of many may be.
ᵍ**elders**—that is, the wise. D. 84 c. 6.
ʰ**Many**—X 1. 29. 21 (*in fine*). I answer that in many men the truth is revealed clearly. Cod. 6. 42. 31; Cod. 7. 14. 3. Thus it appears that, in the absence of ordinance, one should turn to the custom of the place rather than the custom of the Roman Church. D. 12 c. 11; Dig. 1. 3. 32. Others say that one is first to consult the Roman Church, as may be argued from D. 11 c. 11. Ioan. What is to be done is discussed in D. 12 c. 4, and better in D. 1 c. 5.
ADDITION. On this matter, see Cod. 8. 52. 1 [8. 53. 1].⁽⁸³⁾ Archid.

NOTES TO THE DECRETUM

1. Ed. Fried. reads "Law of Nature" for "Divine Law." Ed. Rom. note: "There is great variety at this point in the manuscripts. Sometimes no title is found here; sometimes it reads *Concerning written and unwritten law and what it governs, the authors of laws, and the choice between two evils or dispensation.* Or: *And first concerning the law of natural, divine, and human enactments.* Or: *Concerning the law of nature and human enactment,* which is known to Dominicus de Santo Geminiano [*Super Decretum Volumine Commentaria* (Venice, 1587), fol. 2ᵛ] and found in some ancient manuscripts. Or: *Concerning the law of nature and enactment,* the title that seems to agree most with Gratian's usage, who often refers to this heading, as at the beginning of DD. 5, 7, 8, & 15, and before C. 11 q. 1 c. 26, where he writes, referring to this whole section, *Refer to the beginning, where the difference is given between natural law and the law of enactment.* Nevertheless, with such great variety, it could be proposed to avoid further conjecture that Gratian placed no rubric here. Thus it seemed adequate to keep the common reading and indicate the others."

2. Isidore of Seville, *Etymologies*, V, II, 1–2.

3. Isidore, *Etymologies*, V, III, 1.

4. Ed. Fried. reads, "Law is a genus and ordinance is a species of it."

5. Isidore, *Etymologies*, V, III, 2. Here for the first time and later when a rubric is lacking in the text of Gratian, the marginal reference from the Ed. Rom. has been reproduced in brackets.

6. Isidore, *Etymologies*, V, III, 3, cf. II, X, 2; cf. Ivo Pan. 2. 161, Tri. 3. 7. 1 [3. 8. 1], D. 4. 200.

7. Ed. Rom. note: "In Isidore the following passage comes first: *Usage is custom approved by age or unwritten ordinance. For ordinance* [lex] *gets its name from reading* [legendo], *because it is written. Usage, however, is long-continued custom.*"

8. Isidore, *Etymologies*, V, III, 3–4, cf. II, X, 2–3; cf. Ivo Pan. 2. 161, Tri. 3. 7. 1 [8. 1], D. 4. 200; cf. Dig. 1. 32. 1; cf. Tertullian, *De Corona*, IV, 5 (R. Arbesmann tr., p. 239).

9. Ed. Rom. marginal note: "When 'law' is used in the strict sense, as something promulgated for the future; but when custom is placed in writing and made authoritative by a public authority, so that there can be no question about it or need of another authority, it remains custom."

10. Isidore, *Etymologies*, V, IV, 1; cf. Dig. 1. 1. 2.

11. Isidore, *Etymologies*, V, IV, 1–2; cf. Dig. 1. 1. 3. On the much-debated relationship between natural law and divine law in Gratian, see the brief summary of scholarly opinion in Stanley Chodorow, *Christian Political Theory and Church Politics in the Mid-Twelfth Century* (Berkeley: Univ. of Calif. Press, 1972), pp. 99–102; or, more extensively, Rudolf Weigand, *Die Naturrechtslehre der Legisten und Dekretisten von Irnerius bis Accursius und von Gratian bis Johannes Teutonicus* (Munich: Heuber, 1967). Scholarly debate focuses on whether Gratian considered natural law and divine law as identical. That this question posed problems for medieval readers may be seen by comparing the gloss on *natural* in *Dicta Gratiani ante* D. 1 c. 1 and the gloss on *Natural law* in D. 1 c. 7.

12. Ed. Rom. note: "In three manuscript codices of Isidore and some of Gratian, it reads *the having and rearing of children* and this accords with Dig. 1. 1. 3, which seems to be its origin."

13. Isidore, *Etymologies*, V, v, 1; cf. Dig. 1. 1. 9.

14. Isidore, *Etymologies*, V, vi, 1.

15. Ed. Fried. reads "peace treaties" for "treaties, armistices."

16. Isidore, *Etymologies*, V, vii, 1–2.

17. Ed. Fried. omits "to combat."

18. Isidore, *Etymologies*, V, viii, 8; cf. Dig. 1. 1. 9.

19. Isidore, *Etymologies*, V, ix, 1.

20. Ed. Rom. note: "Previously this read, *either trusteeships or contracts*. It has been corrected from printed and manuscript versions of Isidore. Ulpian [Fragments], title 22, explains what 'cretion' is, as does Isidore, *Etymologies*, V, xxiv, 9." Ed. Fried. reads "trusteeships" for "cretion."

21. Cf. Instit. 1. 2. 3.

22. Isidore, *Etymologies*, V, x, 1, cf. II, x, 1; cf. Instit. 1. 3. 4.

23. Isidore, *Etymologies,* V, xi, 1; cf. Instit. 1. 3. 4.

24. Isidore, *Etymologies,* V, xii, 1; cf. Instit. 1. 2. 5.

25. Isidore, *Etymologies,* V, xiii, 1; cf. Instit. 1. 2. 6.

26. Isidore, *Etymologies*, V, xiv, 1; cf. Instit. 1. 2. 8.

27. Isidore, *Etymologies*, V, xv, 1–2.

28. Ed. Rom. note: "Previously this read *Papius and Pompeius* here and then *Papian and Pompeian* later. This has been amended from manuscript exemplars of Isidore. [Andrea] Alciati, *Dispunctionum Libri Quattuor*, III, iii [(Basil, 1582), VI, 206], noted this error in the printed versions. In the Capitoline Tablets for a.u.c. 761 from the Julian Calendar these consuls are given as M. Papius and Q. Poppaeus." Ed. Fried. reads "Pompeius" and "Papian-Pompeian."

29. Ed. Rom. note: "This reading is not in Eusebius's *Chronicle* as translated into Latin and expanded by Jerome (from which it seems that Isidore took it) nor is it in Dig. 35. 2. 1 where the law itself is given. Nevertheless, this is the text found in the manuscript versions of Isidore."

30. Isidore, *Etymologies*, V, xvi, 1.

31. Ed. Rom. note: "In some manuscript versions of Gratian and one of Isidore it reads 'stuffed' [*satura*]; about which [Sextus Pompeius] Festus [*De Verborum Significationum* (Leipzig, 1913), pp. 416–17], says: *A 'stuffed' food is prepared from a variety of ingredients, and the word is used of an ordinance put together from many different ordinances. And so it was legally declared, 'Neither overturn nor diminish through stuffing.' "* A "stuffed" act in Roman law was one in which unpopular legislation was included with popular legislation in a single act so as to get it passed; the practice was forbidden by the *Lex Caecilia Didia* (98 B.C.).

32. Isidore, *Etymologies*, V, xvii, 1.

33. Isidore, *Etymologies*, VI, xvi, 1; Anselm, proem.

34. Isidore, *Etymologies*, VI, xvi, 1; Anselm, proem.

35. Isidore, *Etymologies*, V, xviii, 1.

36. Ed. Rom. note: "Cicero, *On the Laws*, III, [xix, 44,] says this: *Our ancestors did not want laws to be made about private individuals, that is, what are called 'privileges.'* [Guillaume] Budé [*Annotationes Priores et Posteriores* (Paris, 1556), fol. 48ʳ] and others have noted, however, that this was not the usual meaning of the word."

37. Isidore, *Etymologies*, V, xix, 1; cf. Dig. 1. 3. 7.

38. Isidore, *Etymologies*, V, XX, 1.

39. Isidore, *Etymologies*, V, XXI, 1; Ivo Pan. 2. 142, Tri. 3. 6. 10 [3. 7. 10], D. 4. 168.

40. Ed. Rom. note: "Previously this read, 'as a protection against deception.' The correct reading has been restored from the manuscript codices of Isidore [*Etymologies*], V, XXI, [1], and from the printed editions where the same text is found in ibid., II, X, and from the old exemplars of Gratian where the word 'protection' is missing. A similar phrase is found in [Julius] Paulus, *Sententiarum*, V, XXXIII, 2, where he says, *Lest anyone be deceived by the words given for security*." Ed. Fried. omits "deception."

41. Augustine, *De Vera Religione*, XXXI (58) (Burleigh tr., p. 254–55); Ivo D. 4. 169, Pan. 2. 148, Tri. 3. 6. 11 [3. 7. 11].

42. Ed. Rom. note: "In the printed texts there follows after this word: *adopt the practice of fasting and abstain from meats and delicacies*; but nearly all the manuscripts have it as it has been restored."

43. Ed. Fried. reads "archbishop."

44. *Decretales Pseudo-Isidorianae*, Telesphorus, I, 1, p. 109–10 (with omissions); Ivo D. 4. 25, Pan. 2. 174; Anselm 3. 29, 7. 156; Polycarp 3. 2. 5. 1, 5. 1. 8.

45. Ed. Rom. marginal note: "Or, 'from meat and delicacies.' "

46. Ed. Fried. omits "to the Lord."

47. Ambrose? *Sermones,* XV, 2 (PL 17:654); Anselm 7. 184; Polycarp 3. 25. 6. See *Clavis Patrum*, p. 34, on this collection of sermons, some of which appear to be authentic. Ed. Rom. note: "In the Vatican Library at Rome and in the Library of the Monastery of St. Ambrose at Milan, are found manuscripts of sermons carrying the name of Ambrose, among these is a sermon for Sexagesima Sunday that begins *The time has arrived*, from which this capitulum has been taken."

48. [Pseudo-]Gregory, *Registrum Epistolarum* (ed. Maur.), appendix 13, cf. JE 1987; Ivo Tri. 1. 53. 69, D. 4. 29.

49. Ed. Rom. marginal note: "According to Gregory, in C. 25 q. 1 c. 13."

50. Ed. Rom. note: "The common reading was, *Now, however,* [*let us return*] *to the doctrine*; it has been corrected from old codices and the beginning of D. 15, where this is repeated."

51. Ed. Fried. omits "immediately."

52. Gregory I, *Registrum Epistolarum,* XI, LVI[a], 8 (Barmby tr., pp. 77–78); Bede, *Hist. Ecc.,* I, XXVII, 8 (Colgrave tr., p. 91); cf. Nicholas I, *Epistola*, Ad Res Orientales Pertinentes, XCIX, 65; On the authenticity of this correspondence, see Paul Meyvaert, "Les Responsiones de s. Gregoire le Grand et s. Augustin de Cantorbéry," *Revue d'histoire ecclésiastique* 54 (1959), 879–94.

Rom. Ed. note: "Paleas have been treated completely in the Preface. This text, the first to which the word palea is attached, is found even in the exemplar manuscripts (except for two at the Vatican), and in four of these it is connected to c. 2 which follows, with the word *For* added at the beginning, as it is sometimes found in Gregory."

The number of days given in the *dicta Gratiani* (40 and 80) were arrived at by combining the time a woman was unclean (7 days for a male, 14 for a female) with the wait before the performance of purification rites (33 for a male, 66 for a female). The total "days of purification" were thus 40 and 80. The palea, c. 1, gives only the waiting period (33 or 66 days). Medieval writers often associated the 40 and 80 day periods of Leviticus with Aristotle, *History of Animals*, VII, III (BK 583[b] 1–9), which gives the time between conception and the entry of the human soul into the fetus as 40 days for a male and 80 days for a female.

Gratian's treatment of female impurity in this canon is remarkable for its rejection of the traditional restrictions. In this he contrasts with many of his western contemporaries, like

Hildegard of Bingen, *Scivias*, I, II, 21, and with the eastern churches, who continue to uphold, at least in theory, the ritual impurity of women during menstruation and after childbirth to this day. On the Eastern Orthodox, see Eve Levin, "Female Impurity," in *Sex and Society in the World of the Orthodox Slavs, 900–1700* (Ithaca, N. Y.: Cornell Univ. Press, 1989), pp. 169–72; on the controversy in the west, see J.-L. Flandrin, *Un Temps pour embrasser* (Paris: Edition du Seuil, 1983), pp. 11, 73–82; cf. James A. Brundage, *Law, Sex, and Christian Society in Medieval Europe* (Chicago: Univ. of Chicago Press, 1987), p. 239. Eastern Christians imposed penances for any nocturnal emission, see Levin, pp. 208–9, cf. D. 6, below.

53. Gregory I, *Registrum,* XI, LVI[a], 8; Bede, *Hist. Ecc.,* I, XXVII, 8 (Colgrave tr., p. 91); cf. Nicholas I, *Epistola*, Ad Res Orientales Pertinentes, XCIX, 68; Ivo Tri. 1. 55. 70.

54. Ed. Fried. reads "woman" for "mother of all."

55. Gregory I, *Registrum*, XI, LVI[a], 8; Bede, *Hist. Ecc.,* I, XXVII, 8 (Colgrave tr., p. 91); cf. Nicholas I, *Epistola*, Ad Res Orientales Pertinentes, XCIX, 65; Ivo Tri. 1. 55. 71, D. 1. 62; Polycarp 3. 10. 24.

56. Ed. Rom. note: "From here up to the word *lest* has been added from the blessed Gregory." Ed. Fried. omits this passage.

57. Gregory I, *Registrum*, XI, LVI[a], 8 (Barmby tr., p. 78); Bede, *Hist. Ecc.,* I, XXVII, 8 (Colgrave tr., p. 91–93); cf. Nicholas I, *Epistola*, Ad Res Orientales Pertinentes, XCIX, 58, p. 588; Ivo Tri. 1. 55. 72, D. 8. 88.

58. Ed. Fried. marks from here to the end of the paragraph as a palea.

59. Ed. Rom. marginal note: "Or, 'coming up humbly'." Ed. Fried. adds "humbly."

60. Ed. Fried. omits "Lord's."

61. Gregory I, *Registrum*, XI, LVI[a], 9 (Barmby tr., p. 79); Bede, *Hist. Ecc.*, I, XXXVI, 9 (Colgrave tr., pp. 99–101); Burchard 5.43; Ivo Pan. 1.159, Tri. 1.55.76; Polycarp 3.16.19.

62. Ed. Fried. omits "before the Lord."

63. Ed. Rom. note: "In many codices of the blessed Gregory and in the collection *Concilia Generalia et Provincialia* (Cologne, 1530), one reads, *vain*; but in other codices of Gregory, *various*; but because of the gloss this is left unchanged."

64. Ed. Fried. omits "in the vicinity."

65. Ed. Fried. reads "ministry" for "mystery."

66. Ed. Fried. reads "by impure thoughts" for "by the impure emission."

67. Ed. Rom. note: "Nearly all the exemplar manuscripts of Gratian have *or*. But here there is great variety among the other collections and the codices of Bede and the blessed Gregory. In the manuscript collection of Isidore, it is: *In this matter, one thing is clear: the mind itself is not guilty, nor is it free in respect to its will.* So, on account of the variety found in the codices nothing in this passage has been changed."

68. Ed. Fried. omits "and, on account of such pollution, it is fitting to abstain from the sacred mystery."

69. Gregory I, *Registrum*, XI, LVI[a], 9 (Barmby tr., pp. 80–81); Bede, *Hist. Ecc.*, I, XXXVI, 9 (Colgrave tr., pp. 101–03); Burchard, 5.43; Ivo D. 2.52. Ed. Rom. note: "From here to the end is missing from the codices of the blessed Gregory and Bede, nor is it found in the three oldest exemplars of Gratian. But it is in Burchard, Ivo, the *Panormia*, and Polycarp." Ed. Rom. note: "This palea is not only missing from the first and tenth Vatican manuscripts but also from others that have some paleas. The heading is missing from all. In those cases, when we look for a heading, we find the text joined to what is above, as it is in Burchard and Ivo."

70. Ed. Rom. note: "This has been corrected from the original, from which Ivo also differs; previously it read: *Much discernment is necessary between suggestion and delight, and between delight and consent; let the mind act as its own judge.* Burchard: *let the mind, as its own judge, act.* Others more or less follow Gratian. But in Bede: *and between suggestion and*

delight, and delight and consent, let the mind act as its own judge. In the Isidorian Decretals: *and much discernment is necessary between suggestion, delight, and consent that the mind show itself to be its own judge.*"

71. Ed. Rom. note: "In the witnesses we find great variety from this point on. The shortest sufficiently intact reading is that in the version found in St. Gregory, *Epistolae* (Paris, [1508]): *But if he was a captive, he was not fighting, but he was fighting although he was not a captive. So you see. . . .*"

72. Isidore, *Sententiarum Libri*, III, XIII–XIV; Ivo Tri. 3.18.2 [3.19.2], D. 9.112.

73. Ed. Fried. omits "like the lamb."

74. Ed. Fried. omits "in Genesis."

75. Ed. Rom. note: "The Ordinary Gloss [on the Bible] has from Alcuin on this passage: *a great oppressor and killer of the men he had picked out to build the tower against God.*"

76. Isidore, *Etymologies*, V, I, 1–3; Anselm 12. 62 [56]; Ivo Pan 2. 63, Tri. 3. 3. 26 [3. 4. 26], D. 3. 194.

77. Ed. Fried. adds, "for the Greeks."

78. Isidore, *Etymologies*, V, I, 4–7; cf. Ivo Pan. 2. 144, D. 4. 170.

79. Ed. Rom. marginal note: "Isidore continues in the same place."

80. These "codes" represent the three attempts to codify imperial enactments prior to the collections of Justinian. The Gregorian was published in 291 and represented the legislation of Diocletian and his predecessors. It was soon supplemented by the Hermogenian collection, which consisted mostly of supplementary imperial legislation from between 293 and 294. It was probably the work of the legist Hermogenianus. Neither of these collections was "official" and neither exists today. The next collection, however, was official, being issued with the authorization of the emperor Theodosius II in 438. This consisted of legislation by the emperors from Constantine I to Theodosius himself. It is extant. Justinian's codifiers drew on these works to create his first code (529). This no longer exists because it was replaced in 534 by a revised version, which became (along with the Digest, Institutes, and Novels) the *Corpus Iuris Civilis.*

81. Augustine, *Tractatus in Evangelium Ioannis,* VI, XXV–XXVI (Rettig tr., I, 151–53); Anselm 12. 62; Ivo D. 3. 194, Pan. 2. 63, Tri. 3. 3. 26 [3. 4. 26]; Polycarp 7. 5. 30.

82. Ed. Rom. note: "This word is not in the text of St. Augustine. He was acting against the Donatists, who questioned whether the estates seized by them belonged to the Catholic Church according to the emperors' laws. That is why, when the Donatists were saying, *They have taken our estates, they have taken our fields,* to prove to them that they had not had and did not have a right to them, he added the following, *By what law do you defend the estates, divine.* . . . And below at C. 11 q. 1 c. 26, where Gratian cites the beginning of this chapter, the word *Church's* is also lacking. It is however found in Anselm, Ivo, and in the *Panormia.*"

83. Ed. Rom. marginal note: "Original: 'Therefore by human law means by the emperors' law. Why?' "

84. Ed. Rom. note: "Since the gloss prevents us from adding and correcting this completely, and since there are certain things to be added, it seemed suitable to add the entire passage from Augustine. In him after the word *human* in the preceding paragraph, there follows: *Do you want us to read the ordinances of the jurists and treat the estates according to them? If you wish to possess according to human law, we will examine the emperors' laws; let us see if they allow anything to be possessed by heretics. But what is the emperor to me? According to his law you possess the land. But destroy the laws of the emperors, and who would dare say, that estate is mine, or that slave is mine, or this house is mine? So, in order to possess these things, people accept the laws of kings. Do you want us to examine these laws for your benefit, because one favors you and you, being as meek as a dove, will not cite*

it, or because it permits you to reside there? For the ordinance clearly says, where the emperors command. . . ."

85. Cf. Cod. 51. 5. 4; *Codex Theo.* 16. 5. 43, 52, 54.

86. Augustine, *Confessions*, III, VIII, 15 (Pine-Coffin tr., p. 65); Ivo Tri. 3. 7. 15, D. 4. 178.

87. Nicholas I, *Epistola*, De Causis Rothadi, LXXX; Ivo D. 4. 203, Pan. 2. 164, Tri. 3. 7. 4 [3. 8. 2]. Ed. Rom. note: "This chapter is from the letter of Pope Nicholas which begins, *The letter of Your Beatitude*; it exists along with his and different pontiffs' other manuscript letters in the library of the Dominican monastery at Rome. Its attribution is taken from there."

88. Ed. Fried. reads "evil" for "dangerous."

89. Ed. Rom. marginal note: "Or, 'vain.' "

90. Augustine, *De Baptismo*, III, VI (9) (King tr., p. 439); cf. 1 Council of Carthage, c. 30 (Libosus of Vaga) and c. 68 (Felix of Buscalani); Ivo Pan. 2. 165, Tri. 3. 8. 8, D. 4. 208; cf. D. 8 c. 6.

91. Cf. 1 Council of Carthage, c. 30.

92. Cf. D. 8 c. 8.

93. Urban II? Ivo Pan. 2. 166, Tri. 3. 8. 9, D. 6. 213. It appears that this text is actually an otherwise unwitnessed letter of Pope Urban II. On this, see the Robert Somerville, "Papal Excerpts in Arsenal MS 713B: Alexander II and Urban II," in the forthcoming *Proceedings of the Ninth International Congress of Medieval Canon Law, Munich* (13–18 July 1992). Ed. Rom. note: "Some manuscripts and Ivo read *Gregory VII*. During his pontificate Guitmund, bishop of Aversa, wrote against Berengar on the Lord's Body and Blood in a book that still exists." Ed. Fried. reads: "Gregory VII."

94. Augustine, *De Baptismo*, III, V–IX (8–11) (King tr., pp. 438–39); Ivo Tri. 3. 7. 4 [3. 8. 14], D. 4. 234; cf. 1 Council of Carthage, c. 28.

95. Cf. 1 Council of Carthage, c. 28 (Zosimus of Tharassa). Ed. Rom. note: "In the blessed Augustine, Ivo, and the *Panormia*, we read, *let error yield* [*to truth*]. But Augustine certainly gathered from the words of Zosimus that he had labelled custom as error. For he said: *He did not want to call this custom, but error. Nevertheless, when he said, 'because Peter also, who had first been practicing circumcision, yielded to Paul who was preaching the truth,' this was enough to show, that something else was customary in the case of baptism.*"

96. Ed. Rom. note: "The text, from this word to the end, has suitably been added in Ivo and Gratian, repeating the words of Felix [of Buscalani] which are reported above in D. 8 c. 4."

97. Augustine, *De Baptismo*, IV, V (8) (King tr., p. 438); Ivo Tri. 3. 8. 18, D. 2. 94; cf. Cyprian, *Epistola* LXXIII, 13.

98. Cyprian, *Epistola* LXXIV, 9, 2 (Clarke tr., IV, 75–76).

99. Cyprian, *Epistola* LXXIII, 13, 1–2 (Clarke tr., IV, 61); Anselm 9. 5.

100. Ed. Rom. note: "In the blessed Cyprian it reads, *For one can be ignorant* and it is preceded by the text of D. 8 c. 7, up to the words *Holy Spirit*."

101. Cyprian of Carthage, *Epistola* LXIII, 14, 2 (Clarke tr., III, 106); Anselm 9. 8; cf. Matt. 17:5.

102. Augustine, *Epistola* CLXXXV, 8 (Parson tr., III, 148–49); Ivo Pan. 2. 154, D. 4. 184. Ed. Rom. note: "In old exemplars of Gratian, where there are few or no paleas, we find here only the text from *Therefore* to *reward* [i. e., the second paragraph]. In others, however, where this is present, the whole chapter is found without the indication it is a palea. The whole is found in the text of Augustine."

103. Ed. Fried. reads "will" for "truth."

104. Ed. Rom. note: "In Ivo and the *Panormia* the order of Augustine's words is changed, placing the clause on punishment last and the clause on reward first."

105. Ed. Rom. marginal note: "Original: 'the true God'."

106. Isidore, *Sententiae*, III, LI, 1–2; Burchard 15. 42; Ivo Tri. 3. 29. 15 [3. 30. 15], D. 16. 43. Ed. Rom. note: "In some old exemplars this capitulum is lacking, in others it is joined to the preceding one and lacks a heading." Ed. Fried. marks this capitulum as a palea.

107. Augustine, *De Trinitate,* III, Prologue (McKenna tr., p. 96); Ivo Pan. 2. 120, Tri. 3. 7. 4, D. 4. 71.

108. Ed. Rom. marginal note: "Exemplars: 'What you did think to be certain.'"

109. Augustine, *De Anima et eius Origine*, II, I (Homes tr., p. 353); Ivo Tri. 3. 6. 6 [3. 7. 6], D. 4. 73.

110. Augustine, *Epistola* LXXXII, 3 (Parsons tr., I, 392); Ivo Pan. 2. 119, Tri. 3. 6. 7 [3. 7. 7], D. 4. 74.

111. Ed. Rom. marginal note: "Original, Ivo, and the *Panormia*: 'I firmly believe that none of their authors made any error in their composition.'"

112. Ed. Rom. note: "So it reads in the manuscripts and in the gloss. In Augustine it is, *canonical authors or probable arguments.* The text is not much different in Ivo. It seemed satisfactory to indicate the other variants in the margin."

113. Jerome, *Epistola* LXXI, 5 (Fremantle tr., p. 157). Ed. Rom. note: "The words of this chapter are from the blessed Jerome to Lucinius Baeticus, letter 28, but the heading has not been changed on account of the gloss on *Greek.*"

114. Augustine, *Epistola* XL, 3 (Parsons tr., I, 173); Ivo Tri. 3. 7. 10 [3. 8. 10], D. 4. 215.

115. Augustine, *De Baptismo*, II, III (4) (King tr., p. 427); Ivo Tri. 3. 7. 12 [8. 3. 12], D. 4. 227; Polycarp 3. 21. 1.

116. Augustine, *Epistola* XCIII, 35 (Parsons tr., II, 90–91); Anselm 4. 56; Ivo Tri. 3. 7. 16. 1 [3. 8. 16], D. 4. 236.

117. Ed. Rom. note: "Previously this read, *or from Cyprian and Agrippinus before the Donatist faction separated.* The correct reading has been restored from Augustine, some exemplars of Gratian, and Ivo. For Cyprian and Agrippinus died long before the schism of the Donatists broke the unity of the Church. On this the author of the gloss has erred." Ed. Fried. omits "of the united Church, such as."

118. Ed. Rom. note: "So it reads in the original, Ivo, and some versions of the New Testament. But in St. Augustine, *On John,* V, XLV, LIII, XCVIII, and almost always elsewhere, it reads, *will reveal.* The Greek is ἀποκαλύψει."

119. Augustine, *Epistola* CXLVIII, 15 (Parsons tr., III, 235–36); Ivo Tri. 3. 7. 17 [3. 8. 17], D. 4. 237.

120. Augustine, *De Civitate Dei*, I, XXII, 2 (Bettenson tr., p. 33); Ivo Tri. 2. 50. 27; Polycarp 1. 27. 1. Ed. Fried. gives the title as: "*Also, to Casulanus* [Marcellinus, *The City of God*, I, XXII, 2]."

121. Nicholas I, *Epistola*, De Causis Rothadi, LVII, pp. 355–64; Anselm 12. 34; Burchard 15. 10; Ivo Pan. 2. 138, D. 4. 87; Polycarp 1. 29. 9, 6. 1. 2. Ed. Rom. note: "This chapter is taken from a letter of Nicholas which is extant in a codex in the Dominican library, concerning which comment was made at D. 8. c. 3. The salutation of this letter reads, *Nicholas, Servant of the Servants of God, to our most reverend and holy brethren, the metropolitans, bishops, and other bishops of the various provinces and cities, who have gathered at the manor of Convicinum near the city of Senlis.* The same letter has recently been published in [Marguerin de La Bigne,] *Appendix Bibliothecae Sanctorum Patrum* [(Paris, 1579)]."

122. Ed. Rom. note: "In Nicholas there follows immediately, *To show this. . . .* But in Gratian, though not in Polycarp or Anselm, there is inserted here, *Imperial ordinance is not above the ordinance of God, but below it.* This is taken from Burchard and Ivo who have it from the decretals of Pope Pius, c. 3; it is also had in the capitulary, adjoined to c. 17, while

the rest is found as below in this capitulum beginning at '*You see that ecclesiastical laws. . . .*'" Cf. Burchard 15. 10; Ivo Pan. 2. 139, D. 16. 11.

123. Gregory I, *Registrum*, IX, XXXIX (Barmby tr., p. 65); Innocent I, *Epistola* XVIII, 2; Ivo Pan. 2. 140, D. 4. 187.

124. Symmachus I, *Praeceptum Regis Theodorici (Epistola VI)*; Anselm 3. 87; Burchard 5. 8; Ivo Pan. 2. 141, Tri. 3. 29. 1 [3. 30. 1], D. 4. 231; Polycarp 6. 1. 15. This synod was the occasion of a number of works by Ennodius of Pavia (*c.* 473–521) defending the prerogatives of the papacy. Ennodius's defense of Pope Symmachus in this letter and in his work quoted at *dicta Gratiani post* D. 17 c. 6 are among the earliest elaborations of the implications of the papal primacy. In them, Ennodius also strongly advocated the restriction of the title "pope" to the bishop of Rome alone.

125. Felix III, *Epistola* XIII; Anselm 4. 11; Polycarp 1. 20. 1.

126. *Capitula Angilramni*, XXXVI; Anselm 3. 89; Burchard 15. 9; Ivo D. 5. 38, 16. 10; Polycarp 1. 29. 10.

127. Nicholas I, *Epistola*, Ad Res Orientales Pertinentes, LXXXVIII, pp. 454–87; Ivo Tri. 1. 62. 70; cf. D. 96 c. 8.

128. Gregory of Nazianzus, *Oratio* XVII, 8; Ivo Tri. 2. 14. 6, D. 5. 5.

129. Augustine, *Contra Litteras Petiliani*, II, LVIII [132] (King tr., p. 563); Ivo Pan. 2. 153, Tri. 3. 6. 16 [3. 7. 16], D. 4. 183.

130. Ed. Rom. note: "The author of this rubric reads this chapter as treating ordinances of the emperors passed in favor of the Church, but the blessed Augustine is here conceding to Petilian and the Donatists that they can invoke the ordinances of the emperors on their behalf, but only if they do not do so in the deceitful way he proved them to have done before."

131. Nicholas I, *Epistola*, Ad Res Orientales Pertinentes, LXXXVIII, pp. 454–87; Ivo D. 4. 188; cf. D. 96 c. 6. Ed. Rom. note: "In the printed versions the following title is given to this capitulum: *Cyprian to the Emperor Julian*. But this is chronologically impossible. In all the manuscripts, except the eleventh of the Vatican, the word *Emperor* is lacking, just as in Ivo. The ninth has *to Bishop Julian*. Another, very old, has *to Jubaian*. This entire capitulum is found in the letter of Nicholas to the emperor Michael which begins, *We had established. . .* , from which D. 96 c. 6 below is taken, along with more of the same letter of which this is a section. It has also been taken from Gelasius I, *On the Penalty of Anathema* [XI (Thiel ed., p. 568)]."

The text of the case in the gloss presupposes that this letter is actually addressed to the emperor Julian the Apostate (360–63), who attempted to reestablish paganism and combined the imperial office with the ancient pagan priesthood of pontifex maximus.

132. Ed. Rom. note: "In the original there is, *desiring that those be raised up by the medicine of humility*. Ivo has it as Gratian does here in many codices. In some, however, is found, *desiring that what are his be raised up by the medicine of humility*, just as in D. 96 c. 6 below. In Gelasius, the same passage reads, *desiring that his own be saved by the medicine of humility and human pride not begin anew, divided the proper offices of both powers, according to their proper activities and distinct dignities, so that Christian. . . .*"

133. Leo IV (fragment), JE 2642; Ivo Pan. 2. 149, D. 4. 176. Ed. Rom. note: "This letter has not been found; and it seems that this part of the text is corrupt and has caused the author of the gloss to fall into the error of thinking that he had spoken of the Christian emperors who had been Lothar's predecessors as Isidore says the pagans did, that is, that they were accustomed to call their emperors pontiffs. Gelasius deals with this very well in *On the Penalty of Anathema* [XI], and in D. 21. c. 1. In Ivo it reads, '*of you and of our predecessor pontiffs.*' In the *Panormia, of us and of our pontiffs and predecessors*. But perhaps other texts

of Gratian have it correctly, inasmuch as before the word *predecessors* is added the conjunction *and*, as it is also in the *Panormia*. Now this would indicate that the emperors were accustomed to issue capitula when they had assembled the bishops of the realm in council, which is quite correct. Certainly what was written by Leo seems to refer to the capitula of Charles and Louis that Lothar ordered to be obeyed in all of Italy. So in the *Lombard Laws*, III, XXXV. It is reported that Lothar had so established, *It pleased us that the capitula which we have excerpted from the capitulary of our glorious lord Charles, of blessed memory, and of our father Louis, the most unconquered emperor, are to have force of law and be obeyed as ordinance by everyone here, by our vassals, and by all the members of the holy Church in the kingdom of Italy; and whoever is found in contempt of these capitula, is to be fined sixty shillings.* It displeased the Roman people very much that they were forbidden to follow the ancient Roman law, as can be gathered from the last capitulum of this distinction, and the rumor spread that the opinion of the people and the pontiff was the same on this. On account of this it seems that Leo wanted to remove this from his letter; nevertheless, afterwards, in order to preserve the Roman civil law, he dealt very carefully with Lothar, as appears from the same final capitulum."

134. John VIII (fragment), JE 3011; Ivo Tri. 1. 63. 7, D. 4. 230.

135. Gelasius I (fragment) JK 658; Ivo Pan. 2. 150, Tri. 1. 46. 28, D. 4. 179; cf. D. 54 c. 11.

136. Gelasius I (fragment), JK 722; Ivo Pan. 2. 151, D. 4. 180.

137. Leo IV (fragment), JE 2637; Ivo Pan. 2. 152, D. 4. 181.

138. Ed. Rom. note: "It seems that Lothar conceded to the Roman people what Pope Leo requested here. For in the *Lombard Laws*, II, LVII, it reads, *since the Roman people requested that they might live according to their law,* followed by this enactment:

"Lothar, Emperor"

"Inasmuch as the entire Roman people has requested to live by their own law, we wish that people live in accord with whatever law they have professed to live by. And let it be announced by them so that everyone, be he judge or duke, or anyone else, know this. And, if anyone commit an offense against the law, let him be subject to that law which he has professed to live by, through our and the pontiff's dispensation."

139. Isidore, *Synonyms* II, XVI; Ivo Pan. 2. 165, D. 4. 207.

140. Nicholas I, *Epistola,* Ad Res Orientales Pertinentes, LXXXVIII, pp. 454–87; Ivo Tri. 1. 62. 14, D. 4. 211.

141. *Decretales Pseudo-Isidorianae*, Julius I, I, p. 461; Anselm 1. 8; Polycarp 1. 19. 3.

142. Ed. Rom. note: "This sentence has been expanded from the original and Anselm." Ed. Fried. omits: "delight in these, arm yourselves with these" and "surrounded, delighted, and armed by these."

143. Cod. 8. 52. 2 [8. 53. 2] (Scott tr., I, 333); Ivo D. Pan. 2. 163, Tri. 3. 7. 3 [3. 8. 3], 4. 202; Polycarp 3. 23. 5.

144. Basil the Great, *On the Holy Spirit*, XXVII, 66 (Jackson tr., pp. 40–42); Burchard 3. 127; Ivo Pan. 2. 159, Tri. 3. 7. 2, D. 4. 69.

Ed. Rom. note: "Earlier this section was cited as *Augustine from the book of the sayings of Basil*. In the version of Vercelli is *Whence Augustine says, or from the sayings of Basil*; and the second part of this has been retained since it is thus cited by Burchard and the author of the *Panormia*. But Ivo cites from Basil, *On the Holy Spirit*, XXVII, which has been indicated in the margin. In addition, it is glossed in so many places that it cannot be emended; thus it seems necessary to give the integral text of Basil according to both the Greek and the Latin:

Τῶν ἐν τῇ ἐκκλησίᾳ πεφυλαγμένων δογμάτων καὶ κηρυγμάτων τα μὲν ἐκ τῆς ἐγγράφου διδασκαλίας ἔχομεν, τὰ δὲ ἐκ τῆς τῶν ἀποστόλων παραδόσεως διαδοθέντα ἡμῖν ἐν μυστηρίῳ παρεδεξάμεθα, ἅπερ ἀμφότερα τὴν αὐτὴν ἰσχὺν ἔχει πρὸς τὴν εὐσέβειαν, καὶ τούτοις οὐδεὶς ἀντερεῖ, ὅστις γε κἂν κατὰ μικρὸν γοῦν θεσμῶν ἐκκλησιαστικῶν πεπείραται. εἰ γὰρ ἐπιχειρήσαιμεν τὰ ἄγραφα τῶν ἐθῶν ὡς οὐ μεγάλην ἔχοντα τὴν δύναμιν παραιτεῖσθαι, λάθοιμεν ἂν εἰς αὐτὰ τὰ καίρια ζημιοῦντες τὸ εὐαγγέλιον, μᾶλλον δὲ εἰς ὄνομα ψιλὸν περιστῶντες τὸ κήρυγμα. οἷον ἵνα τοῦ πρώτου καὶ κοινοτάτου πρῶτον μνησθῶ, τῷ τύπῳ τοῦ σταυροῦ τοὺς εἰς τὸ ὄνομα τοῦ κυρίου ἡμῶν Ἰησοῦ Χριστοῦ ἠλπικότας κατασημαίνεσθαι, τὶς ὁ διὰ γράμματος διδάξας; τὸ πρὸς ἀνατολὰς τετράφθαι κατὰ τὴν προσευχήν, ποιον εδιδαξεν ημας γραμμα; τα της επικλησεως ρηματα επι τη αναδειξει του αρτου τῆς εὐχαριστίας καὶ τοῦ ποτηρίου τῆς εὐλογίας τὶς τῶν ἁγίων ἐγγράφως ἡμῖν καταλέλοιπεν; οὐ γὰρ δὴ τούτοις ἀρκούμεθα, ὧν ὁ ἀπόστελος ἢ τὸ εὐαγγέλιον ἐπεμνήσθη, ἀλλὰ δὲ προλέγομεν καὶ ἐπιλέγομεν ἕτερα, ὡς μεγάλην ἔχοντα πρὸς τὸ μυστήριον τὴν ἰσχὺν ἐκ τῆς ἀγράφου διδασκαλίας παραλαβόντες. εὐλογοῦμεν δὲ τὸ ὕδωρ τοῦ βαπτίσματος καὶ τὸ ἔλαιον τῆς χρίσεως, καὶ προςέτι αὐτὸν τὸν βαπτιζόμενον, ἀπὸ ποίων ἐγγράφων; οὐκ ἀπὸ τῆς σιωπωμένης καὶ μυστικῆς παραδόσεως; τὶ δὲ αὐτὴν τοῦ ἐλαίου τὴν χρίσιν τις λόγος γεγραμμένος ἐδίδαξε; τὸ δὲ τρὶς βαπτίζεσθαι τὸν ἄνθρωπον πόθεν; ἀλλα δὲ ὅσα περὶ τὸ βάπτισμα, ἀποτάσσεσθαι τῷ σατανᾷ καὶ τοῖς ἀγγέλοις αὐτοῦ ἐκ ποίας ἐστὶ γραφῆς; οὐκ ἐκ τοῦ ἀδημοσιεύτου ταύτης καὶ ἀπορρήτου διδασκαλίας, ἣν ἐν ἀπολυπραγμονήτῳ καὶ ἀπεριεργάστῳ σιγῇ οἱ πατέρες ἡμῶν ἐφύλαξαν; καλῶς ἐκεῖνοι δεδιδαγμένοι τῶν μυστηρίων τὰ σεμνὰ σιωπῇ διασώζεσθαι.

"That is: *Of the Church's beliefs and practices, whether generally accepted or publicly enjoined, which have been preserved, some we have from written teaching; others we have received delivered to us 'in a mystery' by the tradition of the apostles; and both of these have the same force in true piety. These no one will question—no one, at least, who is even moderately versed in ecclesiastical laws. For were we to reject such customs as are unwritten, on the ground that they possess small importance, we should unintentionally injure the Gospel at its core; or, rather, should make the name we proclaim a mere word and nothing more. For instance, to take the first and most general example, who is there who has taught us in writing to sign with the Cross those who have trusted in the name of our Lord Jesus Christ? What writing has taught us to turn east during prayer? Which of the saints has left us in writing the words of the invocation at the displaying of the bread of the Eucharist and the cup of blessing? For we are not, as is well known, content with what the Apostle or the Gospel has recorded, but from start to finish we add other words as being of great importance to the mystery, receiving these from unwritten teaching. We bless the water of baptism, the oil of chrismation, and the one who will be baptized. On what written authority do we do this? Is not our authority hidden and mystical tradition? Indeed. By what written word is the anointing of oil itself taught? Whence is the baptized immersed three times? And as to the other customs of baptism, what Scripture orders the renunciation of Satan and his angels? Does this not come from that unpublished and secret teaching that our fathers protected in a well-guarded silence? Well had they learnt the lesson that the awe-inspiring dignity of the mysteries is best preserved by silence.*"

Ed. Fried. gives the heading as: "*Whence Augustine says, or from the writings of Basil.*"

145. Ed. Fried. reads "ministry" for "mysteries."

146. Gregory I, *Registrum*, I, LXXXVII (Barmby tr., p. 99); Burchard 3. 124; Anselm 4. 42; Ivo Pan. 2. 157, D. 4. 66; Polycarp 3. 23. 8. Cf. D. 12 c. 8. Ed. Rom. note: "The words of this capitulum, which were previously attributed to St. Augustine, are found among the decretals of Pius I in *Concilia Generalia et Provincialia*, 3 vols. (Cologne, 1580), as decretal 7. It is also found among the letters of the same Pius in the *Collectio in XVI Titulis*, III, IX. Burchard, Ivo and the author of the *Panormia* quote from there. Nearly all the words of the

letter, however, are found in St. Gregory's *Registrum* as *Epistola* LXXV (from which it is quoted in Polycarp). Those sections that are found in this capitulum are also given in D. 12 c. 8 below." Ed. Fried. gives the heading as: *"Also, to the priest Casulanus."*

147. Augustine, *Epistola* XXXVI (Parsons tr., I, 139); Anselm 4. 43; Burchard, 3. 126; Ivo Pan. 2. 158, Tri. 3. 6. 1 [3. 7. 1], D. 4. 68; Polycarp 3. 23. 10. Ed. Fried. gives the heading as: *"Also, to the same."*

148. Ed. Rom. note: "From here to the end is not found in the letter indicated, but it is given by Burchard, Ivo and the *Panormia."*

149. Cf. Augustine, *Epistola* LIV, 1–2 (Parsons tr., pp. 252–54). Ed. Rom. note: "Today no book with this title exists among the works of blessed Augustine. But in his letter to Januarius, that is, *Letter* CXVIII, 1–2, the same idea is expounded at length."

150. Ed. Fried. reads "instruction" for "arrangement."

151. Augustine, *Contra Faustum Manichaeum,* XI, II (Stothert tr., p. 178). Ed. Rom. note: "In the blessed Augustine's *Against Faustus the Manichean,* II, is read, *You see that in these affairs (he is speaking of the norm of faith) what prevails.* . . . He thinks with good reason, in Letter 165 concerning the schism of the Donatists, that the succession of bishops, above all in the See of Peter, gives very certain evidence for the Catholic faith."

152. Leo I, *Epistola* XVI, 6 (Feltoe tr., p. 30); Anselm 1. 45; Polycarp 1. 19. 8.

153. Innocent I, *Epistola* XXV, 2–3 (Ellard tr., pp. 5–6); Burchard 3. 125; Anselm 1. 41; Ivo D. 4. 67; Polycarp 1. 19. 7, 3. 23. 7. Pope Innocent is writing to Bishop Decentius concerning the practice in Gubbio of reciting the Lord's Prayer before communion in contrast to the Roman practice of reciting it after the Canon. The practice at Gubbio was, in fact, the ancient one. The Roman practice was the actual "novelty." On this famous letter, see R. Cabié, *La Lettre du Pape Innocent I à Decentius de Gubbio (19. III. 416)* (Louvain: Publications Universitaires de Louvain, 1973).

154. Ed. Rom. marginal note: "Or, 'ought to receive its authority or standard from elsewhere' [for 'lacks the authority']."

155. Ed. Rom. note: "As found in the original located in the four volumes of councils, what follows is: . . . *there is no doubt. I would be certain that this is sufficient for instructing and correcting your church (if your predecessors had done anything less or something different), had you not decided to consult us on certain matters*; but because of the gloss, especially on the word *Charity*, it has not been changed." Ed. Fried. here inserts: "there is no doubt."

156. *Decretales Pseudo-Isidorianae*, Callistus I, I, 2, p. 136; Anselm 1. 12; Polycarp 1. 19. 2.

157. Gregory IV, *Epistola* XIV, p. 75; Anselm 1. 20; Polycarp 1. 19. 2; on the genuineness of this letter, see W. Goffart, "Gregory IV for Aldric of Le Mans (833)?" *Medieval Studies* 28 (1966), 22–38. Ed. Rom. note: "This entire chapter is found in a letter of Gregory IV, *To all the bishops situated in Gaul, Germany, Europe, and all the provinces.* It is found in the previously mentioned codex of the library of the Dominican monastery. But the beginning is in the letter of Anastasius II to the Augustus Anastasius, c. 6."

158. Ed. Rom. note: "The words *for the hope of the Roman Church* have been removed. The passage is corrected from the letter itself and from some manuscript codices of Gratian."

159. Leo IX, *Epistola* C, 29; cf. Nicholas I, *Epistola,* Ad Res Orientales Pertinentes, LXXXVI, pp. 447–51; Ivo Pan. 2. 155, D. 4. 223, 5. 44. Ed. Rom. note: "This chapter has been constructed from widely divided passages. Until the words, *if there is* it is taken from Leo IX's libellus against the unheard of presumption of bishops Michael of Constantinople and Leo of Ochrid (Letter I, 29). There, speaking of the Roman Church, he says: *He knows that customs diverse according to time and place are no obstacle to the salvation of believers,*

when one faith doing all the good it can through love commends all to the one God. It is given in nearly this form in Ivo and the *Panormia.* The second part is taken from Nicholas's second letter to Photius, which begins, *Later to the blessed Peter. . . .* There it has: *Concerning the customs which you seemed to be evidencing against us, writing that there are diverse customs in diverse churches, if there is no canonical authority standing against them that requires us to abandon them, we make no ruling nor do we oppose them.*"

160. Jerome, *Epistola* LXXI, 6 (Fremantle tr., p. 154); Anselm 4. 44; Polycarp 3. 323. 1.

161. Nicholas I, *Epistola,* Ad Causis Rothadi, LXX; Ivo Pan. 2. 156, D. 4. 212. Ed. Rom. note: "This is found in the letter written to Hincmar and the other archbishops and bishops governing churches in the kingdom of Charles. It is extant in the earlier mentioned codex of the library of the Dominicans, and from it this chapter has been expanded. Previously it was shorter, as it is in Ivo and the *Panormia.*" In this text, Ed. Fried. omits "in our times we permit the holy Church of God to be slandered and that," and "at will by those wandering from the truth."

162. Instit. 1. 2. 9 (Birks tr., p. 39); Anselm 7. 2; Ivo Pan. 2. 162, D. 4. 219.

163. Ed. Fried. adds "unless they are contrary to an ordinance." On this varient, see B. McManus, "An Interpolation at D. 12 c. 6," *Bulletin of Medieval Canon Law* 18 (1988), 55–57.

164. Cod. 8. 53. 2. 1 [52. 2. 1] (Scott tr., I, 333); Ivo Pan. 2. 162, Tri. 3. 7. 2 [3. 8. 2], D. 4. 201.

165. Ed. Rom. note: "In the original this reads: *lest anything be contrary to long-standing custom.* But since the rubric seems to favor Gratian's reading, which is also found in Ivo and the *Panormia,* it has not been changed."

166. Gregory I, *Registrum,* I, LXXVII (Barmby tr., p. 99); Ivo Tri. 3. 7. 6 [3. 8. 5], D. 4. 204. Cf. D. 11 c. 6.

167. Ed. Rom. note: "This is the reading in some old codices of Gratian and in some codices of blessed Gregory; but the author of the gloss does not seem to have had the word *clerical,* which is lacking also in Ivo, many exemplar manuscripts of Gratian, and some of the editions of blessed Gregory." Ed. Fried. omits "clerical."

168. Gregory I, *Registrum,* IX, CLXXVI (not in Barmby translation).

169. Gregory I, *Registrum,* XI, LVI[a], 3 (Barmby tr., p. 75); Bede, *Hist. Ecc.,* I, XXVII, 2 (Colgrave tr., pp. 81–82); Ivo Tri. 1. 55. 22, D. 2. 80; on the authenticity of this correspondence, see Meyvaert, "Les Responsiones."

170. Augustine, *Epistola* LIV, 1 (Parsons tr., I, 252–53); Polycarp 3. 23. 4.

171. Ed. Fried. omits this sentence and the clause, "in one place no day passes when it is not offered, elsewhere this happens only on Saturday and Sunday, or only on Sunday," from the previous one.

172. Ed. Rom. note: "In this capitulum, as in that which follows, many emendations have been made from the text of the blessed Augustine, and some things have been added. From here to the end, however, nothing has been added since the words of Augustine have been condensed well."

173. Ed. Fried. omits *"or places."*

174. Augustine, *Epistola* LV, 19 [35] (Parsons tr., I, 290–91); Ivo Pan. 2. 168, Tri. 3. 7. 6 [3. 8. 6], D. 4. 206.

175. Ed. Rom. marginal note: "Or, 'such servile works'."

176. Eleventh Council of Toledo, c. 3 (from *Collectio Hispana*); Ivo Tri. 2. 24. 2.

177. Ed. Rom. note: "In a very old codex in the library of the Catholic kings at Lugo and in printed versions of the councils, there is the marginal reading, *pontiffs of the province.* This

reading, which is repeated at the end of the capitulum, seems to be the true reading. But in the text of all the editions of the councils, and in two Vatican codices, it reads, *citizens.*"

178. First Council of Braga, c. 1 (version in *Collectio Hispana*); cf. Fourth Council of Toledo, c. 2.

179. Ed. Rom. note: "In the text of the council itself, published in [*Concilia Generalia et Provincialia*] (Cologne, [1530]), the word *or* is lacking. In other editions it reads thus: *private monastic customs are not to be intermingled contrary to ecclesiastical norms.*"

180. Eighth Council of Toledo, c. 2; Burchard 12. 29; Ivo Pan. 8. 119, Tri. 3. 22. 15 [3. 23. 15], D. 12. 16.

181. Ed. Fried. adds "of death."

182. Gregory I, *Moralia in Job*, XXXII, 20 (Bliss tr., III, 538–41). The text commented on by Gregory is Job 40:10–12 in the Vulgate (Job 40:15–17 in the Hebrew and modern versions): "Behold the Behemoth whom I made with you, who eats like an ox; his strength is in his flanks, and his power is in his belly. He raises his tail like a ceder; the sinews of his loins are entangled." (Vulgate version.)

183. Augustine, *Quaestionum in Heptateuchum Libri*, I, XL; Ivo Tri. 3. 19. 2 [3. 20. 2], D. 9. 117.

184. Leo I, *Epistola* CLXVII, pref. (Feltoe tr., p. 109); Anselm 2. 73; Ivo Tri. 1. 42. 46; Polycarp 7. 14. 1.

185. Ed. Rom. marginal note: "This passage has not been restored because of the gloss; original: 'condition.' " Ed. Fried. reads "condition."

186. Isidore, *Etymologies*, VI, XVI, 2–13; Anselm 2. 73; Ivo Tri. 1. 43. 46. Ed. Rom. note: "This capitulum is located before the preface of Isidore's collection of canons, but not in the codex of the Dominican library; there up till the sentence beginning, *Among other*, it is located, as in other cases, before the Council of Nicaea."

187. Ed. Rom. note: "In many ancient exemplar codices of Gratian and in the printed codex of Isidore, the reading is as it has been emended. But in other manuscript and printed versions of these the reading is, *there remain two natures in Christ, and one person of our Lord Jesus Christ.*"

188. In the translation of this etymology, the English words represent the following Latin originals: company, *comitatus*; caucus, *coetus*; council, *concilium*; counsel, *consilium*; consult, *considium*; convention, *conventus*; congregation, *congregatio*; to convene, *conveniendo*.

Ed. Rom. note: "In Isidore's *Etymologies* this text is corrupt. But in the preface by the same Isidore, in the edition *Conciliorum* [*Quatuor Generalium*] (Paris, [1535]), which has been collated with some old versions, the reading is: *Now the word 'council' is taken from its common purpose, because all there direct their minds' gaze on one thing. Now the eyes have cilia: hence, any who differ among themselves cannot have a council, because they do not think the same. Now a convention or congregation is a 'caucus' from 'to caucus,' that is, from 'to convene as one.' And so a 'convention' is so called because people convene there. So a convention, caucus, or council denominates the association of many as one.* There are many variations in the codices of Gratian, the reading which seemed the best has been retained from these, although something better could possibly be desired."

189. Gregory I, *Registrum*, I, XXIV, p. 36; Anselm 6. 50; Ivo Tri. 2. 10ff., D. 4. 117; Polycarp 3. 20. 4.

190. Ed. Rom. note: "In St. Gregory it reads: *and of every life and action exists; whoever does not hold to them in their entirety, although he thinks himself a stone, lies outside the edifice. The Fifth. . . .* In what follows is mentioned the Three Chapters, on account of which some do not receive the Fifth Synod." Those who refused to accept the Fifth Synod were Nestorians.

191. Ed. Fried. reads "Theodore."

192. *Decretum Gelasianum*; Anselm 6. 204. 15, 17, 27; Burchard 3. 220–22; Ivo Pan. 2. 91, 2. 123, D. 6. 64, 65; Polycarp 3. 20. 2–3. This document, traditionally ascribed to Pope Gelasius I, was probably compiled from earlier materials about A.D. 500 in southern Gaul. Of the original five sections, Gratian has included the fourth and fifth, those concerning received councils and books. On the *Decretum*, see E. Von Dobschütz, "Das *Decretum gelasianum de libris reciendis et non recipiendis*," *Texte und Untersuchengen zür Geschichte der altchristlichen Literatur*, 3. ser., 8. 4 (1912).

193. Ed. Rom. note: "After this in the *Decretum Gelasianum* there follows immediately, *Also, the works of the blessed Cyprian, etc.* But Burchard, Ivo, and the *Panormia* have it as Gratian does. But in this chapter there are so many divergences from the original that it is impossible to determine with certainty what the pure reading of Gelasius is, nor is there to be great surprise if some passages present problems. For this reason, what could be emended by the aid of all the codices has been emended. In other cases, the variants have sometimes been indicated and sometimes, when it would have taken forever to indicate them all, the task of consulting other books has been left to the diligent reader." In the passage that follows, Ed. Fried. omits "Also, the works of the blessed Basil, bishop of Cappadocia" and "Also, the works of the blessed Theophilus, bishop of Alexandria. Also, the works of the blessed Cyril, bishop of Alexandria."

194. Ed. Rom. note: "The section from here to the end of the capitulum is missing from many old codices of Gratian, as even the Archdeacon [Guido of Baysio, *Super Decretum Rosarium* (Lyon, 1549), fol. 17ᵛ)] has noted. It is taken from Gelasius to the words, *In addition, we have decided. . . .* In Burchard and Ivo that appears immediately after the above." Ed. Fried marks the remainder of this capitulum as a palea.

195. Ed. Rom. note: "Previously this read, *Vincent*, the correct reading has been restored from Gelasius, Burchard and Ivo. The blessed Jerome spoke of this Juvencus in his catalogue [*De Viris Illustribus*, LXXXIV]."

196. Ed. Fried. reads "Constantius."

197. Ed. Rom. marginal note: "Original, 'tenth.' "

198. Ed. Rom. note: "In the *Collectio Isidoriana*, it reads, *of Mary and the Midwife*. In Burchard, *and of Mary or the Midwife*. But in Ivo, *and of Saint Mary or of the Midwife of the Savior*."

199. Ed. Rom. marginal note: "Or, 'Lentius,' or, 'Leutius.' "

200. Ed. Rom. marginal note: "Original, 'Passing, that is, the Assumption.' "

201. Ed. Rom. marginal note: "Original: 'Job.' "

202. Ed. Rom. marginal note: "Original: 'which is called the *Lusa* of the Apostles.' "

203. Ed. Rom. marginal note: "Original: 'of Tertullian, apocryphal; the works of Lactantius, apocryphal; the works of Africanus, apocryphal.' "

204. Ed. Rom. marginal note: "Original: 'works of Commodianus, apocryphal.' "

205. Ed. Rom. marginal note: "Original: 'works of Tatius, Cyprian, apocryphal; the works of Arnobius, apocryphal; the works of Tyconius, apocryphal.' "

206. Ed. Rom. marginal note: "Original: 'Frumentus the Blind.' "

207. Ed. Rom. marginal note: "Original: 'Africanus.' "

208. Ed. Rom. marginal note: "Or, 'Calixtus.' "

209. Ed. Rom. marginal note: "Original: 'Julian of Celano.' "

210. Ed. Rom. marginal note: "Original: 'Priscilian of Spain, Nestorius of Constantinople, Maximus the Cynic, Lampedius, etc.' "

211. Ed. Rom. note: "The section from here to the end is found neither in the *Collectio Isidoriana*, nor in any old codex of Gratian that was collated. But from the words, *Some*

appoint the Pentateuch. . . , it is given in Burchard and Ivo without an author's name, and in the *Panormia* as from Gelasius with seventy bishops. Nearly all of it is found there or in the book known as the Roman Ordo."

212. Ed. Rom. marginal note: "In Ivo it reads, *Heptateuch,* so that, beyond the five books, Josiah and Judges are included. Jerome used this word for that set of books when writing to Licinius. But others call it the *Heptaticum,* such as St. Gregory in [*Registrum*], VII, XLVIII (Indiction 2) and X, XXI; and elsewhere both by Rhabanus in the preface to Jeremiah and in the Roman Ordo in the chapter on Septuagesima."

213. The original text gives the scriptural references by the beginning words of each verse, and the Ed. Rom. provides marginal notes indicating the chapter references. We have converted this system into modern chapter and verse citations and suppressed the marginal notes.

214. Ed. Rom. note: "So also Ivo. In the Roman Ordo, in the chapter, 'On the Divine Office from Holy Thursday until Pentecost Octave,' and in Burchard, it reads: *on Psalm 63, which begins, 'Lord hear my prayer when I cry out.'* Also, in the chapter, 'On the Vigil of Easter,' it has *Three from the Treatise of Augustine on Psalm 63.*"

215. Ed. Rom. marginal note: "Ivo: 'Judith, Esther.' "

216. Ed. Rom. note: "The title that precedes the *Canons of the Apostles* in the *Collectio Isidoriana* and in the council of Pope Stephen IV (which is given in great part by Cardinal Deusdedit in his collection) has *issued by* for *handed down through.* Dionysius Exiguus [*Collectio Dionysiana*] makes no mention of this version at all, and certain writers are accustomed to quote the letters of Clement: *From the Sayings of the Apostle Peter put forth through Clement,* as does the author Polycarp and others."

217. *Collectio Hispana,* proem. ; Anselm, proem.; Ivo Tri. 2. proem.

218. *Decretales Pseudo-Isidorianae,* Zephyrinus, I, p. 132; Ivo Pan. 2. 105, D. 4. 107; Polycarp 3. 20. 10. Ed. Rom. note: "This capitulum is in the preface to Isidore's collection of councils, which was copied at the library of Toledo, and sent to Rome. What appears in the common version of Isidore, the beginning of which has been mentioned, seems to read very differently. One should refer to D. 16 c. 4, since that is almost the same as the *Isidoriana.*"

219. Ed. Rom. note: "Ivo and the author of the *Panormia* also have, *sixty.* But the original has this in the margin, in the text it has, *seventy.* Polycarp, *fifty.*"

220. Humbert of Silva Candida, *Responsio in Libellum Nicetae,* XVI; Ivo Pan. 2. 124, D. 4. 105. Ed. Rom. note: "This chapter is taken from the response of Humbert, the legate of Leo IX, to the priest-monk Nicetas's [*Synthesis*] *against the Latins,* [ed. A. Michel (Paderborn, 1924–30)], of which manuscripts exist at Rome in the monastery of Santa Maria Novella and in many private libraries. But it can be correctly cited as of Leo IX because Humbert, who was legate by his authority and command, wrote it."

221. Trullan Synod, c. 2 (Percival tr., p. 361); Ivo Pan. 2. 125, D. 4. 106.

222. *Decretales Pseudo-Isidorianae,* proem., I, p. 17; Ivo Pan. 2. 125, D. 4. 106–7. Ed. Rom. note: "Ivo calls this the 'preface' in his canonical collection. It is given under Isidore's name in his collection of the councils. This is the case even though in the older edition, which contains a purer text of Isidore, certain words are lacking." Ed. Rom. note: "In the *Panormia* this passage is the same as in Gratian. In Ivo and the manuscript codices of that collection it reads: *Isidore Mercator, your fellow servant and father in faith* [Ed. Rom. marginal note on this: "Or, 'faithful father.' "] *in the Lord, greetings.* In the common edition of the councils: *Isidore, a sinner, servant. . . .*"

223. Ed. Rom. marginal note: "Or, 'the seventh synod or council'; or, 'the sixth synod, or in the sixth council.' "

224. Adrian I, *Epistola*, LVII; Ivo Tri. 2. 10ff., D. 4. 122. Cf. *De cons*. D. 3 c. 29. Ed. Rom. note: "This is the reading in the second session of the Seventh Synod in the letter of Adrian to Tarasius. But, there Adrian is giving the text of the synodal letter sent to him by Tarasius. Here Gratian is not giving the words of his letter, which reads in the version in Anastasius the Librarian [*Chronographia Tripartita*]: *We have found contained in the aforesaid synodal letter of Your Holiness, after the profession of the fullness of faith, the sacred Creed, and the six synods, the wonderful report, worthy of all praise and veneration, concerning sacred and venerable affairs. For that reason I also receive the same six synods with all the norms that have been promulgated lawfully and under divine inspiration.* And these last words are even in the very letter of Tarasius, as appears clearly from the Greek version of the council and the new translation."

225. Ed. Rom. note: "In the second and twelfth Vatican versions, it is *sixth*, others have *seventh*; it really was the seventh but on account of the gloss nothing has been changed."

226. Second Council of Nicaea, sessions 4 and 6 (Percival tr., p. 540); Ivo Tri. 2. 10ff., D. 4. 121. Ed. Rom. note: "The words are of Bishop Peter of Nicomedia and Patriarch Tarasius of Constantinople during the fourth session of the Seventh Synod. They are speaking of the 102 canons which were issued in the Trullan Synod at the time of Justinian Rhinotmetus during the second year after his taking the imperial office. From these words of Tarasius it appears that the canons are not properly those of the Sixth Synod, because he says that the canons had been issued four or five years after the conclusion of that synod, when it is completely certain that neither the Roman pontiff nor the original bishops were present. Whatever is to be believed about this chronology should be sought from careful historians like Theophanus (whose own words concerning this problem are found translated faithfully from the Greek, which is extant in the Vatican Library, in Franciscus Turrianus [*De Actis Sextae Synodi* (Florence, 1551)] on the Sixth, Seventh and Eighth synods), Anastasius [*Chronographia Tripartita*], and Georgios Cerdrenus [*Historiarum Compendium*], rather than from Tarasius. They say that it was not four or five years, as Tarasius said, but twenty-seven years from the end of the Sixth Synod, held at the time of Agatho, until this version of the decrees appeared. Their very address to the emperor testifies that those bishops who promulgated them did not want to put them forth as canons of the Sixth Synod, but as a supplement to what seemed lacking in the Fifth and Sixth Synods. And so this should be called a new meeting of the bishops. Thus the Greeks call it, as Balsamon [*In Canones Commentaria*, In Concilio in Trullo, proem. (PG 137:508)], writes, πενθ' ἑκτην, that is the "Quinisex" Synod. Furthermore, Anastasius the Librarian and Humbert, the legate of Leo IX, both of whom know these church matters very well, openly report that those canons were not received by the Roman Church. Humbert [*Responsio in Libellum Nicetae*, XX (PL 143:991–92)], uses these words, *Now I am not amazed if you think Pope Agatho and the holy fathers of the Sixth Synod went mad and corrupted and truncated some capitula, since you would impute delusion even to the Lord Jesus Christ and his Apostles. Since we know that the Sixth Synod was gathered to destroy the Greeks' Monothelite heresy and not to make new enactments for the Romans, we completely reject these capitula you would impose on us by its authority, since the first and Apostolic See has at no time accepted them and does not observe them up to the present.* And Anastasius wrote thus to the Roman pontiff John VIII concerning the Seventh Synod in *Praefatio* [VI (MGH Ep., 7:417)]: *Thus the chief see has introduced into this Seventh Synod the norms, which the Greeks put out as included in the Sixth Synod, in order that none of them that are found to be against earlier canons, the decrees of the holy pontiffs of this see or good morals may be received; because all of them have remained completely unknown among the Latins until this time since they were not translated, and they are not even found in the archives of the other patriarchal sees, although these use the Greek language; and this is*

because none of them promulgated them or consented to them, nor were they even present when they were issued. In spite of this, the Greek fathers who are found to have attended the Sixth Synod put it out that those fathers had done the promulgating, something they have no evidence to prove."

227. Trullan Synod, c. 2 (Percival tr., pp. 359–61); Ivo Tri. 2. 10ff., D. 4. 123. Ed. Rom. note: "Many emendations have been made in this capitulum using canon 2 of those which are attributed to the Sixth Synod, in which it is indicated which councils and authors of canons the Greeks follow. The words of this canon have been given in summary form both in Gratian and Ivo."

228. Ed. Rom. note: "In Greek, it is, τὸ περὶ τῆς πίστεως πατρικῶς διατρανώσασαι μυστήριον, that is, *declaring the mystery of the ancestral faith.*"

229. Ivo Pan. 2. 117, D. 4. 106, 134.

230. Ed. Rom. note: "Ivo has: *we confirm the canons and synods of the holy fathers. . . .* In Greek it is ἐπισφραγίζομεν δὲ καὶ τοὺς λοιποὺς πάντας ἱεροὺς κανόνας τοὺς ὑπὸ τῶν ἁγίων καὶ μακαρίων πατέρων ἡμῶν ἐκτεθέντας, τοῦτ᾽ ἐστιν τῶν ἐν Νικαίᾳ συναθροισθέντων. . . , that is, *placing our seals, we confirm also all the other sacred canons, which have been promulgated by our holy and blessed fathers, that is by those who gathered at Nicaea. . . .*"

231. Ed. Rom. note: "In Ivo there follows, *Constantinople, under Nectarius, and the works of Theodosius (or Theophilus). . . .* In Greek, however, it is, καὶ τῶν αὖθις ἐνταύτῃ τῇ θεοφυλάκτῳ καὶ βασιλίδι πόλει συνελθόντων ἐπι Νεκταρίου τοῦ τῆς βασιλίδος ταύτης πόλεως προέδρου, καὶ Θεοφίλου τοῦ γενομένου ᾽Αλεξανδρείας ἀρχιεπισκόπου, that is, *and of those who again convened in the God-protected and imperial city, under Nectarius, bishop of this imperial city, and Theophilus who was archbishop of Alexandria.*"

232. Ed. Rom. note: "This is approximately what it is in the canon issued in Greek, but earlier it read in Gratian, *Dionysius of Alexandria, bishop and martyr.* But in Balsamon [PG 137:521] and Ivo it reads, just as it has been restored, *Dionysius, archbishop of the metropolis of Alexandria, and Peter of Alexandria, bishop and martyr.* The diligent reader will discover other variants himself."

233. Ed. Rom. marginal note: "Or, 'Germanus.' " Ed. Fried. reads "Germanus."

234. Ed. Rom. note: "There is an error in this part of the canon, because it is known that Cyprian's synod, which he attended with many other bishops of Africa, believed that those who had been baptized by the heretics had not received a true baptism. Blessed Augustine, however, said that there was another tradition of the Apostles, and he testified that the opinion of Cyprian had been nullified by the plenary council of the whole world."

235. *Liber Diurnus,* 83; Ivo Pan. 2. 103, Tri. 2. 10ff., D. 4. 132. Ed. Rom. note: "Cardinal Deusdedit gives the entire profession of faith professed when one is elevated to Roman pontiff in the collection of canons that is preserved in the Vatican Library."

236. Bede, *Chronicon de Sex Aetatibus Mundi,* LXV (MGH Auct. Ant. 14); Ivo Pan. 2. 113, Tri. 2. 10ff., D. 14. 125.

237. Ed. Rom. note: "It is certain that the First Nicene Synod was celebrated in the time of Silvester. But in the darkness of those times it is not surprising that Bede and others erred."

238. Ed. Fried. omits this paragraph and replaces it with "[*Lacking*]."

239. Ed. Fried. reads "Julius."

240. This capitulum and the next are found before the preface to the *Decretales Pseudo-Isidorianae* in some mss. and were printed in *Tomus Primus Quattuor Conciliorum Generalium,* ed. Jean Merlin (Paris, 1524), and in the later Cologne editions mentioned by the Roman Correctors.

Ed. Rom. note: "This capitulum is found in the more recent edition, *Conciliorum* [*Quatuor Generalium Tomus Primus*, ed. P. Crabbe (Cologne, 1538)] and in the older edition (Cologne, 1530), as well as in the manuscript of the collection preserved in the Vatican Library. But it is not in the collection that is in the monastery of the Dominicans. It is placed before the preface which carries the name of Isidore *Mercator* in the manuscripts but of Isidore, *sinner*, in the printed versions. Logically mention is made of only four councils in the preface, since the sixth was held only after the time of Isidore of Spain."

241. Ed. Rom. note: "So it is in both Anselm and Gratian. In the original is *Alexander of Constantinople*. But the incorrupt reading would seem to be a combination of both since he was bishop of Constantinople, and at the time of this synod, the bishop of Alexandria was also called Alexander."

242. Ed. Fried. adds "that of one-hundred-fifty fathers."

243. Ed. Rom. note: "Previously this read, as it does in Anselm, *Nectarius of Alexandria*. It has been emended from the original. But the incorrupt reading in this passage may well have been *Nectarius of Constantinople and Timothy of Alexandria*."

244. Ed. Fried. reads "three hundred."

245. Ed. Rom. marginal note: "Original: 'the Great.' "

246. Ed. Fried. reads "fifteen."

247. Ed. Rom. marginal note: "Or, 'God the Word to be one thing and Christ to be another.' "

248. Ed. Fried. reads "Gregory."

249. Ed. Rom. note: "In the passage quoted from the *Collectio Isidoriana*, it reads, *they wrote eight capitula*, and the words *which are appended below* are lacking. In the councils printed at Cologne, after the session of the Sixth Synod, nine capitula are added from the old codex of the monastery of St. Bavo, and before the first chapter there are the words, *they wrote nine capitula, which are appended below*, which is also found in Anselm."

250. Ed. Rom. note: "The greater part of this capitulum, that is, up to *Nineteenth*, is found in the printed edition of the *Isidoriana* before the preface by the same Isidore; in the Vatican version it goes up to *Twenty-first*. Deusdedit and Anselm place the entire text at the beginning of their collections. This does not seem to be an abbreviation of the same Isidore, since it corresponds neither to his preface nor to his collection, in which other variants occur, many concerning councils in Spain, of which no mention is made here."

251. Ed. Rom. marginal note: "In the common Greek version and in Balsamon [PG 137:1121–96] there are twenty-six canons."

252. Ed. Rom. note: "This has been emended from Anselm, Deusdedit, and the Vatican collection. Previously it read *Antioch*. In the printed edition of Isidore, however, it reads, *Nicaea* but the word *before* is lacking. That this should read as emended is shown by the words that precede the Council of Neocaesarea, οἵτινες δεύτεροι μέν εἰσι τῶν ἐν ᾿Αγκύρᾳ, τῶν δὲ ἐν Νικαίᾳ προγενέστεροι, that is, *the canons that are after Ancyra but before Nicaea*. This passage is corrupt in the printed version of Isidore which has, *These second canons are those which were put forth at Ancyra and Caesarea*. The reading *and Caesarea* is redundant and has been omitted in recent editions of the councils. A similar error is found in the codex of canons at Mainz."

253. Ed. Fried. reads "eighteen."

254. Ed. Fried. reads "seventeen."

255. Ed. Fried. reads "Eustasius."

256. Ed. Rom. note: "In the codex of canons, forty bishops are found to have subscribed, but afterwards is added, *and others, and all the bishops of the various provinces and cities, to the number of 121 subscribed*. Socrates [*Historia Ecclesiastica*], II, xvi, says concerning

the same council, that around three hundred western bishops attended, while seventy-six of those from the East created a schism. Nicephorus [*Chronologia*] *Tripartita*, IX, XII, says the same. Theodoret [*Historia Ecclesiastica*], II, VII, however, says, from old histories, that 250 gathered. From all this the number of fathers and canons has been completely emended. But among the many versions there seems to be a considerable variation, the investigation of which is left to the diligent reader."

257. Ed. Rom. note: "Anselm has it as Gratian. In the collection referred to, it is *Vincent, bishop of Capua and legate of the holy Roman Church were present.* In c. 18 of the council itself, Bishop Januarius is named. But he is not named in the list of subscribers, but rather Vincent of Capua, legate of the holy Roman Church and Calepodius of Naples, legate of the holy Roman Church, are."

258. Ed. Fried. reads "thirty."

259. Ed. Fried. reads "twenty-two."

260. Ed. Fried. reads "fifty-eight."

261. Ed. Rom. note: "Here is listed only the synod of Carthage that is found in the version of the canons treated below at D. 20 c. 1."

262. Ed. Fried. reads "two-hundred-eight."

263. Ed. Fried. reads "two-hundred-twenty-four."

264. Ed. Fried. reads "six hundred."

265. Ed. Fried. omits "four."

266. Ed. Fried. reads "eighteen."

267. Ed. Rom. note: "This is so emended from several manuscripts and the Vatican collection of Isidore. Earlier it read *Empauensis*. Nevertheless, in the printed version of the council of Albon, Caesarius is not mentioned, rather mention is made first of Avitus."

268. Ed. Fried. reads "forty."

269. Ed. Fried. reads "thirty-three."

270. Ed. Rom. note: "Here are listed three councils of Orleans that appear in the printed versions of the councils. At Fifth Orleans, Aurelius of Arles subscribed first. In the first, among others, is found the name of Melanius of Rennes. In the third, Aubin of Angiers subscribed in fourth place."

271. Ed. Fried. reads "Aurelian."

272. Ed. Fried. omits "in the time of King Clovis."

273. Ed. Fried. reads "twenty-five."

274. Ed. Fried. reads "sixty-eight."

275. Ed. Fried. reads "seventeen."

276. *Decretales Pseudo-Isidorianae*, Epistola Athanasii, p. 452; Anselm 1. 59; Ivo Pan. 2. 106, D. 4. 108; Polycarp 3. 20. 6. Ed. Rom. marginal note: "There is much more than what is given here in the letter of Athanasius and all the bishops of Egypt to Pope Mark."

277. Ed. Rom. note: "From these words of Athanasius it would seem that not all the canons of the Synod of Nicaea are extant today in either the Greek or Latin versions. Pope Julius to the Easterners and Innocent to Victricius quote many canons to which they had access that are not in the twenty. Isidore writes about this in the preface that is included in his collection of councils. From a certain letter of Gregory X to the king of the Armenians, which speaks of the Council of Lyon [II, A.D. 1274] (a manuscript of which belongs to [Guglielmo] Cardinal Sirleto), it can be gathered that at that time the text of the entire Council of Nicaea existed in Armenian. He wrote thus: *Since it is in many ways useful that during the celebration of the council we have access to the fullness of the ancient councils, we request and attentively urge your Royal Highness that you send to us with all dispatch as much as possible of the whole council of Nicaea and those other councils that you say you have in the*

Armenian language, along with some expert interpreters. At Tunis and Alexandria, eighty canons ascribed to this council have been found written in Arabic. These are in writing at Rome in the possession of the same Cardinal Sirleto in Arabic and Armenian, and shall soon be translated into Latin and printed."

On the number of canons of Nicaea, see C. Hefele and H. Leclercq, *Histoire des conciles d'après les documents originaux* (Paris, 1907), I, 503–28. The additional canons, four or more, preserved in the Coptic, Syriac, Armenian, and Arabic versions of the council, are not authentic, ibid., I, 511–15.

278. Ed. Fried. reads "seventy."

279. Ed. Fried. reads "thirty."

280. Ed. Fried. reads "thirty."

281. Stephen V, *Epistola* VII; Ivo Pan. 2. 107, D. 4. 232; cf. JL 3443. Ed. Rom. note: "In Ivo D. 4. 232, the beginning of this chapter is more complete: *We do not doubt that the chapters of the Council of Nicaea, in the report of Athanasius, are seventy as a figure of the seventy disciples, of these only twenty are accepted by the holy Roman Church. . . .*"

282. Nicholas I, *Epistola*, Ad Res Orientales Pertinentes, LXXXIII, p. 440; Ivo Pan. 2. 110, Tri. 1. 63. 15, D. 4. 135.

The Council of Sardica was convoked in 342 by the emperors Constans I and Constantius II at the request of Pope Julius I to investigate the deposition of Athanasius of Alexandria and his associates. It rehabilitated Athanasius and issued disciplinary canons regulating ecclesiastical order and reaffirming the right of appealing to Rome (as Athanasius had done). Because of these disciplinary canons the council was never received by many Eastern churches, but it was held in high regard in the West.

283. *Decretales Pseudo-Isidorianae*, Epistola Athanasii, p. 452; Anselm 2. 60; Ivo Tri. 1. 29. 1, D. 4. 240; Polycarp 1. 16. 1. Ed. Rom. note on the heading: "Previously this read, *to Bishop Maxentius*; but, in the collections of the councils, the heading of this letter read, *to Maxentius the Tyrant.* But at the beginning of the letter itself it read, *Marcellus to Maxentius*, which reading it seems should be retained."

284. Ed. Rom. note: "From here to the end is not found in some exemplar manuscripts of Gratian." Ed. Fried. marks the rest of this chapter as a palea.

285. *Decretales Pseudo-Isidorianae*, Decreta Julii Papae, XIII, p. 471; Anselm 2. 47; Polycarp 1. 16. 2.

286. *Decretales Pseudo-Isidorianae*, Decreta Damasi Papae, XXI, p. 508; Anselm 1. 54; Polycarp 2. 19. 5.

287. Pelagius I, *Epistola* LIX, 7; Anselm 12. 42; Ivo D. 4. 239; Polycarp 1. 16. 9. Ed. Rom. note: "Without a doubt this passage is from Pelagius, and is so cited by Anselm and Ivo. There are also many passages in Gratian taken from Pelagius, saying that recourse is to be made to the apostolic sees because a universal synod has established this; and that those not in communion with the apostolic sees are to be especially condemned, as in C. 23 q. 5 c. 42 & 43. In D. 17 c. 4 and C. 11 q. 1 c. 20 the entire letter of Pelagius as given by Anselm can be found. In Polycarp it is cited as by Gregory and in the margin is added, *to the bishops of Mauritania.* Also in the summaries of the capitula of the said pope that are found in Gregory VII, in *Register,* II, among other things we find this: *that no general synod ought to be called without the command of the supreme pontiff.*"

288. Ed. Rom. note: "In Anselm, Ivo, and Polycarp this is added, *to judge a universal synod.* This is what is prohibited here by Pelagius. For there were many at that time who, led astray by ignorance or perversity of spirit, refused to accept the Fifth Synod (on this, Gregory VII wrote in *Registrum*, VII, LIII and many other places), and they preferred their local synods to a universal one or one with apostolic authority. By this capitulum neither Pelagius or

Gregory forbade bishops to hold diocesan synods or metropolitans to hold provincial ones, but rather prohibited that they by themselves pass judgment on universal ones. Thus the rubric has been emended."

289. Ed. Rom. marginal note: "Or, 'learn.' " Ed. Fried. reads "learn."

290. Ed. Rom. marginal note: "Or, 'eradicated.' " Ed. Fried. reads "eradicated."

291. *Decretales Pseudo-Isidorianae*, Epistola Pelagii II ad Omnes Episcopos, pp. 721, 724–75; Anselm 2. 36; Ivo D. 5. 12; Polycarp 1. 16. 7.

' This letter relates to the famous controversy over the use of the title "Ecumenical Patriarch" by John IV the Faster (582–95) of Constantinople. This usage was approved during his reign by a council held in Constantinople. Pope Pelagius II (579–90), who saw this as an attack on papal primacy, violently objected to the usage, and ordered his legate to abstain from communion at John's liturgies. The controversy continued into the reign of Pope Gregory the Great.

292. Capitulum 6 and *dicta Gratiani post* c. 6: Ennodius, *Libellus contra eos qui contra Synodum Scribere Praesumpserunt*, IV; Anselm 2. 57, 3. 105; Ivo D. 4. 242; Polycarp 1. 86.

293. Ed. Rom. note: "In Ennodius's book and in more recent editions this sentence is punctuated as a question. These are the words of Symmachus's enemies, presented as if they were a ludicrous opinion. Symmachus responds to them in what follows beginning, *Have you. . . ."*

294. Gregory I, *Registrum*, IX, CCXXII (Barmby tr., p. 28); Anselm 6. 134 [131]. Ed. Fried. prints this capitulum in italics.

295. First Council of Braga, c. 6; Burchard 1. 55; Ivo Pan. 4. 20, D. 5. 165. Ed. Rom. note: "In a very old codex of Gratian this palea is attached to the end of the preceding distinction, joined to the end of c. 7. The other collections cite it as from the Council of Châlons; but it is found in the Council of Braga, c. 24, the Council of Mileum, c. 13, and the Council of Africa, c. 53."

Unless otherwise noted, the conciliar texts cited in this and the following distinctions follow the recension known as the *Collectio Hispana*, which the Roman Correctors usually refer to as the "Collection of Isidore." This collection of conciliar texts was compiled, probably by Isidore of Seville, in the early 600s. Medieval authors, however, did not attribute the collection to him. On the vast influence of this collection on medieval canon law, see G. Le Bras, "Sur la part d'Isidore de Séville et des espagnols dans l'histoire des collections canoniques," *Revue de science réligieux* 10 (1930), 218–57.

The Roman Correctors also refer to the parallel texts in the collection of Dionysius Exiguus, usually known as the *Collectio Dionysiana*. Dionysius compiled this text in the early 500s and it became the favored canonical collection of the Roman Church until the late Middle Ages. Dionysius also compiled a collection of papal letters, the *Collectio Decretorum*, to which references will also be made.

296. Leo I, *Epistola* XIV, 7 (Feltoe tr., p. 18); Anselm 2. 29; Burchard 1. 43; Ivo Pan. 4. 13, D. 4. 241; Polycarp 3. 19. 4, 1. 17. 7.

297. Council of Nicaea, c. 5 (Percival tr., p. 13); Anselm 3. 13; Polycarp 3. 19. 5. Ed. Rom. note: "This chapter is taken from the version used by Isidore. That text, however, reads, *a pure gift solemn to God*; in Polycarp and some codices of Gratian, it reads, *a pure and solemn gift to God*. The Greek is, ἵνα τάσης μικροψυχίας ἀναιρουμένης τὸ δῶρον καθαρὸν προςφέρηται τῷ θεῷ, that is, *that, having restrained the whole soul, a pure gift be offered to God.*"

298. Council of Antioch, c. 20 (Percival tr., p. 118); Burchard 1. 44; Ivo Pan. 4. 15, D. 5. 154; Polycarp 3. 19.

299. Ed. Rom. note: "Dionysius construes the word ἐπιτελεῖσθαι as *convene.*"

300. Ed. Rom. note: "This previously read, *in the middle of the time between Easter and Pentecost*. It is not much different in Ivo, *that is, in the middle of the time.* . . . But this reading has been restored from many exemplars of Gratian and the collection of Isidore, which has the same reading. Other collections seem to follow what Dionysius has in his collection of canons. Burchard and the *Panormia*, however, have *that is, in the middle of Pentecost*, or *in the middle of Pentecost*, where in the version of Dionysius it has *so that it be the fourth week of Pentecost*. This follows word for word the Greek, ὥστε τῇ τετάρτῃ ἑβ-δομάδι τῆς πεντεκοστῆς." This confusion is the result of the difficulty in translating the Greek word "Pentecost" (literally meaning "fifty") into Latin. The Greek word is used not only for the feast of "Pentecost" on the fiftieth day after Easter but also for the fifty-day period itself.

301. Ed. Rom. note: "This is a literal translation of the Greek. Dionysius, who is followed by Burchard and Ivo, has, *the Ides of October, that is the fifteenth day of the month of October, which the Greeks call Hyperberetaeus*. In canon 37 of the Apostles it is read that the second synod of the year is to be celebrated, ὑπερβερεταῖου δωδεκάτη, that is, *on the twelfth of Hyperberetaeus*. It is clear enough that the Latin months do not at all accord with the Greek. In the *Suida* it says that among the Macedonians, Hyperberetaeus is the same as October; but Galen of Pergamum says that it is the same as September."

302. Council of Laodicea, c. 40 (Percival tr., p. 152); Burchard 1. 47; Ivo Tri. 2. 7. 18, D. 5. 157.

303. Council of Chalcedon, c. 19 (Percival tr., p. 282); Anselm 3. 14; Ivo Tri. 2. 10. 19, D. 4. 243.

304. Ed. Rom. note: "In the collection of Isidore, where there is in general the same text, it reads, *from this it is proved that many.* . . . The same is found in Ivo, with the addition of the particle, *and*. The Greek is, καὶ ἐκ τούτου πολλὰ παραμελεῖται τῶν διορθώσεως δεομέ-νων ἐκκλησιαστικῶν πραγμάτων, that is, *and furthermore, many of those ecclesiastical affairs that require correction are neglected.*"

305. Ed. Rom. note: "So also in Isidore, Ivo, and Anselm. The Greek is, ἔνθα ἂν ὁ τῆς μετροπόλεως ἐπίσκοπος δοκιμάσῃ, καὶ διορθοῦν ἕκαστα τὰ ἀνακύπτοντα, which Dionysius translates, *where the metropolitan bishop may check to correct whatever should perchance require it.*"

306. Second Council of Nicaea, c. 6, in the version of Athanasius the Librarian (Percival tr., pp. 559–60); Ivo Tri. 2. 18. 8, D. 5. 373; cf. First Council of Nicaea, c. 5, Council of Antioch, c. 20.

307. Ed. Rom. note: "The Greek is, καὶ τὸ ἐνδεῶς ἔχειν πρὸς ὁδοιπορίαν, that is, *and are well prepared for traveling.*"

308. Leo IV, *Epistolae Selectae*, XVI, 6. Ivo Tri. 1. 60. 5; cf. JE 2599.

309. Fourth Council of Carthage, c. 21; Anselm 7. 191; cf. Burchard 1. 51 and Polycarp 2. 16.

310. Fifth Council of Carthage, c. 10; Anselm 7. 188; Ivo Tri. 2. 19. 10.

311. Ed. Rom. note: "In the printed versions of the councils it reads, *in a summary* [tractoria]. It has been questioned whether this should not be read, *in a summons* [tractatoria], since the letters by which emperors and kings convoke their subordinates or concede any exemption are called *summonses*. So *Codex Theo.*, VIII, VI, is entitled 'On Summonses and Lodging Places.' Nevertheless, in the printed versions we read, *summaries*, which Charlemagne uses with the same meaning as *summonses* in his *Capitularies*, IV, cc. 30 and 69; and the same usage is found in the Council of Meaux, c. 71. Saint Augustine in chapter 34 of his book after the meeting against the Donatists uses *summonses* for letters of invitation, in these words: *If, however, they had been called by their primate through his summons*. In this canon,

where the calling of bishops to a council is treated, it would be a very apt word. For in the Council of Africa, c. 43, which is included in the codex of canons, where the same text is also found, and in c. 57, § Lucianus and § Alypius, the oldest versions always read *summonses* where the printed versions have *summaries*. In the Greek version of the Council of Carthage it is ἡ συνοδική. But the blessed Augustine also used the form *summary* for what is now submitted for a decision. Speaking concerning bishops who refuse to come to a council when called, when they purge themselves of charges brought, he says in letter 162: *Because, if they did not do this, let their depravity and perversity be known, and let summaries be sent with their names from the churches throughout the whole world where the Church of Christ extends, that they be deprived of communion.* In his second sermon on Psalm 36, we find the same word four times. And in the letter of Syricus that was read in the Council of Telepte these are called *summaries*. Innocent made reference to these in his letter to Exuperius of Toledo, chapter I, *Concerning these things, the clear warnings of that man of blessed memory, Bishop Syricus, go out*; these words seem to indicate that the same Syricus sent his summary not only to the African bishops but to all the provinces. So Pope Leo II, at the end of the Sixth Universal Council, sent his brief summary of that council to the bishops of Spain, so that they might subscribe. What were sent from Spain to Rome were called *summaries* in the manuscript letter of Leo II."

312. Ed. Rom. note: "In the original, it is: *or if after the arrival of the summary some necessity should perchance have suddenly arisen, unless they have presented an explanation of his impediment before their primate, they ought to be separated from the communion of their church.* In Council of Africa, c. 43, the rest follows in the same manner. But at the end it reads, like Gratian, *they ought to be limited to the communion of their own church.* In the Greek version of the Council of Carthage, it reads, ᾽Οφείλειν τοὺς τοιούτους τῇ κοινωνίᾳ τῆς ἰδίας αὐτῶν ἀρκεῖσθαι ἐκκλησίας. A similar penalty is imposed by the same council below at D. 58 c. 2."

313. Theodore of Tarsus, *Canones*, II, III (McNeil tr., p. 200); Burchard 8. 73; Ivo D. 7. 91. Ed. Rom. note: "This palea is missing from all the exemplars in which the palea are very few; it is given below by Gratian from the Council of Tours at the end of C. 18 q. 2 c. 31, as it is by Burchard and Ivo."

314. Second Council of Arles, c. 19; Ivo Tri. 2. 24. 6; as from the Council of *Spalensis* in Burchard 1. 50; Ivo D. 5. 160; and Polycarp 2. 15. 1.

315. Council of Agde, c. 35; Anselm 3. 29; Burchard 1. 49; Ivo Pan. 4. 17, Tri. 2. 28. 34, D. 5. 159.

316. Council of Tarragona, c. 6; cf. Pan. 4. 18.

317. Martin of Braga, *Capita Martini*, XVIII; Ivo Tri. 2. 47. 18; Polycarp 3. 17; but cf. Council of Antioch, c. 20 (Percival tr., p. 118); cf. D. 18 c. 4. Ed. Rom. note: "Gratian here quotes this under the name of Pope Martin I, and later many other texts under the same name. These are all taken from the book of capitula of the Greek synods of Bishop Martin of Braga. (In antiquity bishops were called 'popes.') This man, since he was a Greek, translated the capitula into Latin for the use of the church of Spain, where he had his diocese. In some capitula he added certain things, in others he subtracted, as in this chapter, which he took from the Council of Antioch, c. 20, as above at D. 18 c. 4. He gives other passages from the Council of Toledo in his collection."

318. Ed. Rom. note: "In some old editions of the councils, it reads, *that the causes of those who consider themselves wronged, [can come before] the council. . . .*"

319. On this text, see Ed. Fried. p. 57–58, n. 108. Ed. Rom. note: "This text is found in none of the collated exemplars; rather, the sentence is joined to the preceding chapter, as are the *dicta* of Gratian."

320. Sixteenth Council of Toledo, c. 7.

321. Ed. Rom. note: "In two exemplars of the Sixteenth Council of Toledo, this passage reads, *Then, since everything has been explained publicly in their presence that concerns the things done or decided in the council that year, let them be fully informed.*"

322. Nicholas I, *Epistola*, De Causis Rothadi, LXXI, pp. 393–95; Ivo Tri. 1. 62. 10, 11, D. 5. 33.

323. Ed. Fried. adds "and so are not to be included among the canons."

324. Ed. Rom. note: "This passage has been emended from the same letter of Nicholas that is found in the Roman manuscript, which has recently been published in [Marguerin de La Bigne], *Appendix Bibliothecae Sanctorum Patrum* [(Paris, 1579)], as was said above at D. 10 c. 1. In this letter are many other things touching on the most ancient decretal letters."

325. Pope Innocent I, in Dionysius Exiguus, *Collectio Decretorum*, Decreta Innocenti, XXVII (PL 67:248).

326. Leo I, in Dionysius Exiguus, *Collectio Decretorum*, Decreta Leonis, 5 (PL 67:280). Ed. Fried. marks this paragraph as a palea.

327. *Decretum Gelasianum*; cf. D. 15 c. 3, at "Also, the decretal letters."

328. Agatho (fragment) JE 2108; Ivo D. 4. 238; Polycarp 1. 19. 6.

329. Council of Trebur, c. 30. As of Council of Trier: Burchard 1. 220; Ivo Tri. 3. 8. 6 [3. 9. 6], D. 5. 50. As of Charlemagne: Ivo Pan. 2. 101, Tri. 3. 8. 6 [3. 9. 6]. Ed. Rom. note on the heading: "This has been so emended from some manuscripts and Ivo. [Johannes] Nauclerus [*Memorabilium Omnis Aetatis et Omnium Gentium Chronici Commentarii*], II, XXVII, says that this is one of twenty-three capitula of laws that Charlemagne sent to all his provinces. Burchard quotes it from the Council of Trier, c. 30, where it is still extant."

330. Ed. Fried. omits "with just order."

331. Ivo Tri. 1. 64. 6. The letter, ascribed erroneously to Pope Stephen V in Mansi, XVI, 437–38, is probably adapted from *Decretales Pseudo-Isidorianae*, Stephen I, I, p. 180.

332. Gregory IV, *Epistola* XIV, p. 77; Anselm 2. 21; Ivo D. 5. 11, 5. 349; Polycarp 1. 19. 13. Ed. Rom. note: "This capitulum is in the same letter of Gregory IV that was taken as C. 2 q. 6 c. 11. It is extant in the oft-mentioned codex of the Dominican library."

333. Augustine, *De Doctrina Christiana*, II, VIII, 12 (Robertson tr., p. 41); Anselm 6. 212; Polycarp 1. 27. 8. Ed. Rom. note: "This capitulum reads as follows in the work of the blessed Augustine: *In regard to canonical writings he should follow the authority of the greater number of Catholic churches, among which are certainly those which have deserved to possess apostolic sees and to have received epistles. Accordingly he will observe this rule concerning canonical writings: one will prefer those received by all Catholic churches to those that some do not receive; among those which are not received by all, one should prefer those accepted by the larger number of weightier authority to those held by fewer of lesser authority. If, however, one discovers that some books are received by the greater number of churches, and others by the churches of greater authority (although this will not occur), I think that they are then to be held as of equal authority.* The blessed Augustine's opinion does not concern decretals of the Roman pontiffs but rather the canon of sacred Scripture."

334. Leo I, *Epistola* X, 1 (Feltoe tr., p. 8); Ivo D. 5. 6.

335. Ed. Rom. marginal note: "Or, 'ministry.'"

336. Anastasius II, *Epistola* I, 7–8 (Thiel 8. 622); Anselm 2. 25, 9. 62, 13. 31; Ivo Tri. 1. 47. 1, 2, D. 1. 151; Polycarp 3. 10. 10, 3. 22. 2. The conciliatory Anastasius II followed Pope Gelasius I in 496 and moved to end the so-called Acacian Schism by recognizing Acacius's baptisms and ordinations and by reconciling his followers, in particular the deacon Photinus who represented the bishop of Thessalonica, on easy terms. This "soft" line was the occasion of a schism by more hard-line Roman clergy, during which Anastasius died. The *Liber*

Pontificalis, LII, representing this hard-line view, ascribed the pope's death to divine vengeance and gave birth to the medieval legend of Anastasius II's "apostasy." Dante contributed to this legend by placing Anastasius in hell (*Inferno* XI, 8). On the Acacian Schism and Anastasius II, see P. Charanis, *Church and State in the Late Roman Empire*, 2d ed. (Thessalonica: Kentron Vyzontinon Ereunon, 1974). The notes of the Roman Correctors on this and the following capitulum refer to these events and correct the misinterpretations that gave rise to the medieval legend.

Ed. Rom. note: "It is hardly true that Anastasius thought that those who were ordained by Acacius after he had been excommunicated could properly exercise the offices they had received. This is the case, even if he says in this capitulum that they had received the sure grace of the sacrament from Acacius. This is most certainly correct, since all the other opinions that Anastasius took into his letter from blessed Augustine are true. This same letter of Pope Anastasius II is found in the corpus of canons that the Roman Church has always approved, as is noted below at D. 20 c. 1. Thus Gratian is here criticizing Anastasius without reason." Both Augustine and Anastasius II are here upholding the Catholic position that sacramental efficacy is not affected by the moral quality of the minister against the Donatist heresy that denied this.

337. Ed. Fried. adds "God."

338. *Dicta Gratiani* and c. 9: Alger of Liège, *De Misericordia*, III, 59; c. 9: *Liber Pontificalis*, LII (Duchesne ed., vol. 1, p. 258); Ivo D. 14. 40. On Alger, see R. Kretzschmar, "Algar von Lüttichs Tractatat *De Misericordia et Iustitia* (XII cent.)," *Quellen und Forschungen zum Recht im Mittelalter*, 2, (Sigmaringen: Thorbecke, 1985), p. 146; and Stanley Chodorow, *Christian Political Theory and Church Politics in the Mid-Twelfth Century* (Berkeley: Univ. of Calif. Press, 1972), pp. 138–39.

Ed. Rom. note: "This capitulum concerning the life of Anastasius is taken from the second tome of councils. But it is a complete fabrication, as, from many possible texts, it can be manifestly shown that Acacius died at the time of Felix III (as Nicephorus [*Chronologia Tripartita*], XVI, XII; Evagrius, *Ecclesiastical History*, III, XVIII and following; and, above all, Athanasius the Librarian in the chronology [given in *Praefatio* IX (MGH Ep. 7:424)], all testify). His successor was Gelasius, and his successor was Anastasius, who in the salutation and chapter 1 of his letter to Emperor Anastasius wrote that Acacius was already dead and stood before Christ the Judge along with Felix, something that Gelasius had written even before that, as is found below in C. 24 q. 2 c. 4. How then could Anastasius have dealt with reinstating someone who was already dead?"

339. First Council of Constantinople, c. 4 (Percival tr., p. 179); Ivo Tri. 2. 8. 4. Ed. Rom. note: "From the words of this canon (especially in Greek in the translation of Balsamon [PG 137:328–9]), the *Life of Gregory the Theologian* written by Gregory the Priest, and other writings (Theodoret seems to have treated this carefully), it appears that Maximus was never a bishop and, furthermore, it was rightly ruled that no one had given him episcopal orders, something which could not be asserted of Acacius. Here are the words of the Greek canon: Περὶ Μαξίμου τοῦ κυνικοῦ καὶ τῆς κατ' αὐτὸν ἀταξίας τῆς ἐν Κωνσταντινουπόλει γενομένης. Ὥστε μήτε [τὸν] Μάξιμον ἐπίσκοπον ἢ γενέσθαι ἢ εἶναι, μήτε τοὺς παρ' αὐτοῦ χειροτονηθέντας ἐν οἰῳδήποτε βαθμῷ κλήρου, πάντων καὶ τῶν περὶ αὐτὸν καὶ τῶν παρ' αὐτοῦ γενομένων ἀκυρωθέντων, that is, *Concerning Maximus the Cynic and those things that happened concerning him and his lack of orders in Constantinople. That Maximus neither was, nor is, a bishop, nor are those ordained by him to be reckoned to be in any grade of the clergy; everything done to him or by him, being invalid.* There is ample testimony that the same Maximus was never a bishop in the letter of Pope Adrian written to the emperor Basil, which is found in the first session of the Seventh Synod in a manuscript of Cardinal Sirleto.

Quoting Leo I, he says, *The thundering trumpet, that is Leo, pope of the Apostolic See, whose utterance each and every Catholic takes as a celestial miracle and venerates as an oracle, says, 'Since problems often arise concerning unworthily received office, who would question that what appears not to have been granted is never to be ascribed to them? Nor are we convinced that there is any difference between the adulterer Photius and Maximus the Cynic, condemned by the Second Synod, and between the orders of the former and the latter.'* "

340. Leo IV, *Epistola*, XVI, 14; Anselm 3. 123; Ivo Pan. 2. 118, Tri. 3. 6. 5, 1. 60. 9, D. 4. 72; Polycarp 3. 20. 5.

341. Ed. Rom. note: "This indicates the canons and rules from which the body or collection of canons has been made. It also says in the preface that the Roman pontiffs used them especially in passing judgments. In that collection there are, as Nicholas writes in D. 19 c. 1, no synodal acts, but only canons."

342. Ed. Fried omits: "Antioch, Laodicea, Constantinople, Ephesus, Chalcedon."

343. Ed. Rom. note: "In the collection of canons there is a single Synod of Carthage containing thirty-three canons, which had been collected from various councils held at Carthage. The Apostolic See seems to have approved and used those canons when it entered them in the collection of canons. These same canons are found in Greek in the same order as among the Latins, because they translated them into their language along with many others from African synods. These are the canons that Anselm, Burchard, and Ivo quote using a single numbering; but Gratian, when he employs them, considers them as being from the different councils of Carthage, as he indicates on each occasion. This single synod of Carthage is to be identified with that referred to above in D. 16 c. 11 in the paragraph beginning *The Seventh*, in accord with what has been put forth above as an explanation." On these councils, see H. LeClercq, *L'Afrique chrétienne*, 2d ed., 2 vols. (Paris: Lecoffre, 1904).

344. Ed. Rom. marginal note: "In Anselm and Polycarp, all the names of the Roman Pontiffs are lacking." Ed. Fried. reads: "Hilary, Gelasius, Hormisdas, and Gregory III."

345. Ed. Rom. note: "Anselm, Deusdedit, and Gregory the Priest in Polycarp, have at this point, *who does not receive them all, shows himself to have in no way preserved the Catholic and apostolic faith unto his salvation.*"

346. Nicholas I, *Epistola*, Ad Res Orientales Pertinentes, LXXXVI, p. 450; Anselm 3. 33; Ivo Tri. 1. 64. 16; cf. D. 16 c. 14.

347. Pseudo-Innocent I (fragment) JK 320; *Collectio Hibernesis* 19. 1; Burchard 3. 128; Ivo Tri. 3. 6. 3 [3. 7. 3], D. 4. 76; Polycarp 7. 2. 4. Ed. Rom. note: "This passage is not found among the many extant letters of Innocent I; nor can it be from Innocent II since Burchard and Ivo wrote before him, and it is quoted by them."

348. Ed. Rom. note: "These words are lacking in Gratian, but they are in Burchard, Ivo, and Polycarp; they have been restored from the passage as it is found in Polycarp." Sentence is lacking in Ed. Fried.

NOTES TO THE GLOSS

(1) This text says that the world is ruled by two things: the authority of pontiffs and royal power.

(2) This text says that if a debtor pays one of several debts he owes a creditor without indicating which of them he means to pay, the creditor can decide which debt is discharged provided he makes this decision as he would were he the debtor.

(3) These texts distinguish practices to be observed throughout the Church from those that may vary locally.

(4) Reading "Vivianus" for "Julianus" as the title of the law.

(5) Ed. Rom. says, "Properly speaking, they are not contrary to reason but beyond reason."

(6) Ed. Rom. says, "Reason is either depraved or infirm when it is not helpful for salvation."

(7) Citation is to [C.] 32. q. 7. quid adulterio; c. 16 begins "quid in omnibus peccatis est adulterio."

(8) In this text, Augustine deals with the famous case put by Cicero (*De Officiis* III, xxv, 95) in which a person becomes insane after depositing his sword with another, and then demands it back. According to Augustine, the sword need not be returned to the owner even if its custodian had promised to do so on demand. The gloss (to "furens") explains that all promises have the tacit condition: "provided that matters remain in the same state." This canon law doctrine later passed into secular law and was used to give a contracting party relief when circumstances had changed since he entered into a contract. See R. Zimmermann, *The Law of Obligations: Roman Foundations of the Civilian Tradition* (Cape Town, South Africa: Juta, 1990), pp. 579–82.

(9) According to the comment, ascribed to Gratian, it is not sin to be a soldier.

(10) These texts condemn marriages between Christians and non-Christians or heretics.

(11) These texts contain prohibitions on interference with stipends and other property belonging to the Church.

(12) It is noted in the margin of Ed. Rom. that this gloss is transposed and pertains to the next capitulum.

(13) The citation reads: ff. eo Modestinus. In fact the Rhodian law does not say that those who suffer shipwreck lose everything to the inhabitants. D. 14.2.9 is an ambiguous passage in which those who have been despoiled by the inhabitants of an island where they came ashore appeal to the emperor. The emperor pronounces that the Rhodian law is to be followed. This could be read to mean that they can be despoiled. The author of the Greek version of the law is Maecianus, who is sometimes misidentified as Modestinus.

(14) The citation found in the Ed. Rom. is wrong. It is "extra de biga. altercationis," but there is no capitulum "altercationis" in the title De Bigamis of the Liber Extra. The citation given here in its place (D. 16 c. 6) is found in manuscripts of the gloss (*e.g.,* Vat. Lat. 1367) and makes the point the gloss requires.

(15) This text mentions the four noted in the previous gloss: dogmas, mandates, interdicts, and sanctions.

(16) It is found in Innocent IV, *Super Libros Quinque Decretalium* ad X 5.40.25 ad *Si mos*, fol. 570ʳ no. 4 (Frankfurt, 1570, rpt. Frankfurt: Minerva, 1968).

(17) Reading "Fan." for "Fran."

(18) Gratian is speaking of the Cornelian Act on Murderers and Poisoners, a law punishing homicide and certain related crimes.

(19) The citation is to C. 4. q. 3. non in testibus. There is no capitulum by that name, but c. 3. does contain a section (§ 27) beginning "In testibus" that makes the point needed by the gloss. It speaks of the clarity required by witnesses.

(20) Reading "quidam" for "quaedam" for the title of the capitulum.

(21) Reading "plerique" for "plerumque" as the title of the capitulum.

(22) For the origin of this idea, see Aristotle, *History of Animals* VII, III 583ᵇ 1–9.

(23) A treatise on penitential discipline ascribed to St. Theodore (602–90), archbishop of Canterbury.

(24) Reading "Adhuc" for "Ad haec" as title of the capitulum.

(25) Reading C. 32 for C. 22.

(26) Two types of proceedings in Roman law, either of which could be brought for the restitution of property.

(27) The first of these texts says that a claim can be dismissed when the claimant brings an inappropriate action. The second says that the defendant need not respond unless the claimant specifies the basis of his action.

(28) This text says that the claimant need not name the type of action he is bringing but must specify the facts that entitle him to bring an action.

(29) Reading "de donationibus. cum dilecti filii" for "de dona. et contu. cum dilectus filius."

(30) A gloss to this text (to "potestati") explains that the rule that one must obey the higher authority in preference to the lower is not invariable.

(31) Reading "Vivianus" for "Julianus" as the title of the capitulum.

(32) These texts concern liturgical customs that should not be followed.

(33) This text says that a church asserting a privilege must prove that the privilege was granted. A gloss (to "consuetudines") contains a further discussion of when a proof must be made by producing an original document.

(34) Lucretia was a Roman matron who killed herself after having been raped, according to the famous story told by Livy in his *History of Rome Since Its Foundation*, I, LVII–LVIX. In the passage quoted from Augustine, he was arguing that her example, and that of other Romans who had killed themselves, should not be followed.

(35) This text also says that priests have a greater authority than kings.

(36) This case presupposes the medieval attribution of D. 10 c. 8 as "Cyprian to the Emperor Julian." The glossator assumes that the letter was addressed to the emperor Julian the Apostate (360–63), who had attempted to restore paganism and united in his own person the offices of emperor and pontifex maximus, a pagan priesthood. The problem of attribution is explained in the note of the Roman Correctors on this capitulum.

(37) This text says that acts contrary to imperial ordinances are void.

(38) This text says that one must follow what has been laid down by the Church fathers.

(39) The reference is to Guido de Baysio's Commentary to the Decretum of Gratian to D. 11 c. 5. It can be found in *Archdiaconus Super Decreto* ad D. 11 c. 5, f. 13ᵛ nos. 5–6 (Lyon 1549).

(40) This text condemns those who introduce novelties.

(41) This text says that one should make departures only when there is some clear advantage.

(42) This text, speaking of the security that must be given in lawsuits, says that the provinces must use the same system as the imperial capital.

(43) These texts describe permissible differences in the requirement of clerical celibacy, the rite of baptism, and the frequency of taking communion.

(44) This text says it is "ridiculous" for a man barred from seeking a lower office as a punishment to be able to obtain a higher one.

(45) A kind of bishop appointed to care for people in the countryside.

(46) Reading "contra" for "quae contra" as the title of the capitulum.

(47) This text also requires uniformity in saying Office.

(48) This text says that one who knows that another has sworn falsely should communicate that information to a priest, who can both correct that person and pray for him.

(49) This text says that it is preferable to correct an erring brother secretly than to denounce him publicly.

(50) This text says that not only a thief is guilty but also a person who knows who the thief is and fails to tell the owner of the thing stolen.

(51) This text says that such orders are not valid.

(52) In Roman law, a party who is in default because he has not performed a contractual duty at the proper time is liable for any loss or damage that occurs while he is in default, even if he could not have prevented it. In the text cited, a thief is treated in a similar way. The text says that if he steals a slave, he is liable to the owner even if the slave has died.

(53) This text says that orders received in return for a price or a favor are not valid because those who receive them "do not enter through the door, that is, through Christ, but are thieves."

(54) The first text says that it is wrong for a spouse guilty of the same offense to dismiss the other for fornication. The second says that when husband and wife accuse each other of immorality, and both are guilty, neither can prevail on a claim against the other.

(55) The first of these texts says that what is enacted on account of a need should lose its force once the time of need is over. The second says that a priest or deacon taken in fornication, theft, perjury, or homicide is deposed but not deprived of communion, because God does not judge the same offense two times. The third says that an ancient rule regarding who may be a deacon is too rigorous to be enforced in our times.

(56) This text says that in interpreting canons, consideration should be given to motive, person, place, and time.

(57) The first of these texts takes an indulgent view of the sins of the young. The second takes a strict view of those of the old.

(58) This text says that in doubtful matters, we must do what appears to be most certain.

(59) This refers to the legend that the Apostle's Creed was composed by each Apostle contributing one of its twelve clauses.

(60) This gloss is in error. The form of the creed referred to as that of Nicaea is, in fact, more properly known as that of Nicaea-Constantinople, since it consists of that of Nicaea along with additions made by Constantinople on the nature of the Holy Spirit. So the Western Church did possess the creed to which the text refers. The other creed mentioned, that of Athanasius, more properly called the "Quicumque vult" after its opening words, was not composed by Athanasius; it is an early medieval Latin creed that spells out orthodox beliefs on the Trinity.

(61) Ed. Rom. says that that these books are not apocryphal but canonical, although at one time their status was in doubt.

(62) The glossator is mistaken here. The text does not refer to the canons of the Seventh Council (Second Nicaea, 787), but rather to the canons of the Trullan Synod (691–92), also known as the "Quinisex Council," which issued disciplinary canons to supplement the doctrinal pronouncements of the Fifth and Sixth Councils. These supplementary canons are the subject of D. 16 c. 6 §2. Adrian, however, is here quoting the words of another in order to reject them, as the note of the Roman Correctors explains.

(63) The glossator has misunderstood the Monothelite controversy. The orthodox position, as defined by the Sixth Ecumenical Council, is that there are two wills in Christ, a human will and a divine will. The glossator's distinction between the "rational" and "sensual" wills does not capture the intent of the council since both of these "wills" would be human.

(64) Reading "caecus" for "secus" for the title of the capitulum.

(65) Reading D. 61 for D. 41.

(66) This text says that secular authorities are constituted to protect the Church, widows, and children, and to restrain the wicked; churchmen may admonish secular officials who neglect this task and excommunicate these officials if they continue to do so.

(67) Reading C. 32 for C. 33.

(68) This text is the document subscribed to at Pope Symmachus's other synod.

(69) Reading "quid" for "quis" in the cite.

(70) This text says that when a discrepancy is found in the acts of councils, the more ancient or the stronger authority is to be followed.

(71) That text says that a person who cannot himself appear in court due to illness may not be forced to appoint a procurator to appear for him if his case is serious.

(72) Reading "querelam" for "quaedam."

(73) Ed. Rom. says "This gloss does not appear in some [manuscripts] but it is in the ancient apparatus. Johannes."

(74) The first text says that one may be deprived of communion for leaving Mass before the end. The second says that one may be excommunicated for leaving a synod before it is finished.

(75) Reading q. 2 for q. 3.

(76) The latter text says that if there is doubt whether a decretal is genuine, then, if it is in accord with the common law, a judge should follow it, but if it is not, the judge should consult his superior.

(77) Reading C. 25 for C. 26.

(78) The first text says that one should submit patiently to the Church. The second says that one should never do evil out of obedience.

(79) This text distinguishes between a falsification that is due to the malice of a party and one that is due to the party's simplicity or ignorance. In the former case, the party may obtain no advantage from the proceedings in which the documents containing the falsehood were introduced. In the latter case, he may, provided that the proceedings would have conferred this advantage upon him had the documents not contained the falsehood.

(80) Reading "Nullus" for "Nulli" as the title of the capitulum.

(81) This text says that a sacrament has spiritual effect whether the minister is good or evil.

(82) This text says that one should ask about the qualifications of a preacher but one should not ask about those of a person seeking alms in order to eat.

(83) This text says that one should follow custom.

GLOSSARY

This list of terms is not a complete glossary but a series of notes on some of the words we found difficult to translate. Words with technical meanings that can be found in standard dictionaries are not defined here (e.g. metropolitan). We have also given references where the word is used in this translation of the *Treatise on Laws* or in the Digest or Institutes of Justinian.

act, see ordinance.

canon (*canon*). In the broader sense, any ecclesiastical ordinance (qv). In the narrower sense, an enactment (qv) issued by a Church council. D. 3 c. 1; DD. 15–16.

capitulum (plural: capitula). We have left this technical word for the excerpts from canonical sources included in the *Decretum* in its Latin form. Neither of the usual translations, "chapter" and "canon," are satisfactory. Even when it refers to the Bible, chapter means a much larger division of a text, and most of Gratian's selections are not canons (qv) in the strict sense.

cretion (*cretio*). There is no convenient way to translate this Roman law term. It means the formal declaration by an heir that he will accept an inheritance. This form of acceptance was no longer in use by the time of Justinian. D. 1 c. 12 § 2.

custom (*consuetudo*). A usage (qv) that has been observed for a period of time with the intention that it become normative. It has the same legal force as an ordinance (qv), even though it is neither written nor formally enacted. D. 1 c. 5. DD. 8, 11, 12.

decree (*decretum*). An enactment (qv) by the pope issued by his own authority. *Decretum* is also used as a short title for Gratian's *Harmony of Discordant Canons*. DD. 19–20.

degraded (*infamosus, infamia*). Since "infamous" has taken on a wholly different meaning in English, we have had to make do with this inadequate translation of the penalty of "infamy." It entailed the loss of legal rights and disqualification from office.

deified (*divus*). An honorific given to a Roman emperor who had been declared a god after death. This translation seemed more suitable and intelligible than the traditional "divine." In the Christian period its use can only be explained as inveterate habit. For medieval Christians the word also meant "saint."

decretal letter (*epistola decretalis*). A letter issued by the pope that answers an inquiry concerning some point of law. The letter has legal force. Such letters are sometimes referred to as "decretals." DD. 19–20.

defense (*exceptio*). In Romano-canonical procedure, the defendant's reply to the allegations made by the plaintiff. Made in writing, it does not deny the allegation but adduces some circumstance that would bar the plaintiff's claim. Or, some item of law or fact alleged by the defendant to bar the plaintiff's claim.

edict (*edictum*). In these texts, usually a proclamation by a magistrate or by the emperor issued by his own authority. Occasionally this term refers to the body of rules issued in Roman times by the praetor to extend the remedies allowed under civil law (qv). D. 2. c. 4.

enactment (*constitutio*). This is the most general term for any kind of legislation, ecclesiastical or secular. We have avoided the traditional translation "constitution" because in common usage this refers to the basic law of a state. D. 2 c. 4; Dig. 1. 4.

equity (*aequitas*). The principles of fairness that underlie all law. They may be invoked to qualify or override unreasonable ordinances (qv).

heir, direct (*heres suus*). A Roman law term referring to the son in a father's power who would automatically inherit the estate of an intestate or who is named as heir in a will. One who is outside the father's power but named as heir is an "outsider" (qv). Instit. 1. 6. 1–2; 2. 14; 2. 19; 3. 1.

indiction (*indictio*). A Roman tax cycle of fifteen years, established by Constantine, at the end of which property would be revalued for the next cycle. Although this tax system fell from use the indiction cycle continued to be used in dating documents.

interdict (*interdictum*). In civil law, an order issued by a magistrate in an administrative capacity that will give rise to a formal proceeding if ignored. In ecclesiastical law, a sanction applied to a person (personal), the entire population (general), place (local), or some particular group (partial). It suspends the celebration of most of the sacraments, but does not impose excommunication.

jurists' opinions (*responsa*). Authoritative replies to questions given by the classical Roman jurists that came to have legal force.

law/legal (*ius*). We have chosen to translate *ius* by the noun "law" and the adjective "legal," to distinguish it from *lex*, which is translated as "ordinance" (qv). "Law" in this sense, like *Recht* in German, *droit* in French, and *diritto* in Italian, means a legal system understood as a whole, the general principles underlying a legal system, or the expression of those general principles. We have not used this word for *lex*, which like *Gesetz* in German, *loi* in French, and *legge* in Italian, is the most general word for a written enactment. There are two exceptions to this rule: the phrase, "The Law," meaning the Old Testament, and the aphorism, "Necessity knows no law." In both cases the use of "ordinance" seemed too peculiar. In Gratian, the word has a special connotation of a "human" product in contrast to the "divine" one, which is morality (qv). D. 1 c. 1 § 2; D. 1 c. 2; D. 1 cc. 6–12.

law, common (*ius commune*). Law applicable when there is no local ordinance, custom, or privilege, that is, the Roman law in secular matters, the general canon law in ecclesiastical matters, or both taken together and viewed as a single system. "Common law" seemed to be the only suitable translation even though today that expression is used in English for Anglo-American judge-made law, applicable in the absence of constitutional provision or statute.

law, canon (*ius canonicum*). The legal system of the Church. D. 3., DD. 15–20.

law, civil (*ius civile*). This phrase has three meanings. The legal system of any secular state, the legal system of the Roman Empire as found in the enactments of Justinian, and that section of the Roman law produced by the traditional legislative bodies as opposed to edicts by the praetors (praetorian law). Most commonly in Gratian this phrase refers to secular as opposed to ecclesiastical law, or the Roman law as opposed to that of other secular governments. We have adopted this traditional usage even though today the expression "civil law" is often used to mean either "that law which is not criminal law," or the law of continental legal systems, historically derived from Roman law, as distinguished from the "common law" of England and the United States. D. 1 c. 8; D. 2.

law of nations (*ius gentium*). Generally, that complex of law, both written and unwritten, which is common to the legal systems of all peoples. According to the definition taken by Gratian from Isidore (D. 1 c. 9), it includes the law of war, treaties, ambassadors, and other aspects of what we would call "international law."

law, natural/of nature (*ius naturale/naturae*). Interchangeable words for the unwritten norms of human behavior that follow from human nature and are perceived by reason. Much discussion has been devoted to the question of whether Gratian distinguished it from the divine law. Unlike certain Roman jurists, Gratian does not seem to use these terms for the instinct that governs the behavior of animals (although the Gloss lists this meaning as well at D. 1 c. 7.) *Dicta Gratiani ante* D. 1 c. 1; D. 1 c. 7. DD. 5, 8, 9; Instit. 1. 2, 2. 1.

law, praetorian (*ius praetorianum*). In Roman law, the law that was created by the praetor to supplement the legislation of the traditional assemblies.

law, public (*ius publicum*). That law which is not private law, although for Gratian it seems to be principally that law which concerns the government and its officers, roughly speaking, what we would call administrative law. D. 1 c. 11. Instit. 1. 1. 4.

mandate (*mandatum*). A decree (qv) forbidding certain actions. In Roman law, it also means a contract in which one person agrees to act as agent for another.

morality/moral (*fas*). A difficult word to translate. In one sense it refers to all norms of behavior that have God as their author, as opposed to those that are human creations. It may be extended to all behavior that, everything else being equal, God would approve, or at least not condemn. One might translate it adjectivally as "right" (as opposed to "wrong") but the use of this word as a noun would then allow the confusion of *fas* with "right," meaning what is due one. *Fas* is a broader and more explicitly religious concept than equity (qv). D. 1 c. 1.

ordinance/act (*lex*). Written law, or "statute." It may be divine (like the revealed laws in the Bible) or the product of a human legislator. It is the broadest category of written enactments and is to be distinguished from "law" (qv). In our translation, we have reserved the word "statute" (qv) to translate *statuta*, a word more or less synonymous with ordinance. We have translated *lex* as "act" in the case of specific pieces of Roman legislation identified by their authors, the Falcidian Act (*Lex Falcidia*), following usage for the analogous type of American legislation (e.g., the Sherman Anti-Trust Act). In two cases (explained under "law") we have decided to translate *lex* as "law." D. 1 cc. 2–3; D. 2. c. 1; DD. 7 & 9; Dig. 1. 3. 4.

outsider (*extraneus*). Under Roman law, one not in the father's power who is named as heir in a will.

plebiscite (*plebiscita*). In Roman law, a form of ordinance (qv), obsolete by the time of Justinian, issued by the assemblies of the plebeians. It does not have the modern sense of a referendum by the people. D. 2 c. 2.

postliminy (*postliminia*). In Roman law, the regaining of one's rights in private and public law after return from capture by the enemy. D. 1 c. 12; Dig. 49. 15.

practice/use (*usus*). The most general term for forms of more or less repetitive human activity, not necessarily having legal significance.

prescription (*praescriptio*). The acquisition of ownership by possession of real estate for a period of time in accord with law. See also, "usucaption." The analogous institution in modern American law is "adverse possession."

Quinquagesima (*Quinquagesima*). There is no word for this in English. Strictly, the Sunday before Ash Wednesday (called traditionally "Cheesefare Sunday"); more loosely, the weeks preceding Lent that have a semi-penitential character. It is also used for the fifty days after Easter, Paschal time. D. 4 cc. 4–6.

representative (*procurator*). This term here refers to a representative in a civil action or the individual managing a business, not the Roman official known as a "procurator."

rescript (*rescriptum*). A written answer issued in the emperor's name to a legal or administrative question. Analogous to decretal letters (qv) in canon law.

rule/norm (*regula*). A general term for what governs conduct. For Gratian, it usually applies to ecclesiastical conduct. D. 3 cc. 1–2.

sanction (*sanctio*). A mandate (qv) which includes a penalty.

see (*sedes*). The office of bishop or pope (the "Apostolic See"); or, in the case of a bishop, his diocese.

senate resolution (*senatus consultum*). A decision of the Roman Senate that by the early empire had legislative force. By the time of Justinian, it was obsolete. D. 2 c. 3.

servitude (*servitus*). Land was subject to a servitude when a person, not the owner, had the right to use it in a particular way, for example, the right to pass through it. *Servitus* also means slavery, much as in the English phrase, "to be in servitude."

statute (*statuta*). A word essentially synonymous with "ordinance." Our usage of "statute" and "ordinance" parallels Gratian's usage of *statuta* and *lex*. Ordinance seems broader than statute, but the distinction is not clear.

usage (*mos*). Although the texts cited by Gratian use this word ambiguously, it generally means a long-standing and accepted pattern of behavior that has the potential of becoming a custom (qv) and thus has the force of an ordinance (qv). *Dicta Gratiani ante* D. 1 c. 1; D. 1 c. 4–5.

usucaption (*usucaptio*). There is no convenient way to express this in English. It is the acquisition of ownership of a piece of movable property by possession for a period of time under Roman law. See also, "prescription." Instit. 2. 6; Dig. 41. 3.

JURISTS IN THE GLOSS

As noted in the introduction, the Gloss to the *Decretum* grew over time as jurists added notes in the margins, sometimes supplementing, replacing, or incorporating the notes of others. Sometimes the glosses were anonymous, sometimes signed with an abbreviation indicating the author's name. Sometimes an abbreviation indicating the name of a famous jurist was added later. The same abbreviation can sometimes denote more than one jurist. Even when the meaning of an abbreviation is clear, it is difficult to determine who was the original author. Consequently, on the advice of our editors, the translation of the Gloss reproduces the abbreviations as they appear in the Roman edition.

The following is a list of the jurists mentioned or cited in the Gloss and their common abbreviations, but it must be remembered that there is no way to be sure they wrote the glosses after which these abbreviations appear.

Albericus de Rosiate (d. 1360, abbreviated Albericus) worked as a lawyer in Bergamo, where he reformed the statutes of the city. He wrote a dictionary of civil and canon law and a book on municipal statutes.

"The Archdeacon," Guido de Baysio (d. 1313, abbreviated Archidiaconus, Archid., Arch.) taught in Bologna, where he held the rank of archdeacon, and moved to Avignon when it became the seat of the papacy. His most famous work was the *Rosarium*, a commentary on the *Decretum*.

Bartholomew of Brescia (d. 1258, abbreviated Bartholomaeus Brixiensis, Bart. Brixien., Bar. Brix., Bar., B.) taught in Bologna, and is chiefly famous for reworking Johannes Teutonicus's Gloss to the *Decretum*. More information about him is given in the introduction.

"Cy." Although this is a standard abbreviation for Cinus de Pistoia (d. 1336), who taught Roman law and is known for his commentary on Justinian's Code, it is also appears in manuscripts of the twelfth to thirteenth centuries as an abbreviation for the name of an unknown canonist who wrote glosses on the *Decretum*. See S. Kuttner, *Repertorium der Kanonistik (1140–1234)* (Vatican City: Biblioteca Apostolica Vaticana, 1937), pp. 10, 31, 40.

Huguccio (d. 1210, abbreviated Hugo., Hug., Hu., H.), who became bishop of Ferrara, was perhaps the most important canonist of the twelfth century. He is chiefly famous for his *Summa* of the *Decretum*.

Innocent IV, Sinibaldo Fieschi (d. 1254, abbreviated Innocent), who became pope in 1243, wrote a lengthy commentary on the *Decretals* of Gregory IX.

Johannes de Fantutiis (d. 1391, abbreviated Ioan. de Fantu., Ioan. de Fant., Ioann. de Fan., Ioan. de Fan., Io. de Fant., Ion. de Fan., Io. de Fan.) taught canon law in Bologna and wrote an incomplete commentary on the *Decretum*. His name, as abbreviated, is often confused with that of Johannes de Phintona (see below).

Johannes de Phintona (or de Fintona, fl. 13th cent., abbreviated Ioan. de Fant., Ioann. de Fan., Ioan. de Fan., Io. de Fant., Ion. de Fan., Io. de Fan.) wrote glosses to the *Decretum* that were later attributed to Johannes de Fantutiis.

Johannes Teutonicus (d. 1245/46, abbreviated Ioannes Theutonicus, Ioan. Theutonicus, Ioannes., Ioan., Io.) taught in Bologna and later became provost and then dean of the cathedral chapter in Halberstadt in Germany. He compiled the Ordinary Gloss to the *Decretum*. Further information about him is given in the Introduction.

Laurentius Hispanus (d. 1248, abbreviated Lau., Laur.) taught in Bologna, wrote a series of glosses to the *Decretum*, and became bishop of Orense in 1218.

Petrus Beneventanus (Collivaccinus, active 1210, abbreviated Beneventa., Pet.) prepared a collection of papal decretals, now known as the *Compilatio Tertia*, promulgated under Pope Innocent III.

"Pet." stands for Petrus and can refer to several medieval jurists: *e.g.*, Petrus de Salicis, who was active in the last half of the thirteenth century and wrote a commentary on the *Decretum*; Petrus Beneventanus, described above; or Petrus Blesenis or Petrus Hispanus, twelfth-century canonists who wrote glosses to the *Decretum*.

BIBLIOGRAPHY

ANCIENT AND MEDIEVAL SOURCES

Gratian's Decretum

Ed. Fried.: *Decretum Magistri Gratiani*. 2d ed. Ed. E. Friedberg. Corpus Iuris Canonici, 1. Leipzig: Tauchnitz, 1879; rpt. Graz: Akademische Druck- u. Verlagsanstalt, 1959.

Ed. Rom.: *Decretum Gratiani Emendatum et Notationibus Illustratum una cum Glossis*. Rome, 1582. Our translation is based on the Venice 1595 and Lyon 1606 reprints of this edition.

Liber Extra

Decretales Gregorii IX. 2d ed. Ed. E. Friedberg. Corpus Iuris Canonici, 2. Leipzig: Tauchnitz, 1879; rpt. Graz: Akademische Druck- u. Verlagsanstalt, 1959.

Decretales Gregorii Papae IX suae Integritati una cum Glossis Restitutae. Rome, 1582.

Abbreviations for Patristic and Medieval Texts and Collections:

ACW: Ancient Christian Writers (New York: Newman Press, 1953–)
ANF: Ante-Nicene Fathers, ed. A. Roberts and J. Donaldson (Edinburgh, 1867–72; rpt. Grand Rapids: Eerdmans, 1956)
Anselm: Anselm of Lucca, *Collectio Canonum una cum Collectio Minore*, ed. F. Thaner (Innsbruck: Wagner, 1906–15)
Deusdedit: *Die Kanonessammlung des Kardinals Deusdedit* (Paterborn, 1905; rpt. Aalen: Scientia-Verlag, 1967)
Burchard: Burchard of Worms, *Decretum Libri XX*, PL 140:537–1058
CSEL: Corpus Scriptorum Ecclesiasticorum Latinorum (Vienna: Gerold, 1866–)
CCSL: Corpus Christianorum Series Latina (Turnholt: Brepols, 1954–)
ERP: *Epistolae Romanorum Pontificum*, ed. A. Thiel (Braunsberg: Olms, 1868)
FC: Fathers of the Church (Washington, D. C.: Catholic Univ. of America Press, 1948–)
Ivo: Ivo of Chartres
    D. : *Decretum*, PL 161:54–1022
    Tri. : *Collectio Tripartita* [unedited]
    Pan. : *Panormia*, PL 161:1045–344
JK, JE, JL: *Regesta Pontificum Romanorum*. . . . 2d ed. Ed. P. Jaffé, with F. Kaltenbrun-

ner (JK, an. 90–590), with P. Ewald (JE, an. 590–882), with S. Loewenfeld (JL, an. 882–1198). Leipzig: Veit, 1885

LCC: Library of the Christian Classics (Philadelphia: Westminster, 1954–66)

LFCC: Library of the Fathers of the Holy Catholic Church Anterior to the Division of the East and West (Oxford: Parker, 1850)

MGH. Auct. Ant.: Monumenta Germaniae Historica, Auctores Antiquissimi (Berlin: Weidmann, 1877–1919)

MGH. Ep.: Monumenta Germaniae Historica, Epistolae (Berlin: Weidmann, 1887–1939)

MGH. Ep. Sel.: Monumenta Germaniae Historica, Epistolae Selectae (Berlin: Weidmann, 1883–94)

PG: Patrologiae Cursus Completus, Series Graeca (Paris: Migne, 1857-87)

PL: Patrologiae Cursus Completus, Series Latina (Paris: Migne, 1857–66)

Polycarp: The *Polycarpus* [unedited]

SC: Sources Chrétiennes (Paris: Cerf, 1968–)

SLNF1: Select Library of the Nicene and Post-Nicene Fathers, First Series. (New York, 1886–90; rpt. Grand Rapids: Eerdmans, 1978–79)

SLNF2: Select Library of the Nicene and Post-Nicene Fathers, Second Series. (New York, 1890–1900; rpt. Grand Rapids: Eerdmans, 1952–56)

Corpus Juris Civilis

Instit.: *Justiniani Institutiones*. Ed. P. Krueger. Berlin: Weidmann, 1899. English translation: *Justinian's Institutes*. Tr. P. Birkes and G. McLeod. Ithaca: Cornell Univ. Press, 1987.

Dig.: *Omnia Digesta seu Pandectarum*. Ed. T. Mommsen and P. Krueger. Berlin: Weidman, 1899. English translation: *The Digest of Justinian*. Tr. A. Watson. Philadelphia: Univ. of Penn. Press, 1985.

Cod.: *Codex Iustinianus*. Ed. P. Krueger. Berlin: Weidmann, 1954. English translation: *The Code*. Tr. S. P. Scott. 3 vols. In *The Civil Law*, 12–14. New York: AMS, 1932.

Nov.: *Novellae*. Ed. R. Schoel and W. Kroll. Berlin: Weidmann, 1954. English translation: *The Enactments of Justinian*. Tr. S. P. Scott. In *The Civil Law*, 2. New York: AMS, 1932.

Auth.: *Authenticum Novellarum Constitutionum Iustiniani Versio Vulgata*. Ed. G. E. Heimbach. 2 vols. Leipzig, 1846–51.

ADRIAN I. *Epistolae*. MGH. Ep. 3:567–657, 5:1–57.

ALGER OF LIÈGE. *Liber de Misericordia et Iustitia*. Ed. R. Kretzschmer. Sigmaringen: Thorbecke, 1985.

AUGUSTINE OF HIPPO. *Confessionum Liber XIII*. Ed. L. Verjeijen. CCSL 27. English translation: *Confessions*. Tr. R. Pine-Coffin. Baltimore: Penguin, 1961.

———. *Contra Faustum Manichaeum Libri XXXIII*. Ed. J. Zycha. CSEL 25:251–797. English translation: *Reply to Faustus the Manichaean*. Tr. R. Stothert. SLNF1 4:155–345.

——— . *Contra Litteras Petiliani Libri III.* Ed. M. Petschenig. CSEL 52:3–277. English translation: *Answer to the Letters of Petilian, Bishop of Citra.* Tr. J. King and C. Hartranft. SLNF1 4:519–628.

——— . *De Anima et eius Origine Libri IV.* Ed. C. Urba and J. Zycha. CSEL 60:303–419. English translation: *A Treatise on the Soul and its Origin.* Tr. R. Homes and R. Wallis. SLNF1 5:315–71.

——— . *De Baptismo Libri VII.* Ed. M. Petchenig. CSEL 51:145–375. English translation: *On Baptism against the Donatists.* Tr. J. R. King. SLNF1 4:411–514.

——— . *De Civitate Dei Libri XXII.* Ed. D. Dombart and A. Kalb. CCSL 57–58. English translation: *The City of God against the Pagans.* Tr. H. Bettenson. Harmondsworth, Eng: Penguin, 1972.

——— . *De Doctrina Christiana Libri IV.* Ed. J. Martin. CCSL 32:1–167. English translation: *Christian Instruction.* Tr. J. Gavigan. FC 2: Augustine, vol. 4, pp. 19–235.

——— . *De Trinitate Libri XV.* Ed. W. Mountain. CCSL 50–50a. English translation: *On the Trinity.* Tr. S. McKenna. FC 45.

——— . *De Vera Religione Liber I.* Ed. K. Daur. CCSL 32:169–260. English translation: *Of True Religion.* Tr. J. Burleigh. LCC 6: Augustine, *Earlier Writings,* pp. 281–83.

——— . *Epistolae.* Ed. A. Goldbacher. CSEL 34 i–ii; 44; 57; 58. English translation: *Letters.* Tr. W. Parsons. FC 12, 18, 20, 30, 32: Augustine, vols. 9–13.

——— . *Quaestionum in Heptateuchum Libri VII.* Ed. J. Fraipont. CCSL 33:1–377.

——— . *Tractatus in Evangelium Ioannis.* Ed. R. Willems. CCSL 36. English translation: *Tractates on the Gospel of John.* Tr. J. Rettig. FC 78, 79, 88, 90.

BASIL THE GREAT. Περὶ τοῦ ἁγίου πνεύματος. *Traité du Saint-Esprit.* Ed. and tr. into French B. Pruche. SC 17. English translation: *The* De Spiritu Sancto. Tr. B. Jackson. SLNF2 8:1–50.

BEDE THE VENERABLE. *Chronicon de Sex Aetatibus Mundi.* Ed. T. Mommsen. MGH. Auc. Ant. 14.

——— . *Historia Ecclesiastica.* Ed. and tr. in *Ecclesiastical History of the English People.* B. Colgrave. Oxford: Clarendon Press, 1965.

Capitula Angilramni. In *Decretales Pseudo-Isidorianae,* pp. 757–69.

Collectio Hispana. La Colección Hispana. Madrid: Consejo Superior de Investigaciones Científicas, 1966–84. English translations of early councils: SLNF2 14.

The Collection in Seventy-Four Titles: A Canon Law Manual of the Gregorian Reform. Ed. and tr. J. Gilchrist. Medieval Sources in Translation, 22. Toronto: Pontifical Institute of Medieval Studies, 1980.

CYPRIAN OF CARTHAGE. *Epistolae.* Ed. W. Hartel. CSEL 3. English translation: *Letters.* 4 vols. Tr. G. W. Clarke. ACW 43, 44, 46, 47.

Decretales Pseudo-Isidorianae et Capitula Angilramni. Ed. P. Hinschius. Leipzig: Tauchnitz, 1863.

Decretum Gelasianum de Libris Recipiendis et non Recipiendis. Ed. E. von Dobschütz. In *Texte und Untersuchungen der Geschichte der altchristlichen Literatur*, 38.4 (1912).

DIONYSIUS EXIGUUS. *Collectio Decretorum Paparum Romanorum*. PL 67:238–376.

———— . [*Collectio Dionysiana*:] *Die Canonumsammlung des Dionysius Exiguus in der ersten Redaktion*. Ed. A. Strewe. Berlin: Gruyter, 1931.

ENNODIUS. *Libellus contra eos qui contra Synodum Scribere Praesumpserunt*. CSEL 6.

FELIX III. *Epistolae*. Ed. A. Thiel. EPR 223–77.

GREGORY I. *Moralia in Librum Job*. PL 75:509–1162. English translation: *Morals on the Book of Job*. Tr. J. Bliss. LFCC.

———— . *Registrum Epistolarum*. Ed. D. Norberg. CCSL 140–140a. Partial English translation: *Letters*. Tr. J. Barmby. SLNF2 12–13.

———— . "Homilies on the Gospels." PL 76:1075–1312. English translation: *Forty Gospel Homilies*. Cistercian Studies, 123. Tr. D. Hurst. Kalamazoo, Mich.: Cistercian Publ., 1990.

GREGORY IV. *Epistolae*. MGH. Ep. 5.

GREGORY VII. *Registrum Epistolarum*. Ed. E. Casper. MGH. Ep. Sel. 2. Partial English translation: *The Correspondence of Gregory VII*. Records of Western Civilization. Tr. E. Emerson. New York: Columbia Univ. Press, 1932.

GREGORY OF NAZIANZUS. *Orationes*. PG 35–36. Latin version of Rufinus: CSEL 46. English translation: *Select Orations*. Tr. C. Brown and J. Swallow. SLNF2 7:203–434.

HUMBERT OF SILVA CANDIDA. *Responsio sive Contradictio in Libellum Nicetae*. PL 143:983–1004.

INNOCENT I. *Epistolae*. PL 20:463–608. English translation of *Epistola ad Decentium*. Tr. G. Ellard. *Theological Studies* 9 (1948), 3–19.

ISIDORE OF SEVILLE. *De Lamentatione Animae Peccatricis* [*Synonyma*]. PL 83:825–56.

———— . *Etymologiarum sive Originum*. 2 vols. Ed. W. M. Lindsay. Oxford, 1911. English translation of Book 2: *Isidore's* Etymologies, *Book II*. Tr. P. Marshall. Paris: Belles Lettres, 1983.

———— . *Sententiarum Libri III*. PL 83:537–738.

JEROME. *Epistolae*. CSEL 54–56. Partial English translations: *Letters*. Tr. E. Fremantle. SLNF2 6:1–192. *Letters 1–21*. Tr. E. Meriow. ACW 33.

LEO I. *Epistolae*. PL 54:593–1218. English translation: *Letters*. Tr. C. Feltoe. SLNF2 12.

LEO IV. *Epistolae Selectae*. MGH. Ep. 5:585–612.

LEO IX. *Epistolae*. PL 143:591–788.

Leges Longobardorum. MGH Leges, 4. Hannover, 1868. English translation: *The Lom-*

bard Laws. Tr. K. Drew. Philadelphia, 1973.

Liber Pontificalis. Bibliotheque des Écoles françaises d'Athenes et de Rome. 3 vols. Ed. L. Duchesne. Paris: Boccard, 1955. Partial English translation: *The Book of Pontiffs (Liber Pontificalis): The Ancient Biographies of the First Ninety Roman Bishops to A.D. 715.* Tr. R. Davis. Liverpool, U.K.: Liverpool Univ. Press, 1989.

Liber Diurnus Romanorum. Ed. H. Foerster. Bern: Francke, 1958.

MARTIN OF BRAGA. *Capita Martini.* Ed. C. Barlow. In *Opera Omnia*, pp. 123–44. New Haven: Yale Univ. Press, 1950.

NICHOLAS I. *Epistolae.* MGH. Ep. 6:257–694.

PELAGIUS I. *Epistolae quae Supersunt.* Ed. P. Gassó and C. Battle. Montserrat: Abatia Montisserrati, 1956.

STEPHEN V. *Epistolae.* PL 129:785–822.

SYMMACHUS. *Epistolae.* ERP 641–736.

———— . *Praeceptum Regis Theodorici.* MGH. Act. Ant. 12:399.

TERTULLIAN. *De Corona Militis.* CSEL 70:125–52. English translation: *The Chaplet.* Tr. R. Arbesmann. FC 40:231–70.

THEODORE OF TARSUS. *Canones Theodori.* Ed. P. Finsterwald. Weimer: Bohlaus, 1929. English translation: *The Penitential of Theodore.* In *Medieval Handbooks of Penance.* Records of Civilization, 29. Tr. J. McNeil and H. Gamer. New York: Columbia Univ. Press, 1965.

FOR FURTHER READING

This list makes no pretense of completeness; the literature on the *Decretum* alone is vast and constantly increasing. It merely suggests some places to start.

Bibliography

Bulletin of Medieval Canon Law.

COING, HELMUT. *Handbuch der Quellen und Literatur der neureren europäischen Privatrechtsgeschichte*, 1. Munich: Beck, 1973.

Medioevo latino: Bulletino bibliografico della cultura dal secolo VI al XIII.

Revue d'histoire ecclésiastique.

Gratian, the *Decretum*, and the Gloss

DE GHELLINCK, JOSEPH. "Gratien." *Dictionnaire de Théologie Catholique* 6:2 (1920), col. 1727–51.

FRANSEN, GERARD. "La Date de Décret de Gratien." *Revue d'histoire ecclésiastique* 5 (1956), 521–31.

KUTTNER, STEPHAN. "The Father of the Science of Canon Law." *The Jurist* 1 (1941), 2–19.

———. *Harmony from Dissonance: An Interpretation of Medieval Canon Law.* Wimmer Lecture 10. Latrobe, Penn.: Archabbey Press, 1960. Reprinted in *The History of Ideas and Doctrines in the Middle Ages.* London: Variorum, 1980, pp. 1–16.

———. "Research on Gratian: Acta and Agenda." *Proceedings of the Seventh International Congress of Medieval Canon Law, Cambridge.* Ed. P. Linehan. Monumenta Iuris Canonici, Series C: Subsidia 8. Vatican City: Biblioteca Apostolica Vaticana, 1988, pp. 3–26.

———. "Zur Frage der Theologische Vorlagen Gratians." *Zeitschrift der Savigny-Stiftung für Rechtsgeschichte, kanonistische Abteilung* 23 (1934), 243–68.

LANDAU, PETER. "Gratian (von Bologna)." *Theologische Realenzyklopaedie* 14:1/2, pp. 124–30.

———. "Neue Forschungen zu vorgratianischen Kanonessammlungen und den Quellen des gratianischen Dekrets." *Ius Commune* 11 (1984), 1–29.

LE BRAS, GABRIEL. "Les Écritures dans le Décret de Gratien." *Zeitschrift der Savigny-Stiftung für Rechtsgeschichte, kanonistische Abteilung* 27 (1938), 47–80.

———. "Inventoire théologique du Décret et de la Glose ordinaire." In *Êtres et mondes invisibles: Mélanges Joseph de Ghellinck, S. J.* Museum Lessianum, Section historique 14. Gembloux: Duculot, 1951, II, 603–16.

LENHERR, TITUS. "Arbeiten mit Gratians Dekret." *Archiv für katholisches Kirchenrecht* 151 (1982), 140–66.

MELNIKAS, ANTHONY. *The Corpus of Miniatures in the Manuscripts of the Decretum Gratiani.* 3 vols. Subsidia Gratiana 16–18. Rome: Istitutum Gratianum, 1975.

NOONAN, JOHN T., JR. "Gratian Slept Here: The Changing Identity of the Father of the Systematic Study of Canon Law." *Traditio* 35 (1979), 145–79.

PENNINGTON, KENNETH. "Prolegomena." In Johannes Teutonicus, *Apparatus Glossarum in Compilationem Tertiam.* Monumenta Iuris Canonici, Series A: Corpus Glossatorum 3. Ed. K. Pennington. Vatican City: Biblioteca Apostolica Vaticana, 1981, pp. xi–xxx.

———. "Johannes Teutonicus." *Dictionary of the Middle Ages* 7 (1986), 121–22.

SCHELLHASS, KARL. "Wissenschaftliche Forschungen unter Gregor XIII für die Neuausgabe des gratianischen Dekrets." In *Papsttum und Kaisertum: Forschungen zur politischen Geschichte und Geisteskultur des Mittelalters.* Ed. A. Brackmann. Munich: Brackmann, 1926, pp. 674–90.

VETULANI, ADAM. "Autour du Décret de Gratien." *Apollinaris* 41 (1968), 43–58.

WOJTYŁA, KAROL (POPE JOHN PAUL II). "Le Traité 'De Poenitentia' de Gratien dans l'abrégé de Gdansk Mar. F.275." *Studia Gratiana* 7 (1959), 355–90.

Canon Law

BALDWIN, JOHN W. *The Scholastic Culture of the Middle Ages.* Lexington, Mass.: Heath, 1971.

DONAHUE, CHARLES. *Why the History of Canon Law is Not Written.* Selden Society Lecture. London: Selden Society, 1986.

FOURNIER, PAUL, AND GABRIEL LE BRAS. *Histoire des collections canoniques en occident depuis les Fausses décrétales jusqu'au Décret de Gratien.* 2 vols. Paris: Sirey, 1931–32.

FRANSEN, GERARD. *Les Collections canoniques.* Typologie des sources du moyen âge occidental 10. Tourhout: Brepols, 1973/1985.

GARCIA Y GARCIA, ANTONIO. *Historia del Derecho Canonico I: El Primer Milenio.* Salamanca: Instituto de Historia de la Teología Española, 1967.

KUTTNER, STEPHAN. "Quelques observations sur l'autorité des collections canoniques dans le droit classique de l'Église." In *Actes du Congrés de droit canonique, Paris 22–26 Avril 1947.* Paris: Letouzey et Ané, 1950, pp. 305–12.

———. "The Revival of Jurisprudence." *Renaissance and Renewal in the Twelfth Century.* Ed. R. Benson and G. Constable. Cambridge, Mass.: Harvard Univ. Press, 1982, pp. 299–323.

LE BRAS, GABRIEL, with CHARLES LEFEBRE and JACQUELINE RAMBAUD. *L'Âge classique, 1140-1378: Sources et théorie du droit.* Histoire du droit et des institutions de l'Église en occident 7. Paris: Sirey, 1965.

MUNIER, CHARLES. *Les Sources patristiques du droit de l'Église.* Univ. of Strasbourg dissertation, 1954. Mulhouse: Salvator, 1957.

REYNOLDS, ROGER E. "Law, Canon, to Gratian." *Dictionary of the Middle Ages* 7 (1986), 395–413.

STICKLER, ALPHONSO M. *Historia Iuris Canonici Latini: Historia Fontium.* Turin: Libraria Pontificia Athenaei Salesiani, 1950.

VAN HOVE, ALPHONSE. "Prolegomena." *Commentarium Lovaniense in Codicem Iuris Canonici*, I/1. 2d ed. Louvain and Rome: Dessain, 1945.

VAN DE WEIL, CONSTANT. *History of Canon Law.* Louvain: Peeters, 1991.

Roman Law

BELLOMO, MANLIO. *L'Europa del diritto comune.* Rome: Il Cigno Galileo Galilei, 1991. English translation: *The Common Law* (Ius Commune) *of Europe.* Tr. L. Cochrane. Studies in Medieval and Early Modern Canon Law. Washington, D.C.: Catholic Univ. Press of America, [forthcoming].

DAWSON, JOHN P. *Oracles of the Law.* Ann Arbor: Univ. of Mich. Law School, 1968.

NICHOLAS, BARRY. *An Introduction to Roman Law.* Oxford: Oxford Univ. Press, 1962.

NÖRR, KNUT. "Institutional Foundations of the New Jurisprudence," in *Renaissance and Renewal in the Twelfth Century.* Ed. R. L. Benson and G. Constable. Cambridge, Mass.: Harvard Univ. Press, 1982, pp. 324–38.

Legal Theory

BERMAN, HAROLD J. *Law and Revolution: The Formation of the Western Legal Tradition.* Cambridge, Mass.: Harvard Univ. Press, 1983.

CHODOROW, STANLEY. *Christian Political Theory and Church Politics in the Mid-Twelfth Century: The Ecclesiology of Gratian's Decretum.* Berkeley: Univ. of Calif. Press, 1972.

GAUDEMET, JEAN. "Équité et droit chez Gratien et les premiers décrétistes." In *La storia del diritto nel quardro delle scienze storiche.* Atti del I Congresso internazionale della Società italiana di storia del diritto. Florence: Olschki, 1966, pp. 269–91.

――――. "La Doctrine des sources du droit dans le Décret de Gratien." *Revue de droit canonique* 1 (1950), 5–31.

TIERNEY, BRIAN. "*Natura id est Deus*: A Case of Juristic Pantheism?" *Journal of the History of Ideas* 24 (1963), 307–22.

――――. " 'Only the Truth has Authority': The Problem of 'Reception' in the Decretists and in Johannes de Turrecremata." In *Law, Church, and Society: Essays in Honor of Stephan Kuttner.* Ed. K. Pennington and R. Somerville. Philadelphia: Univ. of Penn. Press, 1977, pp. 69–96.

――――. " 'Sola Scriptura' and the Canonists." *Studia Gratiana* 11 (1967), 345–66.

WEIGAND, RUDOLF. *Die Naturrechtslehre der Legisten und Dekretisten von Irnerius bis Accursius und von Gratian bis Johannes Teutonicus.* Münchener theologische Studien, kanonistische Abteilung 26. Munich: Hueber, 1967.

Canon Law and Protestantism

HECKEL, JOHANNES. "Das Decretum Gratiani und das evangelische Kirchenrecht." *Studia Gratiana* 3 (1955), 483–538.

HELMHOLTZ, R. H. *Canon Law in Protestant Lands.* Berlin: Duncker & Humblot, 1992.

PINCHERLE, A. "Graziano e Lutero." *Studia Gratiana* 3 (1955), 451–82.

REULOS, MICHEL. "Le Décret de Gratien chez les humanistes, les gallicans, et les réformés français du XVI siècle." *Studia Gratiana* 2 (1954), 677–96.